W9-DAU-149

GOOD AND MAD

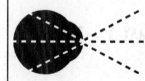

GOOD AND MAD

THE REVOLUTIONARY POWER OF WOMEN'S ANGER

REBECCA TRAISTER

THORNDIKE PRESS
A part of Gale, a Cengage Company

Farmington Hills, Mich • San Francisco • New York • Waterville, Maine
Meriden, Conn • Mason, Ohio • Chicago

Copyright © 2018 by Rebecca Traister.
Thorndike Press, a part of Gale, a Cengage Company.

**LIBRARY OF CONGRESS CIP DATA ON FILE.
CATALOGUING IN PUBLICATION FOR THIS BOOK
IS AVAILABLE FROM THE LIBRARY OF CONGRESS**

ISBN-13: 978-1-4328-6370-8 (hardcover)

Published in 2019 by arrangement with Simon & Schuster, Inc.

Printed in Mexico
1 2 3 4 5 6 7 23 22 21 20 19

For Bella and Rosie

Do not put such unlimited power into the hands of the husbands. Remember, all men would be tyrants if they could. If particular care and attention is not paid to the ladies, we are determined to foment a rebellion, and will not hold ourselves bound by any laws in which we have no voice or representation.

— ABIGAIL ADAMS

The Feminine
Is not
Dead
Nor is she
Sleeping

Angry, yes,
Seething, yes.

Biding her time;

Yes.
Yes.

— ALICE WALKER

CONTENTS

INTRODUCTION

When I was hosting my CNBC show, it was ten years ago [2008] during the crisis. I was counseling people daily who'd lost every penny. It was heartbreaking and intense. I had on the head of the SEC at the time and asked him some pointed questions about his department's lack of oversight. I got pulled into the executive producer's office after we wrapped — was forced to sit and watch the segment, then lectured about how I looked "angry." All I did was not smile. My jaw was tight. My eyes, maybe burning a bit. My response: "I was and am angry." Soon after, another host has a meltdown on the floor of the stock exchange, screaming in anger, *male,* and he's lauded as starting the Tea Party. I mean . . . *Fuck it!*

— Carmen Rita Wong

"Get your fucking hands off me, goddamn it!" bellowed Florynce Kennedy, enormous peace sign earrings flying, her head wrapped in a red turban. "Don't touch me, you motherfucker!"

It was an electrifying interaction in the midst of the 1972 Democratic National Convention in Miami. Kennedy, the black feminist and lawyer, was aiming all her ire at a bunch of white network news guys, including CBS's Mike Wallace and Dan Rather, who were taking a break on the mostly empty convention floor; for the most part, the men were showing little interest in Kennedy's fury. But one was trying to calm her and persuade her to back away by putting his hands on her. "The next son of a bitch that touches a woman is gonna get kicked in the balls," she vowed.

In 1972, Shirley Chisholm — the first black woman ever elected to Congress —

had run for the presidency and made it all the way to the convention. The party's national gathering had been a wild one, thanks in no small part to the participation of the National Women's Political Caucus, which had been founded the previous year by Chisholm, Kennedy, and other feminists and civil rights leaders including Gloria Steinem, Betty Friedan, and Dorothy Height.[1] In Miami, they'd convened and argued: over Chisholm's candidacy; over the eventual nominee, George McGovern; over the Equal Rights Amendment; and over a controversial abortion plank proposed for the party's platform.[2] And as it was all unfolding, they'd gotten almost no television coverage.

This was what had led Kennedy and a group of other women that included Sandra Hochman — a white feminist poet, who had been given $15,000 by independent film producers to make a documentary about feminists at the convention — to storm the TV crews and reporters gathered on the convention's floor during a down moment.

The powerful newsmen had sat, silent and amused, some not looking up from their newspapers, as the scrum of women had berated them. The women's fury had only built in response to the men's inattention to

18

it, bubbling over at the couple of guys who'd tried to hush them.

Hochman's camera crew had recorded it all for her documentary, which would be called *Year of the Woman*. The film captured so much of the gendered derision and dismissal that was provoking those women to scream their heads off: footage of the news crews who wouldn't cover Chisholm, instead falling all over Liz Renay, a beautiful stripper and actress; a Democratic power broker telling Hochman that there *were* women working on George McGovern's campaign, "so far mostly in the childcare centers and things like that"; McGovern's dashing young campaign manager, Gary Hart, then two years away from his own bid for the Senate, telling Hochman that his boss wouldn't pick a female vice presidential candidate because there was no "satisfactory woman candidate . . . qualified to be president of the United States." (Chisholm, then in her second congressional term, had already worked to expand the food stamp program as well as the Special Supplemental Nutrition Program for Women, Infants, and Children; she had pushed a $10 billion subsidized childcare bill, a version of which would be introduced by Walter Mondale and passed by Congress before Richard

19

Nixon vetoed it. For his running mate, McGovern would wind up selecting Thomas Eagleton, a senator from Missouri who had not disclosed his previous history of depression treatments and had to resign from the ticket eighteen days after having been chosen.)

Hochman's movie played for five nights in New York City's Greenwich Village to sold-out crowds in 1973, and then, except for a handful of screenings, mostly disappeared from public view for forty-two years. In 2004, the *Washington Post* described *Year of the Woman* as having been "too radical, too weird, and too far ahead of its time for any distributor to touch."[3] When, in 2015, I was assigned to write about it as a feminist journalist heading into the 2016 presidential election, I immediately understood what had made it so charged and dangerous, what had made it *too much:* it was a celluloid time capsule, its wholly unfiltered view of women's outrage, acute and strange to contemporary ears and eyes, trapped in amber.

"We are people that have been left out!" Hochman shouts in the film, and it's hard to disagree with her frustration, although it's also hard not to notice that she is wearing a papier-mâché crocodile mask while screaming. "People don't take women seriously. They make them into freaks. So I say, as a poet, be a freak." The whole documentary is filled with women activists acting, from a 2015 vantage point, like freaks: wearing sparkly eyeglass frames, snorkeling masks, and Mickey Mouse ears. They sing an anthem to the tune of the "Battle Hymn of the Republic," appropriated by the feminist songwriter Meredith Tax, via the Black Panthers.[4]

Mine eyes have seen the glory of the flame
    of women's rage
Kept smoldering for centuries, now burning
    in this age
We no longer will be prisoners in that same
    old gilded cage
That's why we're marching on . . .
You think that you can buy us off with
    crummy wedding rings
You never give us half the profit that our
    labor brings
Our anger eats into us, we'll no longer
    bend to kings,
That's why we're marching on . . .

This view — of anger burning raw and hot, profane and freakish; of the men who controlled the national popular narrative

21

about women, politics, and power; who tried to get Flo Kennedy to stop yelling by putting their *fucking hands* on her — brought a jolting realization when I first saw it three years ago: that the freakishness was, as Hochman noted, a by-product of unadulterated fury. A desperate *rage* at being manhandled, ignored, sidelined, and not taken seriously was driving this group of revolutionaries — some of them leading public figures in the still-coalescing second-wave feminist movement — to behave outlandishly. Their frustration at the seeming impossibility of their project was being disgorged, superseding common sense about decorum and polite discourse. They would do *anything* to get people to really hear how livid they were, lizard cosplay its own furious reflection of the amusement and contempt with which these powerful men regarded them.

Back in that summer of 2015, when I watched these giddy scenes of cascading female wrath, wrath aimed at men — who demeaned and diminished and degraded women, who ignored them and touched them against their will, who bullied and insulted them and refused to take them seriously — they felt retro, like a relic of an angry second-wave past. Here we were, in the second term of our first black president, on the verge of actually *running* a woman for the presidency who was by all estimations the favorite, a woman whose future as president of the United States of America, we were repeatedly assured, was so inevitable that its history-making character was barely discernible. It felt a world away from the era in which cameras wouldn't even cover Shirley Chisholm's convention speech.

While I understood, and made my living writing about, the persistent — and in many ways expanding — inequities faced by all kinds of Americans, especially those who were not white men, the outward signs of progress were so visible, so indisputable, that it was hard to conceive of being so belligerent. Privately, I yearned for such open, unapologetic confrontation of the men, and the male-designed systems, that until now had kept women from ever becoming president — or from holding any comparable share of political, social, or economic power — but I understood that they would feel anachronistic, theatric, and unnecessary in an age in which there were more women in colleges and graduate schools than men and our next president was probably going to be a woman.

Yet just two and half years later, while taking the subway home from the second annual Women's March, protests conceived in response to the inauguration of President Donald Trump, I scrolled through images on my social media feeds and saw another cascade of wrath. There were pictures of the marchers, middle fingers raised in vivid loathing at buildings owned by the president, who was of course *not* a woman, but rather a white supremacist, admitted sexual harasser, and businessman who'd capitalized on the fury of white America and male America to defeat a woman and replace the black man who'd previously held the job.

Some of the women I'd stood near at this 2018 march had held an effigy of Trump's testicles in the air, decorated with a poof of orange hair. Others had depicted him as a pile of excrement. I looked at homemade signs from across the nation, where protests had, for the second year in a row, taken place not just in New York and Los Angeles and Washington, but in Bangor, Anchorage, Austin, and Shreveport: "Fuck you, you fucking fuck," read one of my favorites. "Feminazis against Actual Nazis," "Fuck the Patriarchy," and "Angry Women Will Change the World" were other examples. One woman had cut out a hole for her head and written around it, "Resisting Bitch Face."

Many others held aloft signs that read "#metoo" — in one case: "me *fucking* too" — the phrase a reference to activist Tarana Burke's campaign against pervasive sexual violence inflicted on women and girls, now describing the reckoning with workplace sexual assault and harassment that had burned through the media in preceding months, a conflagration in which many powerful men had been relieved of their jobs. The #metoo movement had felt almost like a forty-five-year-late return on Flo Kennedy's promise that "The next son of a bitch that touches a woman is gonna get kicked in the balls."

And then, on the Instagram feed of a friend in San Francisco, I saw her, like something out of a 1972 fever dream: a woman riding BART, wearing enormous lizard slippers strapped above her sandals and socks, a soft, sparkly, green reptilian boob-bib across her front, and a sharp-toothed lizard's mask over her head. She was carrying a sign.

"Goddess-zilla got woke. Watch out."

This is not an emotional exploration of women's anger. There are already long,

25

fascinating volumes about the psychology and resonance of anger within our personal relationships, with more writers out there wrestling with the internal dimensions of the rage women are feeling and expressing anew. Some posit that women are inherently angry, others that women need to harness more of their fury. There are self-help books and also critical examinations of the ways in which women's anger at their subjugation plays out within their families, partnerships, friendships, and at work. This is not that book, though it will certainly touch on how personal rage and frustration have felt to many women, and the ways that they are echoed in political discourse, keeping in mind that for women, the personal is indeed always political.

But more broadly: this is about the specific nexus of women's anger and American *politics,* about how the particular dissatisfactions and resentments of America's women have often ignited movements for social change and progress. It is an exploration of how an impulse that many women have taken pains to hide or disguise or distance themselves from — the impulse to be really mad — has been crucial in determining their political power and social standing, how women's rage has played parts in

26

revolutionary social movements, and how it has shaped how women leaders and political candidates have been received.

In the United States, we have never been taught how noncompliant, insistent, furious women have shaped our history and our present, our activism and our art. We should be.

These stories exist in other cultures. *Lysistrata* is an ancient yarn about women so angry at their husbands' propensity for combat that they withhold sex until the fighting stops (a particularly self-defeating approach to female satisfaction, but one that emphasized women's power with its assurance that "no man is ever going to get satisfaction if the woman doesn't choose that he should"). The Greeks also tell the tale of Thaïs, a courtesan and companion of Alexander the Great, who urged her lover to burn down the temple of Persepolis as revenge for Persian king Xerxes's destruction of the Temple of Athena during his attack on Athens one hundred and fifty years earlier. In real life, it was Parisian women, furious and starving, who rioted over the high price of bread, leading a march to Versailles in October of 1789 that would help kick off the French Revolution and ultimately dethrone King Louis the XVI. In

27

2003 in Liberia, after fourteen years of civil war, a group of the nation's women — Muslim and Christian, indigenous and Americo-Liberian — joined together, their anger at the ravages of war put to work in a call for its end. "In the past we were silent, but after being killed, raped, dehumanized, and infected with diseases . . . war has taught us that the future lies in saying NO to violence and YES to peace!"[5] the Liberian activist Leymah Gbowee declared to a crowd of raging women at the start of their crusade. It took two years of protest, but in 2005, the women's mass action ended with the election of the nation's first female president, Ellen Johnson Sirleaf.

While we in the United States may not have been told the stories, our nation, too, has been transformed by women's anger — in response not just to sexism, but also to racism, homophobia, capitalist excess, to the many inequities to which women and those around them have been exposed. In *A Place of Rage,* a 1991 documentary about black women activists and artists, the poet June Jordan, whose writing was a tender chronicle of rage at having her liberties restricted "because I am the wrong sex, the wrong age, the wrong skin," recalled the event that brought her to her political and

28

ideological sensibilities. In her childhood in Bedford-Stuyvesant in Brooklyn, a young man in her neighborhood was beaten on his roof by the police in a case of mistaken identity. "To see this boy I idolized, who belonged to us, in the sense of our block . . . disfigured by these strangers who came in with all this force and license to use that force was really terrifying. And also it hardened me early on in a kind of place of rage."

It's crucial to remember that women's anger has been received — and often vilified or marginalized — in ways that have reflected the very same biases that provoked it: black women's fury is treated differently from white women's rage; poor women's frustrations are heard differently from the ire of the wealthy. Yet despite the varied and unjust ways America has dismissed or derided the rages of women, those rages have often borne substantive change, alterations to the nation's rules and practices, its very fabric.

This book is about women so angry at slavery and lynching that they risked their lives and reputations and pioneered new forms of public expression for women, including speeches in front of mixed-gender and mixed-race audiences; about women so

29

furious at their lack of a franchise that they walked 150 miles from New York City to Albany to petition for the vote, went on hunger strikes, and picketed outside the White House. Women so angry that they stayed angry for the decades — their lifetimes — it took to get the right to vote, first via the Nineteenth Amendment and then the Voting Rights Act, their rage leading them to acts of civil disobedience — marches and sit-ins and voting when it was not legal to do so — for which they would be jailed, beaten. Women who took conversations that had historically been whispered and chose instead to broadcast them via open-air rallies and in the pages of newspapers and in lawsuits and in front of political conventions and judiciary committees.

Anger has often been the sparking impetus for long-lasting, legal, or institutional reform in the United States. It is, in fact, the founding, canonical narrative of the nation's revolutionary rupture from England. Yet somehow the rage has rarely been acknowledged as righteous and patriotic when it has originated with women, though women have often taken pains to mimic or reference the language and sentiments of America's founding while making their own angry demands for liberty, independence,

30

and equality. So this is a book about the impulse that led an enslaved Massachusetts woman known as Mumbet, and later as Elizabeth Freeman, to hear the revolutionary rhetoric in the home in which she labored, and — in angry response to abuses she suffered at the hands of her owners, including being hit with hot kitchen implements — to apply ideas of liberty to her own circumstances and petition for her freedom; her case was instrumental to Massachusetts's abolition of slavery in 1783.

It's about how young girls laboring in the Lowell mills in the 1830s saw in their own situation a similar reflection of the insurgent rhetoric of the American Revolution, declaring that "as our fathers resisted unto blood the lordly avarice of the British ministry, so we, their daughters, never will wear the yoke which has been prepared for us," as they staged the walkouts that were one of the first iterations of what would become the American labor movement.[6] And how seventy years later, a twenty-three-year-old labor organizer named Clara Lemlich, who'd already been beaten for her participation in earlier strikes, grew impatient with all the talk from men at a meeting at Cooper Union in 1909, and stood up to call for a general strike that became the great uprising of twenty thousand shirtwaist workers, and resulted in new labor agreements with all but a few shirtwaist factories in New York. Triangle, one of the shirtwaist shops that did not give in to the strikers, burned two years later, killing 146 people inside, the vast majority women. That deadly fire would provoke the wrath of other activists, women who would in turn be driven to remake America's workplace safety regulations.

This book also aims to show how this anger — so instrumental to the nation's growth and progress — has never been celebrated, rarely even been noted in mainstream culture; how women are not lauded for their fury, and too often have had their righteous passions simply erased from the record. We aren't taught that Rosa Parks, the perfectly demure woman whose refusal to give up her seat kicked off the Montgomery Bus Boycott in 1955, was a fervent antirape activist who had once told a would-be attacker that she'd rather die than be raped by him and who, at ten years old, threatened by a white boy, picked up a piece of brick and drew it back to strike him if he approached. "I was angry," she'd later say of that youthful act of resistance. "He went his way without further comment."[7] We are

32

never forced to consider that rage — and not just stoicism, sadness, or strength — were behind the actions of the few women's heroes we're ever taught about in school, from Harriet Tubman to Susan B. Anthony. Instead, we are regularly fed and we regularly ingest cultural messages that suggest that women's rage is irrational, dangerous, or laughable.

This book is about how anger works for men in ways that it does not for women, how men like both Donald Trump and Bernie Sanders can wage yelling campaigns and be credited with understanding — and compellingly channeling — the rage felt by their supporters while their female opponents can be jeered and mocked as shrill for speaking too loudly or forcefully into a microphone. This is about women, some of whom have been angry for a long time, but didn't have an outlet for it, didn't realize how many of their neighbors, their coworkers, their friends and mothers and sisters, felt the same, until someone yelled, loud and fierce and ugly, and everyone heard her. It's about women who found themselves at the Women's March holding signs, and experienced a kind of awakening there — one third of those women had never been to a political protest before — and wondered

33

for the first time how on earth they'd been lulled to sleep in the first place.[8]

Which means that this is also a story about women's anger at one another: at the kinds of privileges and incentives certain women — white women — have been offered in exchange for shutting off or turning down their anger, and about the price other women — nonwhite and especially black women — have paid, always having *had* reasons to be angry and having rarely been offered reprieve or reward for the act of suppressing it.

In her book *Anger and Forgiveness,* the philosopher Martha Nussbaum argues that anger in both personal and political contexts is an inherently vengeful impulse, and is therefore punitive and counterproductive. But not all political anger is about a drive to get even; it's not necessarily about seeing a president and his cronies rot in the jails they put so many struggling Americans in; it's not just about those who want to lock *him* up. It can also stem from a straightforward objection to injustice, a desire to free those who've been unjustly constrained or harmed. For women, who have long had their anger censured, vilified, ridiculed, tsked as incivility, the pressure to *not be angry,* to bottle up their resentments, or

34

conversely, the pushback they've encountered when they've chosen to express themselves, has often been the vengeful, punitive act to begin with.

As another philosopher, Myisha Cherry, has recently argued, "I want to convince you that there are types of anger that are not bad." In particular, she is interested in anger at injustice, regarding it as a wholly appropriate response to inequity. "Here are some of the features of the anger at injustice: it recognizes wrongdoing. This recognition is not mistaken; this person is not delusional or making this up in their head. It is not selfish. So when someone is angry at injustice they're not just concerned with themselves but also other people . . . this anger does not violate other people's rights and most importantly, it desires change."[9]

As Cherry makes clear, political anger — which can stem from personal fury and be felt individually, but which is distinct from a personalized and punitive anger — can be, and in many cases has been, far more expansive and optimistic in its goals than the anger Nussbaum describes; it can be a communicative tool, a call to action, engagement, and collaboration between ideological compatriots, who, without first having made their ire loud and public, would not

35

have known that they had the numbers to form an army, or to see past differences and toward powerful cooperation.

This is a book that seeks to identify the warmth and righteousness of women's rage, but not simply to cheer it. Because it does have limits, perils; of course it can corrode. Anger at injustice and inequality is in many ways exactly like fuel. A necessary accelerant, it can drive — on some level *must* drive — noble and difficult crusades. But it is also combustible, explosive; its power can be unpredictable and can burn.

In an era of renewed rage, an age of women who are as mad as hell, this is a volume that examines how this emotion has functioned in our past — what it has brought us and what damage it has wrought — at the same time that it questions where it will take this nation next. On some real level, it is bananas that women's rage has never been given its proper due, its historical credit, that too few historians and journalists have noticed the catalytic role that furious women — speaking alone or working together against tyranny or oppression or injustice — have played in shaping and reshaping this country, in moving it closer to where it must be if it is to fulfill its patriotic, and yet unmet, promise of equality.

But it also posits that there is a lesson in how hard the powerful — very often the white and the male — have worked to shut up angry women, to divert attention from them. In 1964, the civil rights activist Fannie Lou Hamer began to give her testimony before the Democratic National Convention's credentials committee about how she had been arrested and then badly beaten by police after attempting to register voters in Mississippi. The president, Lyndon B. Johnson, concerned that Hamer's speech would alienate white voters, held an impromptu press conference about the nine-month anniversary of John F. Kennedy's death, forcing the news networks to turn away from Hamer's words and instead broadcast his own. Johnson knew that Hamer's anger would be meaningful and sought to draw America's attention away from it.[10]

On some level, if not intellectual than animal, there has *always* been an understanding of the power of women's anger: that as an oppressed majority in the United States, women have long had within them the potential to rise up in fury, to take over a country in which they've never really been

37

offered their fair or representative stake. Perhaps the reason that women's anger is so broadly denigrated — treated as so ugly, so alienating, and so irrational — is because we have known all along that with it came the explosive power to upturn the very systems that have sought to contain it.

What becomes clear, when we look to the past with an eye to the future, is that the discouragement of women's anger — via silencing, erasure, and repression — stems from the correct understanding of those in power that in the fury of women lies the power to change the world.

I am a white woman who has been angry in my life and my work, occasionally on my own behalf but more often about politics, about inequity, and the grotesque *unfairness* of the world, this country, how it was built and who it still excludes and systematically diminishes. Some of that rage has become the driving force of my professional life. For fifteen years I have written, as a journalist, about women in media and politics and entertainment from a feminist perspective; that work itself has been rooted in anger, and in turn often strengthened by critics who got mad at me, and forced me to reconsider my perspective and think differ-

38

ently and more rigorously about race and class and sexuality and identity and opportunity. I value my own rage and the rage of others, especially of women.

But I also live in the world. I have, for years, made the rage that guided my work appear palatable. I'd absorbed the message that open anger was needlessly overdramatic and unattractive — that it would be too *much,* really — and I had worked to accommodate these assumptions, tempering my fury in my writing. As thoughtful as I tried to be about contemporary gendered, racial, and economic inequality, I'd nevertheless, on some level, swallowed the myth that circumstances were no longer so severe that they called for, or could be effectively addressed by, livid public display. I had soaked in the admonition — implicit from the moment I was first taught about a version of Martin Luther King, Jr. that was never angry, that I first understood that to be called a Dworkinist (as I was by some commenters on my stories who compared me to the radical feminist Andrea Dworkin) was a bad thing — that women who talked too loudly and too aggressively were considered immensely unappealing, sexually and intellectually, by the men whose opinions still shaped the world. That to be openly angry was a bad idea. That even when things were bad, a nonconfrontational approach was preferable, for strategic, aesthetic, and moral reasons.

So I was funny! And playful, cheeky, ironic, knowing! I worked to make it clear that I am a fun person who enjoys friends and beer and laughter. I took great care to be nice and respectful to opposing viewpoints. To full-throatedly express my ire would have been alienating, tactically unsound. I have watched as my peers have made similar choices. When feminism came roaring back to life, those of us who were engaging its new idioms and locutions were careful to distance ourselves from the angry ghosts we'd been assured haunted feminism's past. It is ironic that the generation that I, in some unconscious way, worked to distance myself from is now the generation that thrills me in its bonkers rage: the women who yelled at men and gave every direct indication that they had had it with their bullshit. Yet when I was younger, it was important that I made every effort to differentiate my wise-but-cool, sharp-but-easygoing critique from that past radicalism.

But all the good humor and in-jokes can't cover for the reality of wrath, the thing that makes you want to hit a wall or smash a glass or throw something, the electric impulse that occasionally streaks across our brains, making reason fuzz out, and our insides light up like firecrackers, in a way that does not permit hearty laughs over cold beers. Many of us who may have covered our fury in humor have occasionally found ourselves exploding.

In 2014, I was writing a semiregular column for the *New Republic.* One day, I was tired. I was pregnant. I was mad at my workplace for a variety of reasons having to do with my pregnancy and my economic status in relation to my gender. I read some things in other publications that pissed me off: a patronizing story by a man congratulating women over forty on suddenly being "hot"; a piece about the constant appraisals of Hillary Clinton's facial expressions; a story about teenaged boys speculating over a young woman's HIV status; the tale of a sixteen-year-old Houston girl who'd been drugged and assaulted and then had photos of her naked, limp body posted on social media; a *New York Times* investigation of a college's botched handling of a sexual assault case. This was the summer when a woman had been jailed and separated from her child for using meth while pregnant, and a mother had been arrested for letting her nine-year-old play alone while she worked her McDonald's shift; the Supreme Court had decided that corporations could elect not to cover birth control for their employees based on religious belief, and also that abortion clinic protesters were free to get close-up into the faces of women seeking reproductive health care and offer their jeering judgment.

The column I wrote, quickly, was its own meta-reflection on my willingness to get mad in public: in it, I expressed my yearning for a world in which women's worth was no longer measurable on scales fashioned by men, be they cultural, legal, legislative . . . or expressive. For a moment, I felt completely done with — temporarily unable to tolerate — the male-determined metrics of female acceptability, and in my exhausted ire, I did something that I had previously understood to be unacceptable: I wrote out of acidic and untempered anger, drawing on a remembered moment recalled in the comedian Tina Fey's memoir, in which she'd described how fellow comedian Amy Poehler had once unexpectedly wheeled around on a male colleague who'd told her that her vulgar jokes weren't cute and said "I don't fucking care if you like it." Perhaps

42

for the first time in my writing life, I myself did not fucking care if readers liked that I was mad.

I didn't know, then, about what Rosa Parks had reportedly told her terrified grandmother after explaining why she'd raised that brick at the boy who'd been threatening her: "I would rather be lynched than live to be mistreated and not be allowed to say 'I don't like it.' " I had no idea how old and deep and urgent was women's impulse to sometimes just let their fury out without a care to how it would be evaluated, even if that expression of rage put them at risk: in young Rosa Parks's case, at the risk of death; in my case, at the risk of being mocked on the internet.

To my surprise, that column quickly became the most popular I'd ever written; it went viral; someone made T-shirts reading "I don't care if you like it"; my friend from an evangelical midwestern community told me that her religious childhood friends were posting it on their Facebook pages. There had been something in my eruption that had worked, communicatively.

It's not a formula I have ever tried to replicate; explosive fury cannot be faked. But I have permitted myself more often in the years since to write out of anger when I

43

felt it and to express it in speeches and on television. Sometimes — once, memorably, at the height of #metoo — an editor has advised me not to publish, and I have heeded the advice, because I am all too sensitive to the ways in which anger can backfire strategically. But then, during the fall of 2016, after the presidential debate to which Donald Trump had brought women who had accused Hillary Clinton's husband of sexual misconduct, I went onto a cable news show, shaking and red-faced with rage at the degradation directed toward the first female candidate for the presidency. That clip, too, went briefly viral, and I got hundreds of messages from people telling me how much it had meant to them to hear someone say out loud what they'd been longing to yell.

What I have glimpsed, in the moments when I have let myself give voice to the deep, rich, curdled fury that for years I tried to pretty up and make easier on everyone's stomach, is that for all the care we take to bottle it up, rage can be a powerful tonic. It is a communicative tool, which speakers and writers and activists not only find freeing, but which acts as a balm to listeners and readers struggling with their own subsumed vexations.

44

We must come to recognize — those of us who feel anger, who have in our lives taken pains to disguise it, who worry about its ill effects, who rear back from it and try to tamp it down in ourselves for fear that letting it out will hurt our goals — that anger is often an exuberant expression. It is the force that injects energy, intensity, and urgency into battles that must be intense and urgent if they are to be won. More broadly, we must come to recognize our own rage as valid, as rational, and not as what we're told it is: ugly, hysterical, marginal, laughable.

I first decided to write this book as a means to channel and make sense of my own rage: how I've suppressed it or cloaked it in more officially attractive stuff. After the 2016 election, and two years of having been assured every day by the political press, by popular culture, by my friends and by those on the right and the left that there was no reason for women to be angry — that sexism would not be a factor in the candidacy of Hillary Clinton, that she was in fact the candidate with the disproportionate share of power; that the impulses guiding the support of Donald Trump were not sexism, racism, or xenophobia but rather economic anxiety; that it was the anger of *his* sup-

45

porters that we needed to be paying attention to and that *in fact,* it was the overheated expressions of feminism and civil rights activism that had provoked white America into this Trumpian frenzy to begin with — I felt as though I might lose my mind with the rage I'd not been able to give full voice to.

I had to look into women's rage in America: how it has been suppressed, discouraged, discounted, when I felt very surely that it was central to our growth and history as a nation. When I began to tell people I was writing about women's anger and social change, I began to understand the depth and breadth and desperation of other women's desire to talk about their fury. Women told me they *needed* to read, and to write themselves, and to talk about their anger, even if it was in an email to me or in a tweet or conversation with their friends. They couldn't hold it in anymore, to keep it bottled up one more second would make them explode. What did they hope to gain from letting it out? I asked many of them. Validation was the answer I got, over and over again.

Here's the validation that I hope it can offer: that those who are furious right now are not alone, are not crazy, are not unattractive. That in fact, female rage in America has a long and righteous history, one that we have, very pointedly, never been taught.

But also, crucially: the women who are *suddenly* angry, newly angry, and are discombobulated by the intensity of their rage, are not the first to have felt this way. They did not invent rage at injustice, and in addition to realizing that they are in good company, they will find excellent models for activism and expression in the women around them who have never *not* been angry, and who have done so much work already to change things in America for the better.

We've got to think about these things — history and future — because we are in the midst of a potentially revolutionary moment: not one in which all wrongs will be righted or errors fixed. But one with the potential for a big alteration in who has power in this country. Progress in America takes a punishingly long time; but it also happens in fits and bursts, sometimes in reaction to terrible, deadening, deeply damaging setbacks. We are in one of those moments now, and we need to pay attention, to be aware of what is possible if we think hard about what we're angry about, and what needs to change. Because change *can*

47

happen quickly.

At the height of the #metoo-inspired movement around sexual harassment in early 2018, I sat at a family holiday table listening to my mother and my aunt tell stories of their early days in academia, in the 1960s and early 1970s. Sisters from a farm in northern Maine, both women went on to get PhDs from the same graduate school and go into the same field. My mother, just five years older than my aunt, recalled going on the job market after earning her degree and seeing interview postings that read "We will not be hiring a woman for this position." At one interview, she was told as she walked in the door, "We're not considering women, but I thought it was unfair that they didn't get practice interviewing, so you can have a trial run." At another, she was told, "You're very good, but we already have one of you in the department." By the time her sister came along, just five years later, these hiring practices were not only frowned upon, they were illegal.

They were illegal in part because those years in which women, mad at how they were discriminated against and harassed, had expressed their fury, had brought lawsuits. Some had become lawyers them-

48

selves, and some of these, including Eleanor Holmes Norton and Ruth Bader Ginsburg, went to work advocating for women. A willingness to be mad as hell changed the legal system and provoked legislative changes and protections, including the Civil Rights Act, altering the professional landscape for my aunt, in ways that would have been inconceivable to even her older sister.

That same week in 2018, again talking about the frankly terrifying intensity of the #metoo movement, my friend Esther Kaplan, an editor of the Investigative Fund at The Nation Institute, told me that the furor had made her think back to the era of feminist consciousness raising, of how women in the 1970s had gathered together in suburban homes and city apartments, had talked about liberation and equality and sexuality. They had learned to look at their own bodies and lives in new ways, to recognize the ways in which their domestic arrangements subjugated them, to question what they'd always been taught was the way things were.

"Those women *left their husbands*," Esther marveled to me, noting with wonder that "social movements have the potential to radically change us, not just radically change the world." What she was pointing

49

out was that this contemporary wave of women's rage in the early twenty-first century — over sexual assault and harassment and workplace discrimination and political power imbalances — *also* entailed a wholesale reevaluation of women's pasts, a remaking of their perspectives, on themselves and on gendered power and its abuses. And of course it was happening at unprecedented speed, thanks to the internet. "This kind of thing can be culturally explosive, radical, out of control." She meant this, and I understood it, positively. But for some, the eruptive velocity is too much.

She's right, the fury can upend institutions, cut through our bedrock assumptions, and remake the geography of possibility. Not only did the consciousness raising of the 1970s result in a massive spike in the divorce rate, it also created a next generation that wanted to avoid the pitfalls of broken marriages that their parents had experienced, a population of women who expected more from the institution and so delayed marriage, or didn't marry at all, and instead expanded the possibilities for women to enjoy economic, social, and sexual independence. Those women's lives were remapped. Generations of women moved forward at new speed, their dependency not just on marriage but on men wholly revised. The anger of the second wavers, anger that has been used to caricature them as retrospectively unappealing, had blown off the doors for their daughters and their granddaughters.

The black feminist Audre Lorde famously argued in her germinal essay "The Uses of Anger," which is about women responding to racism, including the racism of other women, that "every woman has a well-stocked arsenal of anger potentially useful against those oppressions, personal and institutional, which brought that anger into being. Focused with precision it can become a powerful source of energy, serving progress and change." Lorde was very firm that she did not mean temporary, cosmetic change, not simply "the ability to smile or feel good." Rather, she argued, well-aimed anger from women can lead to "a basic and radical alteration in those assumptions underlining our lives."

On February 14, 2018, a gunman who had stalked an ex-girlfriend shot and killed seventeen people at Marjory Stoneman Douglas High School in Parkland, Florida. That afternoon, in response to a tweet from Donald Trump, offering "prayers and condolences" to the families of victims, one of the survivors of the shooting, sixteen-year-old Sarah Chadwick, tweeted "I don't want your condolences you fucking piece of shit, my friends and teachers were shot. Do something instead of sending prayers. Prayers won't fix this. But gun control will prevent it from happening again." Chadwick's livid message was retweeted 144,000 times before it was made unavailable; the rage it expressed would help to set the furious tone for what would become the Parkland students' righteous crusade to alter the gun laws in the United States.

The day after her tweet, Chadwick returned to Twitter under a different handle, and again addressed the president, making clear that while she had been chastised for her profanity, she had no intention of backing away from the rage that had undergirded it, the rage that would continue to drive her and her classmates toward changing the nation. "I apologize for the profanity and harsh comment I made," she wrote. "I'm a grieving sixteen-year-old girl who lost friends, teachers, and peers yesterday. I was and am still angry. I am apologizing for my comment but not for my anger."

We cannot afford to dismiss or fetishize or marginalize or rear back from women's anger any longer if we want this moment to be transformative. We have to look at it straight, stop hemming and hawing around it or trying to disavow it or worrying that it might offend and discomfit. It must be and always has been at the heart of social progress.

PART I
ERUPTION

PART 1
ERUPTION

I remember the first time I got angry. I was about ten. We were at McDonald's with our family friends, who were African American. I'm really light-skinned, my mom has light skin, so a lot of people don't always recognize that we are Mexicans. But our friends were very dark-skinned. The woman who was at the counter — who in retrospect was almost certainly herself a Mexican immigrant — let us play in the ball pit but didn't let our friends play. My mom fucking flipped her shit. She screamed like a banshee at this woman in the McDonald's. My mom said "I will never come back. I will tell all my friends never to come here. Give me the number of *your* manager; is there a regional manager? I'm going to call corporate headquarters." She just blew a gasket. Then she took us all out for ice cream and we all got gigantic sundaes that we had no business eating. I remember watching her and thinking: She's doing the right thing.

— Jessica Morales

CHAPTER ONE:
SLEEPING GIANT

The contemporary reemergence of women's rage as a mass impulse comes after decades of feminist deep freeze. The years following the great social movements of the twentieth century — the women's movement, the civil rights movement, the gay rights movement — were shaped by deeply reactionary politics. When Phyllis Schlafly led an antifeminist crusade to stop the ratification of the Equal Rights Amendment — the twenty-four-word constitutional amendment that would have guaranteed equal rights regardless of gender — finally succeeding in 1982, it was a sign that the second-wave feminist movement of the 1970s, and the righteous fury that had ignited it, had been sidelined.

More broadly, the Reagan era, in which increasingly hard-right reactionary politics had joined with a religious "moral majority," gave rise to a cultural backlash to all sorts of social progress. Under sharp attack were the benefits, rights, and protections that afforded poor women any stability, as well as the parts of the women's movement that had produced legal, professional, and educational gains for middle-class women, better enabling them to live independently, outside of marriage, the patriarchal institution that had historically contained them and on which they had long depended.

The right wing of the 1980s was driven to restrict abortion access and deregulate Wall Street while simultaneously destroying the social safety net, which Ronald Reagan had made sure was embodied by the specter of the black welfare queen. A 1986 *Newsweek* cover story, meanwhile, blared the news that a single woman at forty was more likely to get killed by a terrorist than get married. That later-debunked study was a key point of Susan Faludi's chronicle of the era, *Backlash,* in which she tracked the varied, suffocating ways in which women's anger was muffled throughout the Reagan years: how feminist activism was blamed for the purported "man shortage"; the day-care that enabled women to work outside the home vilified as dangerous for children.

Popular culture showed liberated white career women as oversexed monsters, as in *Fatal Attraction,* or as cold, shoulder-padded harpies who had to be saved via hetero-union or punished via romantic rejection (see Diane Keaton in *Baby Boom,* Sigourney Weaver in *Working Girl*). There was far too little space afforded to black heroines, and even some of the most nuanced were often crafted to serve male creators' investments in how women's liberation might serve their messages: Spike Lee's view of the sexually voracious Nola Darling in the 1986 film *She's Gotta Have It* and Bill Cosby's Clair Huxtable, the successful matriarch who, given the context of Cosby's own racial politics, served as a repudiation of black women who were *not* wealthy hetero-married mothers with law degrees.

Who wanted to be a feminist? No one. And the anxiety about the term wasn't about any of the *good* reasons to be skeptical of feminism — like the movement's racial exclusions and elisions — but because the term itself, the idea of public and politicized challenge to male dominance, had been successfully coded as unattractively old, as crazy, as ugly. Susan Sarandon, the rare celebrity who actually maintained her publicly left politics through the 1980s and 90s, once explained why even she of the unrelenting commitment to disruptive political speech preferred the misnomer "humanist" to calling herself a "feminist": "it's less alienating to people who think of feminism as being a load of strident bitches."[1]

To be sure, there were eruptions of fury, coming from people — often from women — who were waging battles against inequities. In 1991, the law professor Anita Hill testified in front of an all-white, all-male Senate Judiciary Committee that Clarence Thomas, her former boss at the Equal Employment Opportunity Commission, then a nominee for the Supreme Court, had sexually harassed her. Many women were taken aback by the way the committee insulted, dismissed, and ultimately disbelieved Hill, confirming Thomas to the court, where he sits today.

"It was so stark, watching these men grill this woman in these big chairs and looking down at her," Patty Murray, senator from Washington state, has recalled. Murray and a lot of other women were so outraged by the treatment of Hill that an unprecedented number of them ran for office in 1992. Four, including Murray, won Senate seats; one of them, Carol Moseley Braun, became the first-ever African-American woman elected to the Senate. Twenty-four women were elected to the House of Representa-

62

tives for the first time, more than had been elected in any other previous decade.

These years sometimes included violent rage in response to racism: in 1992, after four white cops were acquitted by a mostly white jury in the brutal beating of African-American taxi driver Rodney King in Los Angeles, the city erupted in fury. Angry protesters looted stores and set fires; sixty-three people died. At the time, the news media and local politicians were quick to describe the events as riots, throwing around the term "thugs."

But one Los Angeles Democratic representative saw something else in the riots: "There are those who would like for me . . . to tell people to go inside, to be peaceful, that they have to accept the verdict. I accept the responsibility of asking people not to endanger their lives. I am not asking people not to be angry," said first-term congresswoman Maxine Waters, who represented a big part of the South Central Los Angeles neighborhood where much of the unrest was unfolding. "I am angry and I have a right to that anger and the people out there have a right to that anger."[2]

Waters spent days tending to her constituents, bringing food, water, and diapers to Angelenos living without gas or electricity;

she also pushed to charge the police officers civilly, and objected to Mayor Tom Bradley's use of the word "riot" to describe events. Instead, she saw the politically rational frame for the resentments being expressed, calling it "an insurrection."[3]

Eventually, Los Angeles Police Chief Daryl Gates was fired, and two of the police officers were convicted for violating Rodney King's civil rights.[4] There were other moments of political protest: those against the World Trade Organization in Seattle in 1999 and marches against the invasion of Iraq in 2003, for example. But much of the spirit of mass, brash, sustained political fury that had animated the 1960s and 1970s was muffled in the 1980s and stayed that way for decades.

The journalist Mychal Denzel Smith has written of how this suppression worked itself out around expressions of black rage in the years in which he'd grown up, noting that during most of the 1990s, "there was no longer a Reagan or a Bush to serve as an identifiable enemy," and that a pop commitment to "multiculturalism" permitted the illusion that racial progress had been achieved, so rage as a mass impulse had subsided.[5]

There had been a brief revival during the

64

second Bush administration, Smith argued, recalling how, in the wake of the derelict response to Hurricane Katrina, rapper Kanye West had yelled that George W. Bush "doesn't care about black people." But that surge of fury had been quieted by the presidential campaign of Barack Obama. Obama's historic drive had relied in part on his ability to reassure white voters that he was not an angry black man, that he was cut from a different cloth than some of his more bellicose black predecessors, including Jesse Jackson and Al Sharpton, and did not in his demeanor threaten white supremacy. But Obama's reputation for cordiality was gravely imperiled by the appearance of old-style black rage, when Reverend Jeremiah Wright, the man who had married the Obamas, became a campaign story, along with his much-played sermon, during which he'd exhorted, "God *damn* America!" The specter of Wright's version of confrontational blackness was enough to remind America of Obama's outsider status, and thus Obama was forced to quash it, becoming, in Smith's words, "the first viable black presidential candidate to throw water on the flames of black rage." The anger expressed by Wright, Obama would say in his famous speech on race, "is not always

65

productive; indeed, all too often it distracts attention from solving real problems."

But partway through the Obama administration, some political fury had begun to bubble over and break through this veneer of calm, in part driven by, or in ways that meaningfully sidelined, the angry voices of women.

ANGER RIGHT AND LEFT

Perhaps the most politically effective strike came from the right, with the Tea Party protests that began in 2009, soon after President Barack Obama took office. In response to Obama's plan to bail out some homeowners who'd been caught in the housing crisis, cable news reporter Rick Santelli angrily called on television for the "Tea Party" to object. The reference, of course, was to the 1773 revolutionary protest of colonists who threw tea in Boston Harbor to register their objection to being taxed by Britain, which was using tariffs not to support the colonies but to stabilize its own floundering economy, and had imposed them on colonists who had no representation in British Parliament.[6]

The contemporary version was portrayed as a leaderless grassroots movement, though almost from its start, right-wing mega

66

donors the Koch brothers had been funding its protests and its candidates. In theory, the agitation was in response to the far right's view that Barack Obama's administration was misusing taxpayer money, but the Tea Party was also driven by a wave of revanchist rage and racial resentment toward Barack Obama; no amount of non-confrontational rhetoric could convince overwhelmingly white Tea Partiers he wasn't a threat to their status and supremacy.

Though the public face of the Tea Party protesters was that of furious white men — often dressed in colonial-era tricorn hats in their early gatherings — some polls indicated that the majority of the faction's supporters were women. Its most audible early female voice belonged to former vice-presidential candidate Sarah Palin, who in one address to activists called the movement "another revolution." In 2010, a number of Tea Party–affiliated female candidates ran; Palin, who'd cast herself as a pit-bullish hockey mom, dubbed them "Mama Grizzlies." And while the movement's theatrics — funny hats and grizzly bears — were reminiscent of some of the performative exertions of the Second Wave, its mission was the precise opposite, more of a callback to the Schlafly-led antifeminist crusades of the 1970s and 80s.

Somehow, as with Schlafly, these women voicing their anger and throwing around their political weight weren't caricatured as ugly hysterics; instead they were permitted to cast themselves as patriotic moms on steroids, some bizarro-world embodiment of female empowerment, despite the fact (or, more precisely, *because* of the fact) that what they were advocating was a return to traditionalist roles for women and reduced government investment in nonwhite people. Once they landed in the United States Congress, their obsessive mission was to vote to take away the federal funding received by family planning programs, to outlaw abortion, to punish Planned Parenthood, and to reduce government safety net programs such as food stamps and what remained of welfare.

"Conservative women have found their voices and are using them, actively and loudly," Tea Partier Rebecca Wales told *Politico* in 2010. Another Tea Partier, Darla Dawald, put it this way: "You know the old saying 'If Mama ain't happy, ain't nobody happy'? When legislation messes with Mama's kids and it affects her family, then Mama comes out fighting — and I don't mean in a violent way, of course."[7]

As more moderate Republicans got knocked out of their seats by Tea Party candidates, and those who remained moved further right, an angry protest in New York was drawing crowds of agitators from the other side. In the fall of 2011, in Zuccotti Park in downtown Manhattan, young people gathered to voice their fury at economic inequality, the widening gap between rich and poor, the rampant deregulation of and tax breaks for corporate America and Wall Street, and the steady gutting of social welfare programs.

Occupy Wall Street's impact on the American left was crucial and long-lasting; the movement helped to popularize the view of economic inequality that set the 99 percent against the nation's richest 1 percent. It was both a symptom and a fomenter of increased interest in socialist economic policy. That interest would help push the Democratic Party — which had for decades run screaming from the notion of even "liberalism" — further left, boosting the profiles and fortunes of politicians including Elizabeth Warren, who was elected Senator for Massachusetts in 2012, and Bernie Sanders, an independent who'd served in Congress for twenty-six years and would mount an electrifying campaign for the presidency in 2016.

Many different types of people participated in Occupy — estimates varied, but reportedly around 40 percent of the protesters were women, and 37 percent identified as nonwhite, making it *far* closer to representative of the United States than, say, Congress.[8-10] Yet despite the fact that its structure was consciously collaborative and nonhierarchical, it was nevertheless a movement dominated publicly by the voices and ideas of white men. There were enough allegations of rape, groping, and sexual assault at Zuccotti Park that after several weeks, women-only tents were set up. Kanene Holder, an artist, activist, and black woman who served as one of Occupy's spokespeople, told the *Guardian* that even within this progressive space, "white males are used to speaking and running things. . . . You can't expect them to abdicate the power they have just because they are in this movement." Eventually, Occupy had to adopt special sessions in which women were encouraged to speak uninterrupted.[11]

More than that, some of the righteously radical men who dominated Occupy were reportedly inhospitable to internal feminist critique. As one activist, Ren Jender, wrote

70

after a proposal to better address sexual assault allegations was met with defensive anger from some of these radically progressive men, "I wasn't angry with only the people who . . . said stupid, misogynistic shit . . . I was angry with the greater number of people who hadn't confronted the misogyny."[12] Occupy was a reminder to many who agreed with its principles that the left was no more free of gender hierarchies and power abuses than the rest of the country.

Then, in 2013, in the wake of the acquittal of George Zimmerman in the murder of seventeen-year-old Trayvon Martin, the longtime progressive activist Alicia Garza wrote a note on Facebook, which concluded with the sentences, "Black people, I love you. I love us. We matter. Our lives matter." The artist and activist Patrisse Khan-Cullors appended a hashtag to it, #Black LivesMatter; the writer and community organizer Opal Tometi helped to push the message out over social media.

A movement — born of grief, horror, and unleashed fury at the persistent killing of African Americans by the state, by the police — was born. And while it, like Occupy and the Tea Party, was purposefully nonhierarchical in its internal structure, it had been founded by women, and many of

71

the most prominent voices of the movement belonged to women, including Brittany Packnett, Johnetta Elzie, Nekima Levy-Pounds, and Elle Hearns. Khan-Cullors later wrote of how black liberation movements of the past had been led largely by straight men, "leaving women, who are often queer or transgender, either out of the movement or in the background to move the work forward with little or no recognition. As younger organizers, we recognized a need to center the leadership of women."[13]

Black Lives Matter increased national awareness of common racist policing practices that had remained largely invisible, especially to white eyes, but which millions of Americans now understand to be a systemic reality. The movement, which spread across the country and the world, staged days of protest in Ferguson, Missouri, after the police killing of Michael Brown; activists pioneered a new age of public demonstration, staging "die-ins," in which protesters laid on the ground in recognition of African Americans gunned down in the streets. In 2015, in the wake of the mass killing of black churchgoers by a white man in Charleston, activist Bree Newsome scaled the flagpole at the South Carolina State House, removing the Confederate flag that had long hung there, an act that provoked a wave of removal of statues of Confederate leaders throughout the South.

So in the years leading up to the 2016 election, there was a building, public rage — rage that had an impact on politics, on civic structures, on public spaces. More than that, there were women finding contemporary ways to broadcast their powerful, desperately felt anger to the nation. And, at least on the left, they were doing it in a way that specifically challenged patriarchal, male-dominated histories of movement-building.

But in mainstream feminism, there was a different spirit. Hot fury — expressed through public acts of protest, mass movements to the streets, or defiant profanity bellowed loudly at the powerful — was simply not the main mode of feminist expression. And it's not that feminism itself was in remission.

FEMINIST COOL

What used to be called "the women's movement" had found energetic new life in the media in the first decades of the twenty-first century. After years of backlash, feminist journalists and bloggers had revived a conversation about gender, and many of us

73

who participated in that conversation were angry — angry about sexism, and racism, and economic inequality, and how all of these injustices were woven together. But, perhaps anxious to differentiate ourselves from our spitting-mad forebears, many contemporary feminists (including me) had worked to make the expression of our frustrations sound agreeable, relatable, and inviting to others, including to the very men who might have a hand in oppressing us.

The popular feminist site Feministing used the ironic image of a sexy mudflap girl flipping the bird as its mascot; young feminists traded in jokey signifiers of man-hating: mugs and T-shirts reading "I bathe in male tears" and "misandry." The hashtag #banmen conveyed frustration with bad men in a way that strenuously mocked the absurd notion that feminists hated *all* men. And while plenty of men's rights activists did not see these sentiments as funny or ironic, the exaggerations radiated reassurance: that a truly abrasive challenge to patriarchy wasn't a real political threat, rather the stuff of screen-printed punch lines.

There *was* a heated movement to combat sexual assault on campus, and, in 2011 and 2012, a string of vibrant street protests, dubbed Slutwalks, in which women furiously objected to the victim-blaming to which they were so often subjected. The Slutwalks were, perhaps, the first sign that a more raw grade of feminist fury was about to erupt. But they too trafficked in a kind of winking, eroticized irony: the reembrace of a degrading but sexualized word, the "I [heart] sluts" buttons, the marchers dressed in short skirts and garters; it was all in line with another aspect of revived feminism: its exuberant positivity about sex.

"Sex positivity" was a theory that had sprung up in response to anti-porn activists during ideological wars waged by another generation; it endorsed the idea that any kind of sexual behavior, from celibacy to kink, might bring women pleasure, and not on terms laid out by a misogynistic culture. In the hands of a new generation, however, it had become a kind of shorthand for boosterism, as opposed to a censor, of sex: all sex, as long as it was consensual. And it could sometimes feel as though the eagerness to express a feminist sexual appetite was a strategic attempt to obscure or distract from more unpleasant challenges to male power. So while plenty of writers weighed in powerfully on gendered and racial injustice, many were also penning essays defend-

75

ing a feminist prerogative to wear makeup and sky-high heels and scanty outfits. And that was fine; it just also sent a direct message: that when it came to clashing with male sexual expectation, this wave of feminism wasn't so spiky, wasn't so aggressively rigid and confrontational. New, mainstream feminism was funny, hip, enthusiastic about sex . . . and kind of cool.

And, not for nothing, it worked! In the years leading up to 2016 feminism was becoming a bit trendy. There were all-women reboots of *Ghostbusters* and female Jedis and powerful female leads all over television — tough and complicated women created by Shonda Rhimes, feminist heroines like *The Good Wife*'s Alicia, and the stoned, raunchy heroines of *Broad City* — whose stories exposed the limitations still put on women by the patriarchy. But a lot of the critique was at a remove — analytical and observed, not vulgar, not *animal.* Not angry.

In 2013 Facebook mogul Sheryl Sandberg published *Lean In,* a book looking at the disadvantages still faced by women in the workplace; it focused largely on individual behavioral strategies to get around inequities, earning sharp, fair criticism for not focusing more on systemic overhaul. This

76

incomplete but unapologetic expression of feminist complaint, from someone who had risen within the system, became a massive bestseller.

The next year, Beyoncé performed at the MTV Video Music Awards, backed up by a recording of Chimamanda Ngozi Adichie's TED Talk "We Should All Be Feminists": "We teach girls to shrink themselves, to make themselves smaller. We say to girls 'You can have ambition, but not too much. You should aim to be successful, but not too successful. Otherwise, you will threaten the man.' " Then up came a giant bright sign, "FEMINIST," and Beyoncé, glittering like a disco ball, stood in front of it.

It was pop culture, packaged and polished to a high gloss. But it was also a feminist assertion — all too prescient, as it would turn out — delivered by a woman of color, citing another woman of color, a crucial but powerful correction to the ways in which media had historically (and falsely) presented the project of women's liberation as having been led by white women. Here was a woman who had amassed enough power — had become, arguably, the most powerful person in pop music — to create her own narrative: she was not left at the margins to yell at media about what they were getting

77

wrong or ignoring. Beyoncé had certainly made compromises with power structures; bell hooks had described her as "this super rich, very powerful black female" who had worked "in the service of imperialist, white supremacist capitalist patriarchy."[14] But she also seemed to have delivered on the promise of what a new, less furious, less confrontational approach to feminism could achieve: broad, attractive appeal.

And that was it, wasn't it? The loud angry battles waged by earlier generations of women had produced some dramatic results. An admittedly small number of women who had gained unprecedented power — within colleges and graduate schools, in business, in entertainment, in media, in politics — had begun to enjoy opportunity and power that had historically been denied. And if those women wanted to move forward, they couldn't afford to behave in the confrontational, angry ways that had marked a past approach to a fight for something closer to actual equality. Because that challenge, that fury, would designate them as outsiders, as marginal. To have climbed within the system was to agree not to tear it down, not to remind America too aggressively of its gender and racial inequities or distract from the cheery view of progress and empowerment.

Anyone who wants power within a white male power structure has been asked to quell anything that sounds like wrath, to reassure that they come in cooperative peace and are not looking to mete out repercussion against those who have oppressed or subjugated them. Women signaling fury — by cursing, organizing, marching, yelling, threatening retribution — would have been marked as unstable forces, exactly what couldn't happen going into a 2016 election in which there seemed for the first time in American history to be a chance that the country would elect a woman and protect the legacy of the nation's first black president.

As Hillary Clinton geared up to run for the presidency, the stakes were far too high for the kind of anger that had been so openly and defiantly expressed by the activists — in suffrage, abolition, civil rights, feminism — whose achievements had, ironically, made her candidacy possible. Female power was visible at the Video Music Awards, it was the COO of Facebook. It was in the *Ghostbusters* reboot and a slick, funny feminist media, and the inevitable presidential candidate. What was there to complain about?

Any hint of truly angry, truly challenging feminist resentment behind a political movement would get written off as performed. Senate Majority Leader Mitch McConnell had already called it playing "the gender card," like it was a move in a game, a put-on. Authentic expressions of resistance — marches, hunger strikes, demonstrations, sit-ins — had been useful for getting attention, banging down doors, forcing women's way in. But the public antics and outpourings of vivid fury at an unequal system that had been useful in eras when women were so far from the inside would work against those who'd *gotten* inside, making them look and sound like outsiders once more.

CHAPTER TWO:
THE GRAND ILLUSION

Of course women weren't *really* inside. And you could tell because the ones who looked to be had actually walked into the most ingenious trap of all: the one in which their insider status, the illusion of their assured claim to political power, gained after centuries of exclusion, would be the very thing that worked to disqualify them.

The fact is that when Hillary Clinton began her second campaign for the presidency, not only had we not elected a single woman president in 226 years of presidential history, we had not elected a single woman *vice* president. Despite the more than two hundred women who had thrown their hats in, the country had never managed to make a woman a major party *nominee* for the presidency. Congress was still only 19 percent female and had only ever elected one black woman to the Senate. And all of these representational gaps existed in

81

a country in which women's bodies were ever more heavily legislated and their wages and economic stability were under new attacks from the right.

Yet the climate was one in which furious displays of anger on behalf of women's equality had been ceded and replaced by some milder forms of agitation coming from the few who *had* worked their way to power, permitting the propagation of the myth that centuries of gendered and racial discrimination were over, that things were pretty much even, that those who had been barred from power historically now possessed an equal share of it.

That myth — the fantasy that racism and sexism were stages through which the country had successfully passed, leaving new kinds of people, like President Barack Obama and "inevitable" next president Hillary Clinton, in charge — had unleashed another kind of anger. The rage that was alight, and openly, eagerly expressed in the years before the 2016 election was the rage of those *already* on the inside: the greedy anger of the kind of Americans who had been, over centuries, afforded the disproportionate share of political, economic, social, and sexual power, and who were explosively furious at the perception that others were grabbing shares away from them.

The political profile of Donald Trump was built on his racist birther campaign, his public claims that Barack Obama's presidency had always been illegitimate. His campaign kicked off with his statements about Mexicans as rapists, promises to build walls and make laws to keep foreign interlopers out. He had once taken out a full-page ad calling for the death penalty for the so-called Central Park Five — the group of young black men arrested for the rape of a white woman jogger and later exonerated. Trump's scorn for women was on prominent display from the start: he called them pigs, dogs, evaluated them on scales of one to ten, had run beauty pageants, been accused by his first wife of rape, and bragged to Howard Stern of never having changed a diaper. He had told a magazine that you have to "treat [women] like shit."

Because of the national illusion that we as a country were too culturally advanced for this kind of retrograde white patriarchal expression, we were regularly assured by political experts that Trump's candidacy would never get off the ground, that these kinds of locutions of racist and sexist resentment and dismissal would make him ineligible for the presidency.

But not only did Trump seem to surge ahead in *spite* of his hatred and dismissal of nonwhite non-men, his supporters seemed to love him *because* of it. Even those who claimed he'd never be president credited him with reaching voters in a visceral way, as having a gift for channeling the rage of a white America which felt it had been left behind, had its privileges stolen by female, nonwhite interlopers — the kinds of people who'd never occupied the White House or held representative numbers of seats in legislative bodies, people who were paid less, taxed more for health care, and denied full control of their reproductive lives, but who had given such a convincing impression of having taken up more than an equal share of space that they were the objects of the resentful ire being channeled by the orange-tinted and toupéed businessman from Queens. The guy who just kept winning primaries.

His rallies were raucous and furious events, stadium-sized yell-ins, with supporters offering "Sieg Heil" salutes and wearing white nationalist insignia. Trump himself encouraged angry violence in his crowds, at one point telling a crowd, as a protester was removed, "I love the old days; you know what they used to do to guys like that when they were in a place like this? They'd be carried out in a stretcher . . . I'd like to punch him in the face." But as he waxed nostalgic for the good old days of quelling protest through brutality, Trump's supporters acted like furious protesters themselves, screaming insults and profanity at anyone they imagined to be challenging their authority: "Build a wall!" "Fuck political correctness!" "Fuck Islam!" In one video report, the *New York Times* recorded Trump supporters responding to the candidate's mention of then-president Obama with "Fuck that n— !"

And then there was the fury with which Trump supporters treated Hillary Clinton: effigies of the candidate in prison garb and coffins were carried at Fourth of July parades in the summer of 2016; Trump's crowds were energized by their hatred for her: "Hillary is a whore!" "Trump that bitch!" "Tramp!" "Bitch!" "Kill her!" "Hang the Bitch!"[15] And always, always the drum beat: "Lock! Her! Up!" And it wasn't just the anonymous crowds. Retired Army Lieutenant General Michael Flynn led the crowd in a chorus of "Lock her up" at the Republican National Convention; at the same gathering, New Jersey Governor Chris Christie, who would soon fall under criminal investigation himself, led a mock trial of Clinton, rousing the crowd on the floor to a writhing, frenzied scream of "Guilty!" that recalled seventeenth-century Salem, as if Clinton were a witch about to be sentenced to death. A month later, at a North Carolina rally, Trump told his supporters that Clinton wanted to take away their guns, telling them, "If she gets to pick her judges, [there's] nothing you can do, folks. Although the second amendment people, maybe there is, I don't know." Trump's deranged syntax didn't effectively cover up the fact that he was hinting at Clinton's assassination. More direct was his advisor on veteran's affairs, a state representative from New Hampshire named Al Baldasaro, who said in a radio interview that Clinton "should be put in the firing line and shot for treason."[16]

The vitriolic hatred of Clinton was sometimes only slightly less muted on the left, in part because of the sticky truth of her position: she *did* have power, she was one of the exceptional women to have risen within a white patriarchal capitalist system that hadn't been built for her, and she'd risen in part by participating in it.

Other women who'd attempted runs for the presidency, from Shirley Chisholm in 1972 to Patricia Schroeder in 1987, had been stopped by their outsider status or their inability to fund-raise or garner enough serious support from the powerful men who ran their party. Clinton had been hell-bent on overcoming these hurdles, but in doing so, had offered her opponents on the left the ammunition to undercut the historic nature of her candidacy. She'd played far too nicely with Wall Street, voted for the invasion of Iraq, and worked too eagerly with Republicans on centrist policy during her time as a senator. She'd supported her husband's neoliberal policies as first lady, including the 1994 crime bill, 1996's disastrous and despicable welfare reform legislation, and the 1996 Immigration Reform and Immigrant Responsibility Act, all of which had done disproportionate harm to poor and nonwhite communities.

The very fact that she had carefully established close relationships with big donors and garnered the support of bigwigs made her part of a political elite and vulnerable to the anti-establishment rhetoric of the men she'd wind up running against; it kept her from being understood or celebrated as the outsider that, as a member of a gender that had been historically denied access to executive power, she was. In figuring out how a woman might *win* within a system that had not been designed with her in mind, Clinton had set herself up to lose.

Clinton's affiliation with the power structure created a terrific incentive for many on the left to support her primary opponent, the genuinely left-wing Democratic Socialist senator from Vermont, Bernie Sanders, a man who had long retained his independence from the Democratic Party. The Sanders campaign turned into its own kind of buoyant social movement, one that had a salutary effect on Clinton's campaign: it pushed her leftward.

But some of the left's loathing for her, and for her supporters, could often seem as though it were about more than simple policy differences or distrust of the establishment. It could be deeply gendered, and it occasionally reeked of condescension and belittlement, as when Sanders's campaign manager, Jeff Weaver, sneered to a political reporter regarding Clinton, "We're willing to consider her for vice president. . . . We'll even interview her." Some progressives — echoing the attitudes of some of the Occupiers who had been the forerunners of the Bernie core — remained inhospitable to feminist arguments on behalf of Clinton, even to the basic claim that it mattered, democratically and representatively, that there'd never been a woman in the White House, much less a liberal woman running on the abolishment of the Hyde Amendment (which barred the use of federal insurance money to pay for abortion, making abortion inaccessible to poor women) and increasing funding for childcare and paid leave programs. "Ppl voting for Hillary for this reason are like southern GOP neighbors wanting GOP for culturally affirming reasons," tweeted the leftist writer Zaid Jilani during the primary, while *Salon*'s Daniel Denvir claimed that Clinton was "getting a free pass as a feminist," waving off "the notion that Hillary Clinton is a feminist choice because she is a qualified woman" as "really very caricatured identity politics."[17]

The frustration that some Sanders supporters felt, as enthusiasm for him grew but Clinton kept winning anyway, prompted some of them to borrow from the vilifying imagery and delegitimizing accusations being lodged on the right, including the propagation of the story that Clinton had rigged the primary. At the Democratic National Convention, *progressive* protesters held up signs saying "Hillary for Prison" and chanted "Lock her up!" while Green Party candidate Jill Stein stoked the rage, promising to urge Sanders to withdraw his

89

endorsement of Hillary, "based on the outright, purposeful sabotage of your campaign by the DNC and by Hillary Clinton."[18]

Of course, lots of Hillary's most vociferous and vivid critics on the left were feminist women, women who described how Hillary's fervid supporters attacked *them* in sexist and degrading terms, calling them gender traitors, diagnosing them as victims of internalized misogyny. As one feminist Sanders supporter, Sarah Jones, wrote "No one's liberated by portraying left-wing women as oppressed automatons incapable of independently formulating political thought."

One of those who was attacked from both sides was Kathleen Geier, who, during the primary, described to the journalist Michelle Goldberg how some of her fellow Berners used a "sanctimonious, lecturing, hectoring tone" when discussing Clinton and feminism. "They're trying to delegitimize any critique of sexist Hillary coverage . . . my politics are with that side, but this ancient left-wing misogyny has risen its ugly head."[19]

While the gender dynamics here were far more nuanced and complex than those on the right, there was no question that there

90

were weird misogynist resentments at play. After Clinton finally beat Sanders and earned the nomination in June of 2016, two of the progressive politicians who had purposefully withheld endorsements came out for Hillary: Russ Feingold and Elizabeth Warren. But it was Warren who was subject to the brunt of the ire from Sanders's supporters; her Facebook page was flooded with messages calling her a hypocrite and "another pseudo progressive we must vote out of office"; graffiti spray-painted on a bridge in Northampton, Massachusetts, read "#JudasWarrenSellout."

On both the right and the left, the kind of foul-mouthed, performative anger that I had gawked at coming from women trying to storm the political gates in earlier eras was in 2016 being directed *at* the woman who had come closer to knocking those gates down than any other before her.

CHAPTER THREE: WE'RE NOT CHEERFUL ANYMORE

"I tried to change. Closed my mouth more, tried to be softer, prettier, less awake."

There was Beyoncé, riffing on a poem by Warsan Shire called "For Women Who Are Difficult to Love" — about a female subject who is with a man who finds her intensity frightening — in her visual album, *Lemonade,* released in April of 2016, the week before Donald Trump would officially become the Republican candidate for president.[20]

In the video, Beyoncé strides jauntily through city streets in a big yellow dress, swinging a baseball bat with which she smashes car windows and takes the tops off fire hydrants, releasing furious geysers of water and causing flames to erupt behind her. In the video, women look on with surprised delight while men stare at her, wary. At the time, the narrative arc, words, and visuals of *Lemonade,* understood to be

Beyoncé's ferocious response to her husband Jay-Z's infidelities, appeared wholly unconnected to politics.

But the shift between the public performance of polished empowerment feminism offered by the pop star just two years earlier, and the unleashed rage at men's bad behavior (and at the women who enable it, including Beyoncé's "Becky," the slang term connoting white women) also marked a certain kind of turning point. Even in Beyoncé's universe — still glossy and gorgeous, still with men near the center — cheerful feminism was gone; in its place a slick wrath, a punitive and righteous rage, presented as having been pent up, like floods and flames, now pouring forth onto the streets. By the spring of 2016, Beyoncé was mad, and at least some of her anger was about men — the husbands and fathers of her lyrics — and how they treated women.

Her rage would turn out to be a harbinger in the months to come, as the reality that Donald Trump was going to be the Republican nominee for president set in and revelations of his vile behavior toward women became better known. Trump found women's bodies and their functions grotesque, called Clinton's trip to the bathroom during a debate "disgusting," made a comment about debate moderator Megyn Kelly having "blood coming out of her wherever," and had once told a lawyer who'd had to take a break to pump breast milk during a meeting, "you're disgusting." It was perfectly clear that when he promised to "Make America Great Again," part of what Donald Trump was promising was a return to a retro version of white masculinity, and all of the misogynist subjugation and objectification it comprised.

That he was the candidate felt absurd, anachronistic in the era we were assured was postfeminist. Yet a postelection study done by Harvard Kennedy School's Shorenstein Center, looked at the nation's leading newspapers and news networks and found that the press covered Donald Trump and Hillary Clinton equivalently, as if they and their faults were legitimately comparable. The ratio of negative to positive coverage of their fitness for office was the same: 87 percent of the stories about each of them were negative, thirteen percent were positive.[21]

This relative parity in coverage, the both-sides-ism that defined media coverage of the race, was a reflection of the lie at the center of everything. Because the reality was that Trump's racist and sexist attitudes were

94

not in fact out of line with contemporary assumptions; they were not disqualifying. They were measured on the same scale that weighed Clinton's real but politically ordinary flaws, because on some level, his biases were still considered legitimate. The idea that the nation had moved beyond retro, macho white attitudes about who could lay claim to political power had always been a fable, one that had worked to quash the dissent and discourage the disruptive fury that might have otherwise had more power to beat back Trump before his rise.

When, a month before the election, it was revealed that Donald Trump had been caught on tape joking about women with Billy Bush — a *Today* show host and member of a family that had produced two American presidents, the cousin of another man who'd run for president against Donald Trump — about how "when you're a star, they let you do it. You can do anything . . . grab 'em by the pussy. You can do anything," people got mad. Women got mad. The night that the *Access Hollywood* tape was made public, a Canadian author, Kelly Oxford, tweeted, "Women: tweet me your first assaults. They aren't just stats. I'll go first: Old man on city bus grabs my 'pussy' and smiles at me, I'm 12." In re-

95

sponse came more than twenty million tweets and visits to her Twitter page, many posting under the hashtag #notokay to signify stories of unwanted sexual contact, many women recalling incidents from when they were children or teens.[22]

The next week, women began to come forward with stories about how Trump himself had kissed or groped them against their will: a former *People* reporter, Natasha Stoynoff, wrote about how years before, while she'd been reporting a story on Trump and his third wife, Melania, he'd taken her into a room alone and "within seconds . . . was pushing me against the wall and forcing his tongue down my throat."[23] Stoynoff recalled her surprise at the incident, how when she got back to the hotel room, her "shock began to wear off and was replaced by anger. I kept thinking, 'Why didn't I slug him? Why couldn't I say anything?' " Another woman, seventy-four-year-old Jessica Leeds, recalled to the *New York Times* how, on a flight three decades earlier, she had been seated next to Trump, and he had groped her, touching her breasts. "He was like an octopus," Leeds told the *Times*. "His hands were everywhere."[24] She had changed airplane seats and not reported the incident, she said, because she was

96

groped so frequently back then. "We accepted it for years," she told the paper. "We were taught it was our fault." But hearing Trump deny on television, in response to the *Access Hollywood* tape, that he had ever grabbed a woman against her will, Leeds said, "I wanted to punch the screen."[25]

Michelle Obama — the nation's first lady, who had been caricatured during her husband's 2008 campaign as an angry black woman and had worked relentlessly to battle that perception — roared to furious life, making a remarkable speech, in which she called out the "hurtful, hateful language about women" that Trump had been deploying on the campaign trail and described how the flood of stories from women about abuse and harassment had "shaken me to my core in a way that I couldn't have predicted." It was a critical speech, in part because it had been Obama who that summer had issued the left its directive during the Democratic Convention, after a week of unreconstructed racism and sexism at the Republican Convention in Cleveland. "When they go low, we go high," she had admonished, advising her side to behave with the assuredness that morality would surely win the day.

Now Obama was mad. And crucially,

97

while so much of the angry reaction to Trump's abhorrent trespasses had come on behalf of *white* women, she was ensuring that the white experience of coercion and harassment was not the only one that would be heard in a country in which black women are even less likely to be believed as victims of assault, and far less likely to be treated with respect. Obama called out the press for its inattention to women's anger, chiding those who were "treating this as just another day's headline, as if our outrage is overblown or unwarranted."

Powerfully, Michelle Obama argued that there was something to *do* with this outrage, urging all the women out there who were livid to take action. "While our mothers and grandmothers were often powerless to change their circumstances, today, we as women have all the power we need to determine the outcome of this election. We have knowledge. We have a voice. We have a vote."

Many women took Obama's words to heart. We were furious; I heard from friends who were rounding on their street harassers for the first time, yelling back at them. Men, including a former senator, told me of how shaken they were to hear from their wives and friends and mothers and coworkers

98

about the ubiquity of sexual assault and harassment, how they had had their hair blown back by the anger they hadn't even known had been pent up. Women took some of Trump's sexist words and worked to re-appropriate them — turning the phrase "nasty woman," which he'd called Clinton in a debate, into a T-shirt slogan, and printing up all manner of Etsy merchandise promising that soon "pussy" would "grab back." Millions of women, and some men, rushed to join the Clinton-supporting internet group Pantsuit Nation. But in a season in which Clinton supporters were still being lectured by many in their lives on the right *and* the left, the group was private, visible only to its members on Facebook.

There was a creeping fear that this explosion was too little, and perhaps too late. The week before the election, I traveled to Boston to speak to a group of women, most of them lifelong feminists. One former National Organization for Women (NOW) chapter president in her fifties expressed her anxiety to me: why were these groups secret? She recalled how furious her friends had been over the treatment of Anita Hill in 1991, how in her memory, women had left their office buildings and stormed outside en masse to show that they had indeed had

99

enough. How their public show of anger — the current of outrage and desperation to express it — had eventually led to women's electoral run on Washington the next year. Why weren't women taking to the streets? she asked me with concern. I didn't know, I replied, but I hoped that perhaps it was because they knew that they didn't have to; as Michelle Obama had noted, now — as had not been possible in 1992, as had never been possible before — they knew they could walk out the door on an upcoming Tuesday and vote for a woman for president.

The weekend before the 2016 presidential election, an old family friend and political science professor joked to me, "I'll see you in our female-led future." I looked at him, pretending to hold my breath with fear. "Be kind to me in the reeducation camps," he said with a smile. This was an optimistic joke. So many were optimistic.

But the optimism was part of the trick: the reaffirmation of the myth of Clinton's power. On an episode of *Saturday Night Live* that followed the release of the "pussy tape," comedians portraying debate moderators Anderson Cooper and Martha Raddatz introduced the candidates as "Republican nominee Donald Trump and . . . can we say this yet . . . ? Probably fine. . . . *President*

Hillary Clinton."

This surety, that Clinton had already won the presidency, was what prompted so many white people on the right, including white women, to vote against the creeping ascendency of women, especially against *the* woman who'd been so effectively vilified on both the left and the right. It was *also* what disabused women on the left of the purportedly overdramatic notion that the country was still powered by enough misogyny and racism that it would elect an openly hateful bigot, or that they needed to truly stir themselves on Clinton's account in order to combat those biases and beat Trump. In treating her as though she had already beat him, and not like the single tool on the table with which the nation might stop this monstrous racist patriarch, we talked ourselves out of the outrage we should have been mustering. We didn't have to be angry on *behalf* of Hillary Clinton, this seductive song went. If anything, we should be angry *at* her, for not having done enough for us with the power we imagined she had.

After the election, Senator Claire Mc-Caskill of Missouri would tell TV audiences about what she'd heard from women in her state immediately after the election: "I just assumed he wouldn't win," her constituents said in retrospect. "I could have done more. I should have done more."[26] Americans who might have exerted more energy to oppose Trump or support Clinton — especially white women — were goaded into *in*action by the assurance that sexism and racism were things of the past, and that to work themselves up about either would look silly, would be unnecessary exertions on behalf of an imperfect candidate. And of course, many other Americans — including white women — were moved to support Trump for essentially the same reason: what they heard as the *threat* that white patriarchy had lost its grip.

Which is why Donald Trump kept doubling down on the thing that made him purportedly unelectable, alleging that his opponent didn't have the "stamina" to be president, inviting women who had previously accused her husband of sexual misconduct to a debate — *not* in an effort to jumpstart the overdue feminist reassessment of Bill Clinton's sexual improprieties, but rather to humiliate and destabilize Hillary. Trump's primary defense against accusations of assault and harassment was that the women weren't attractive enough to hit on — "Believe me, she would not be my first choice," Trump had said of Jessica Leeds[27]

102

— and he took care to note, after watching Clinton walk in front of him at a debate: "I wasn't impressed."

Clinton's left critics would often comment that she'd lucked out in her draw of opponents, that she'd won — and then blown — a once-in-a-lifetime opportunity to run against such a cartoonishly awful man. What this view failed to acknowledge was that it was the opposite of both luck and accident that this man had been summoned, elected by his party to face down the first woman who was running to be president, the woman we'd been assured *would* be president. To fight her, and her predecessor — another history-making challenge to white masculinity — the Republican Party had chosen a figure who embodied every one of the strains of denigration and disrespect that had historically worked to bar women and nonwhite men from the presidency and to deny them equal access to political power.

It worked. He won.

Chapter Four: The Winter of Our Discontent

The election of Donald Trump over Hillary Clinton for the presidency of the United States in 2016 may have felt like a stinging, agonizing shock to many of us who lived through it. But in the context of American history, it should have been wholly unsurprising. In the wake of a challenge to white supremacy, in the form of two Obama administrations, racism won. Over the threat of a potential female leader, brutal masculinity won.

For older women, the metaphor was quotidian, familiar, the stuff of 80s shoulder-padded boardroom movies like *9 to 5*: the sexist, egotistical, lying hypocritical bigot who gets the big job over the woman, even when he's less qualified, even when he's been reported to human resources. This was not extraordinary; this was just another Tuesday in America.

We'd allowed ourselves to be taken in by

the lie, by the illusion that we had come farther than we had, and in so doing we'd forfeited our right to be furious. We'd permitted those who *had* expressed anger or passion on behalf of Clinton to become the punch lines, and not the prognosticators.

In the months that followed, after the Women's Marches that would take place in January, many people asked where this raucous fury had been *before* November 9. But the truth was that had it been expressed, it would have been laughed off as silly and faddish, performed and unserious. Rage about sexism would have been its own meta threat to a male-dominated political discourse convinced that sexism was a long-eradicated American ghost, that it would have no damaging impact on a woman as powerful as Clinton.

Even in her loss, instead of bracing acknowledgment of the unabated power of racism and sexism and the structural disadvantages faced by non-white non-men in a country that had just elected an openly racist and misogynistic president, there came an outpouring of concern from some on the left who promptly blamed progressives for having been *too* focused on racial and gender disparities. "American liberalism has

105

slipped into a kind of moral panic about racial, gender and sexual identity that has distorted liberalism's message and prevented it from becoming a unifying force capable of governing," wrote Columbia professor Mark Lilla in the *New York Times.*[28]

But in the wake of that loss, there was no longer a tool at hand — no candidate who could beat this man and his administration of white men and racists, men who would be revealed as wife-beaters and harassers and corrupt grifters. It would be years before an election would provide an opportunity to replace or control him, and now the anger poured out like the water in the Beyoncé video, women amassing — not always as smoothly or peaceably as we might wish — and getting into some rough sort of formation.

The night after the election, Teresa Shook, a retired lawyer and grandmother in Hawaii, feeling shattered, made a Facebook page proposing a march on Washington set for the day after Trump's inauguration. By the time she woke up the next morning she had ten thousand replies; in the same days, New York fashion designer Bob Bland — who had made those "Nasty Woman" T-shirts — had had the same idea. It wasn't a fluid organizational process; the white women who'd thought of it first called the event the Million Women March, without being aware that they were appropriating the name of a 1997 demonstration staged by African-American women in Philadelphia. This only heightened the racial resentments that had sprung up with the news that that while *94 percent* of black women had voted for Hillary Clinton, the majority of white women had voted for Donald Trump: *now* white women organizers were going to stage an angry protest, co-opting the name of an event that had been led by black women twenty years earlier?

But within a couple of weeks, organizers from other movements had taken over the event. Tamika Mallory, a gun control advocate; Carmen Perez, who had worked on behalf of criminal justice reform; and Linda Sarsour, a Muslim-rights activist who'd been active on Bernie Sanders's campaign, all joined Bob Bland to organize the millions who would show up not just in Washington, but in cities around the country and the world — including in Antarctica. The Women's March on January 21, 2017 was the biggest one-day political protest in this country's history, and it was staged by angry women.[29]

At one of the only other comparable protests of a presidential inauguration, held at the height of the New Left, to protest the swearing-in of Richard Nixon in 1969, women in the movement had fought for space for two speakers, Marilyn Salzman Webb and Shulamith Firestone. As soon as Webb had begun to speak about abortion, childcare, and how men on the left treated women, the booing from the male crowd had drowned her out; Webb has recalled that "people were yelling 'Take her off the stage and fuck her!' and 'Fuck her down a dark alley!' " She left the stage crying, and decades later she told the historian Annelise Orleck that that was when she knew that women "couldn't build a coalition with the left; women's liberation was going to be its own movement."[30] Firestone, who'd also been unable to give her speech in the face of booing from her ideological brethren, wrote more bluntly after the event: "Fuck off Left! We're starting our own movement."[31]

Forty-eight years later, decades during which the women's movement had exploded and then receded again, and wrestled with its own internal biases and inequities, here was an inauguration protest that spanned all fifty states, led by a young, multiracial coalition of women hoping to lead a new iteration of the movement into the future. It was groundbreaking that these women weren't asking for speaking slots at a left event; they *were* the left, and they were (imperfectly but insistently) situating leftist progressive priorities — including civil rights, reproductive justice, disability rights, immigrant rights, workers' rights, economic equality, and environmental justice — all within a feminist framework.

As the longtime activist Angela Davis said during her speech from the dais in Washington, DC, the event offered "the promise of *feminism* against the pernicious powers of state violence — an inclusive and intersectional feminism that calls upon all of us to join the resistance to racism, to Islamophobia, to antisemitism, to misogyny, to capitalist exploitation."[32]

And when, the morning after the march, ABC anchor George Stephanopoulos had seventeen minutes to interview Trump spokeswoman Kellyanne Conway on his Sunday morning news show, it was Conway herself who brought up the demonstration against her boss, mentioning it twice before she drew a direct question from Stephanopoulos, who asked, thirteen minutes deep: "What did the president think of that march?"[33]

Conway's response was to criticize the "profanity-laced, threatening, vulgar comments" of the celebrities onstage, citing in particular the pop star Madonna, who had said that she dreamt of "blowing up the White House." (In fact, she had said, "Yes, I'm angry. Yes, I am outraged. Yes, I have thought an awful lot about blowing up the White House. But I know that this won't change anything.") Stephanopoulos — who'd talked with Conway at length about the new president's provably false claims that his inauguration crowds had been bigger than Obama's — did not follow up with any questions about the relative size of the Women's March, or about the impact such unprecedented mass resistance might have on the incoming administration. In the next segment, Senate Minority Leader Chuck Schumer told Stephanopoulos that he'd participated in the Women's March in his home state of New York, and Stephanopoulos responded with only one question, in reference to Madonna's profane rage: "Were you comfortable with everything you heard?"[34]

It was such a neat trick, a way to reduce all the strains of righteous anger that had been on display the previous day to a sound bite that could be swiftly rejected as inappropriate. A way to crumple the mass display of resistance into a ball of paper and toss it into the media trash can of public impropriety; Stephanopoulos's hanky-waving was especially irrational after two years of a presidential candidate who encouraged violence, led public calls for incarceration of his opponent, and whose supporters spoke of killing her for treason. Yet Trump was rarely censured by the Beltway press for having made anyone feel uncomfortable.

It was telling that it was *Conway* — the enabler of the president against whom so much of the ire was directed and one of the very few women in his inner circle — who seemed attuned enough to the potential power of what she'd seen on the streets the day before to bring it up with more interest than her interrogator. It was as though a massive political eruption of women had happened, and the male-dominated political media *hadn't even seen it.*

But the shrugging incuriosity displayed by some in the press was better, by some measure, than the shrugging condescension with which other political commentators treated the march. David Axelrod, one of Barack Obama's former advisors, tweeted

111

on January 21, 2017, "This outpouring today is extraordinary and inspiring. But if all this energy isn't channeled into sustained pol action, it will mean little." Micah White, one of the architects of Occupy Wall Street, worried in the *Guardian* that "Without a clear path from march to power, the protest is destined to be an ineffective feelgood spectacle adorned with pink pussy hats."[35] It was enough to recall Madonna's speech itself, in which she had bellowed, "To our detractors that insist that this march will never add up to anything? Fuck you. Fuck you!"

To anyone who actually attended the event, the proposition that it was some casually undertaken dilettante party about hats was nuts. The day before the march I'd been part of a panel about women's resistance at a Washington, DC, bookstore where so many people showed up that they had to bar the door. Inside, the conversation had been urgent, tactical: about promising candidates and which organizations were doing voter registration and fighting gerrymandering. As soon as the march had concluded, its organizers had staged a gathering called "Where do we go from here?" EMILY's List, the political action committee dedicated to electing pro-choice

Democratic women to office, partnering with other organizations designed to get Latinx, gay, lesbian, African-American, Asian-American, and female progressive candidates elected, held a massive candidate training in Washington, DC; its press release read, "This fight may start in the streets, but it's going to end at the ballot box. Let's bring our army to both."[36]

The same day, Planned Parenthood held a political action training session for two thousand people, zeroing in on how to organize around protecting and expanding health care under the incoming administration. Marchers told reporters that they were thinking of running for office, and if they were not thinking of running for office themselves, they were looking at their local- and state-level candidates with an eye toward volunteering, organizing, and donating; they described their new awareness of how many Republicans across the country had been running unopposed and of the need to recruit candidates to challenge incumbents. Marchers spoke of sending postcards and making phone calls to representatives, of lobbying for increased funding to women's health organizations.[37] Women were in it for the long haul. "Immediate outrage and sustained outrage are two different things," a protestor named Sarah Jaffe told *Politico.* "I'm gearing up to be mad as hell for a long time."[38]

But it seemed that there was nothing that women could say, or post on a sign, or yell, or express through organizing or training sessions or strategic planning that would persuade some people that what they were promising, in the context of American history, was revolution. Speaking on *Morning Joe* to Missouri Senator Claire McCaskill, who, in discussion with Mika Brzezinski, had just detailed the marchers' stated commitment to equal pay, women's health care, defending Obamacare, environmental activism, and their plans to run for office and get involved in campaigns as volunteers leading to the midterms, MSNBC analyst Mark Halperin — a man who had spent previous years reporting on the Tea Party's "huge impact on America" — asked her with suppurating condescension, "Senator, [can I] just ask you to be a notch more specific" about how the marchers might "impact what's going on in Washington [this week], not running for [the] school board down the road?"[39]

What happened within the next week was that Donald Trump issued his first version of the travel ban that barred people from

114

several predominantly Muslim nations from entering the country, and it was women who stepped up to oppose him. People rushed to airports; New York congresswoman Nydia Velázquez was one of the first at JFK in New York, demanding the release of immigrants being held there after Trump's executive order barred even those with valid visas and green cards from entry. Lawyers arrived to help those who'd been detained by the ban, and one journalist, Matt Ford, noted the "striking" gender disparity among attorneys who'd sprinted to fight the ban.[40] At Dulles Airport, he tweeted, "Probably 70 percent of lawyers volunteering . . . are young women." In a later story, Ford noted how many of those attorneys were also people of color, an observation that corresponded to the fact that women and people of color are overrepresented in public interest law jobs, and that it was the public interest lawyers who were hurrying to airports.

It was four women judges, and one man, who initially issued stays on Trump's travel ban. These were the fruits of the last furious women's movements, the First and Second Waves, which had opened doors to colleges and law schools, producing a generation of women with law degrees, women who had ascended to the federal bench, and were therefore in the position to block a president's unconstitutional order.

At the rallies objecting to the ban, politicians including Velázquez, New York City Public Advocate Letitia James, Representatives Pramila Jayapal and Nanette Barragán, Senators Elizabeth Warren and Kirsten Gillibrand — the only senator to vote "no" on all but one of Donald Trump's cabinet appointments — joined the leaders of the Women's March, Linda Sarsour and Tamika Mallory, as impassioned speakers. Many of these women had also spoken at the marches the weekend before, conveying that in this moment, those on the inside of the political structure — the senators and elected officials — were *not* going to distance themselves from the angry rabble of activists at the gates. "It is clear that the resistance to Trump's radical agenda will be led by courageous women fighting for our future," tweeted Kamala Harris, the newly sworn-in senator from California, and only the second black woman elected to the body in its history.

In Congress the following Monday, it was Harris and Washington state's Patty Murray who led their caucus in objection to the travel ban, penning a livid letter that expressed their "outrage" at the executive order "and its haphazard implementation," which "run counter to our American values and the Constitution." The letter went on to call Trump's order "unconscionable and unconstitutional."[41] That day, Acting Attorney General Sally Yates sent a letter to Justice Department lawyers, noting that she was unconvinced that Trump's order was lawful, and that "Consequently, for as long as I am the Acting Attorney General, the Department of Justice will not present arguments in defense of the Executive Order unless and until I become convinced that it is appropriate to do so." Yates was fired before midnight, and Trump called her, in a statement, "weak on borders and very weak on illegal immigration."

But of course, what those first days of Trump's administration showed was that women were the opposite of weak in their opposition to the Trump administration; and every attempt to cut them down was taken up as an opportunity for replenishing their fury.

In the week following, Massachusetts Senator Elizabeth Warren voiced her opposition to Trump's appointment of Jefferson Beauregard Sessions III as attorney general by calling on the words of another woman, the late Coretta Scott King. During Sessions's confirmation hearings, Warren began to read the statement that King had sent to the Senate Judiciary Committee, objecting to the 1986 nomination of Sessions to be a federal district court judge. King had detailed Sessions's history of working against voting rights for African Americans, arguing that Sessions "lacks the temperament, fairness, and judgment to be a federal judge."

But when Warren stood on the Senate floor to read the letter, Republican Senate Majority Leader Mitch McConnell ordered her to stop, forcing her to leave the floor. McConnell surely made this move as his own symbolic message to his base: that he was willing and able to shut down a mouthy woman and aggressive challenger to Republican policies. He would later offer this view of his choice, using the interaction — perhaps consciously, to serve his own purposes — as a metaphor for the suppression of female dissent: "She was warned," McConnell said of Warren's attempt to read King's letter. "She was given an explanation. Nevertheless, she persisted."

Whether or not McConnell's base warmed to his performative dickishness, women around the country immediately took to his words with even more fervor than they'd displayed for nasty women or pussies grabbing back; across social media and Etsy shops, "Nevertheless, she persisted" became a phrase appended to images of tough women, from Harriet Tubman to Malala Yousafzai. One woman in Minneapolis persuaded more than a hundred of her friends and strangers to get "She persisted" tattoos, arranging — as if to show the blowhards sure it was *all* about aesthetics that there was more to it than that — that $55 of the $75 cost of the ink would go to an organization that supported pro-choice women running for office.[42] As Warren herself said on cable television, eager to capitalize on the optics with her own base, whose potential power she clearly saw: "They can shut me up, but they can't change the truth."[43]

As had happened in the wake of Trump's election, the perceived vanquishing of one threatening woman was provoking a million more — many of them a million times angrier than they'd ever been before — to raise their own voices.

By June, protesters had so powerfully clogged the phone lines and registered their names in the logs of congressional staffers that progress on undoing the accomplishments of the Obama era had been effectively delayed. They camped out outside the offices of Senate Majority Leader Mitch McConnell, some arriving in their wheelchairs, to protest threats to overturn the Affordable Care Act. One poll revealed that 86 percent of those taking daily action to contact their representatives were women, the majority of them over the age of forty-five. Most of them had been to the women's marches.[44]

Protest took both quotidian — calls and letters — and more theatrical forms: In March, women protested an abortion bill in Texas dressed in the red dresses from the television adaptation of *The Handmaid's Tale,* Margaret Atwood's dystopian novel of authoritarian misogyny run amok.[45] In August, protesters in Boston gathered in the wake of the Nazi march on Charlottesville, Virginia, to counter another march of white supremacists; among the counterprotesters was a group of women dressed in black witches' hats, their faces shrouded by black fabric, carrying signs that read things like "Hex White Supremacy." They were members of W.I.T.C.H. Boston, "an intersectional coven" convened in the spirit of the original second-wave radical group W.I.T.C.H., whose members had dressed as witches and "hexed" Wall Street bankers in

120

the 1960s, and which had originally stood for Women's International Terrorist Conspiracy From Hell or Women Inspired to Tell their Collective History, depending on which witch you asked.[46]

To many commentators, it surely appeared that it was all about Donald Trump. But in fact the fury was in response to many of the varied inequities, injustices, and abuses that Donald Trump's ascendance had made so visible. Patrisse Khan-Cullors would say in 2018, "The fight against 45 is not just against him. It's a bigger fight against white supremacy. It's a bigger fight against patriarchy. It's a fight against classism."[47]

In the fall, Carmen Yulín Cruz, the mayor of San Juan, Puerto Rico, furious at the way the U.S. government was leaving the territory without power in the wake of a disastrous hurricane, responded to Acting Homeland Security Secretary Elaine Duke's remark about hurricane response being a "good news story" by saying, "Dammit, this is not a good news story. This is a people-are-dying story." In turn, Donald Trump called her "nasty."

"I don't give a shit," Cruz told reporters when asked about the president's criticism. "I am done being polite, I am done being

121

politically correct, I am mad as hell." A few months later, Kirsten Gillibrand would invite Cruz to be her guest at Trump's first State of the Union address.[48]

Gillibrand, too, stopped being polite, telling me during a spring 2017 interview that officials are in Washington "to help people, and if we're not helping people we should go the fuck home." In winter of 2018, Illinois Senator Tammy Duckworth, a veteran and an amputee, laid into Donald Trump in a blistering floor speech in the Senate, asserting that "I will not be lectured about what our military needs by a five-deferment draft dodger," and later called the president "Cadet Bone Spurs" in reference to his stated medical reason for evading the military draft of his youth. In January 2018, Hawaii Senator Mazie Hirono began to ask every nominee for the federal judiciary whether they'd been accused of sexual misconduct; when questioned on what she'd say to those who argued that this was a partisan strategy, Hirono responded in the summer of 2018, "Fuck them." And Maxine Waters, still a congresswoman from California, and still staunch in her regard for fury as a rational response to injustice, made a cottage industry of tearing into Trump. "I don't honor him, I don't respect him, and I don't want to be involved with him," Waters said early in the administration, later calling him a "disgusting, poor excuse of a man."

Here it was, an anger that was so intense it blazed its way via stupid hats and foul-mouthed tirades, even from the most official and respectable sources — anything to let people know this: Women. Were. Furious. After the election, everything that had been restrained and secret and muffled could no longer be contained beneath a veneer of "going high," or venting only to the like-minded. "Of all the feelings that have surfaced since January — sadness, depression, hopelessness, rare bits of joy," wrote the feminist journalist Samhita Mukhopadhyay at the end of 2017, "the one that has sustained, motivated and sometimes felt like it was destroying me has been anger."[49]

The anger had spilled out into speech and into streets and into organizing, scrambling the daily schedules of women whose lives had been kick-started by writing postcards and calling their representatives, going to organizing meetings and town halls and making signs on oaktag with smelly markers and spending Saturdays at rallies and learning for the first time about intersectionality (and, too rarely, about those who'd been

123

making the calls and drawing the signs *before* the anger reached their doors). The British feminist Laurie Penny tweeted in July 2017, "Most of the interesting women you know are far, far angrier than you'd imagine."[50]

Women signed up to run for office, in numbers higher than the country had ever seen: EMILY's List put the number at over forty thousand in the year and a half after the election. Many of them spoke openly of how it was their fury at Trump, about the fact that he'd won and what it had shown them about the biases and inequities that still existed, contrary to everything they'd been told, that had motivated them to throw their hats in the ring.

Patricia Russo, the head of the Women's Campaign School at Yale, which had been training women to run for office since the 1990s, spoke of the numbers of women who called her, starting in November and then increasing exponentially after the first Women's March, telling her, "I'm mad, I marched, I want to run." So great a motivating force was the anger that Russo worried to me in the late summer of 2017 that it might inevitably fade, dry up, that soon, all these activated women would wilt with the discomfort and the exhaustion and sorrow of all their rage.

A TIME FOR RAGE

And then, in October 2017, the *New York Times,* followed swiftly by the *New Yorker,* published long, frightening, heavily reported stories about the movie producer Harvey Weinstein and his long history of violent sexual harassment and assault, and about how his abusive, misogynistic behavior had done so much damage to the careers of the women he'd harassed, and how it had been systematically covered up for decades. It was — while grotesque and a long time coming — not *so* different from other stories — about Roger Ailes or Bill O'Reilly or Bill Cosby or Donald Trump himself — that had been published in recent years, stories that had attracted increasing interest, that had been taken, slowly, more seriously, but which had not changed the world or workplaces, or how they continued to function.

But American women were a tinderbox and the Weinstein story was an extremely hot match. Of the reverberations in Hollywood, the *New York Times'* Manohla Dargis wrote, "The movies can break your heart, but this isn't the time only for tears. It is also the time for rage."[51]

Suddenly, the media, not to mention the

125

women making it and consuming it, were newly aflame. Many took to using the hashtag #metoo, which had been pioneered in 2006 by Tarana Burke as a movement to address sexual violence, and using it to tell their stories of harassment and abuse. Women and men broadened the conversation beyond sexual violence, using "#metoo" as a catchall that also encompassed tales of denigration and diminution in the professional sphere. Long bottled-up stories poured forth. Powerful, wealthy men — film directors, high-profile professors, morning show anchors who made millions, senators and congressmen and hotel magnates and radio hosts and editors — were losing their jobs, the institutions that had promoted and protected them for decades suddenly jettisoning them. One year after Donald Trump had faced no repercussion for having admitted to grabbing women nonconsensually, women appeared hell-bent on ensuring that other men *would* be forced — at long last — to accept some consequence.

Women were telling stories they'd never told aloud before, to reporters and to one another. And where moments like this had lasted, in the past, for a few days or weeks, what was most startling, given the seizing, rapid-fire pace of the news cycle under Donald Trump, was that this movement just kept going . . . for weeks, then months, expanding to include debate and acknowledgment of assault, bad sex, domestic violence. Hollywood's interest went beyond dress adornments and lip service; activists were brought onto red carpets; a fund was established to legally support women in less stable industries; Anita Hill signed up to head an entertainment industry commission on how to move forward.

It was a conflagration, an eruption of so much that had been held back, hidden from view, for decades, for centuries. Ijeoma Oluo wrote in *Elle* in January 2018: "To the men scratching their heads in concern and confusion: The rage you see right now, the rage bringing down previously invulnerable men today, barely scratches the surface. You think we might be angry? You have no idea how angry we are."[52] The same magazine would publish a survey in March, finding that 57 percent of women were angrier in 2018 than they had been in 2017, and that a whopping 83 percent of Democratic women were getting furious, particularly at the news, at least once a day.[53]

Those who were anxious about the velocity and intensity of #metoo spoke of dan-

127

gerous category collapse, about how anger in response to rape and assault was mingling with anger about workplace sexual harassment, which in turn melded into anger about plain old bad sex. They weren't wrong, exactly. There was a blurring, there was confusion, in part because what was coming into view was the tie that bound all of these behaviors: sexism, plain and simple. Sexism and the systemic damage that it did; sexism as it mingled with class and race to create unequal opportunities and outcomes. Sexism made suddenly, enragingly clear to lots of people for whom it had long been obscured.

"The antipatriarchy movement," warned presidential advisor Steve Bannon, was building, and aiming to "undo ten thousand years of recorded history . . . You watch. The time has come. Women are gonna take charge of society. And they couldn't juxtapose a better villain than Trump. He is the patriarch. This is a [defining] moment in the culture. It'll never be the same going forward." Bannon, a living embodiment of sexist, racist, white patriarchal impulse, seemed to see the fury that was amassing, and understand its potential power.[54]

"Grab the broom of anger and drive off the beast of fear," wrote Zora Neale Hurston, and I thought hard about that formulation through the fall of 2017, as the fear that Patricia Russo had expressed to me — that the anger was going to fade — itself began to dim. The anger that had propelled women into the streets in January and to the phones and protests and onto ballots through the spring was still burning, alighting on new subjects, picking further fights. Anger was the broom that swept America's newly infuriated women into a new year, 2018, the year in which electoral opportunity provided a new channel for their furious drive.

A REPRESSED MAJORITY

"Female rage is the essential fuel of #metoo," wrote Caitlin Flanagan in the *Atlantic.* "Unchecked it is the potent force that will destroy it."[55] That anger was hot, bubbling, wholly out of control.

Yes, it is out of control. It is a loud and livid objection to the kinds of control that have long been in place in a nation built by white men who, when they angrily broke free of imperialist control themselves, promptly encoded protections of liberty and independence only for themselves, building their new nation on slavery and the oppression of women, on the legal and civic

129

subjugation of that nation's majority.

Social movements are necessarily about challenging social controls. This is what social change is built on, and what America's politics themselves are built on, that political act that Maxine Waters could see twenty-five years earlier when others simply saw "riots" and "thugs": *insurrection.*

Insurrections don't always work; in fact, they don't *often* work, in part — as Flanagan suggested — because the rage that fuels them has the power to burn them up. Which is just part of what makes them scary; the other thing that makes them scary is that they are designed to destabilize power structures, often the ones that have been abusive, but are nonetheless the only ones we've got.

As America approaches its two hundred and fiftieth year since revolution was declared, still just one hundred and fifty years since abolition, a century since some women won the right to vote, and fifty years since African Americans in the Jim Crow South were fully enfranchised — all events that occurred in the wake of *uprisings* of Americans furious at the injustices they faced — women in America are coalescing in anger again. It is messy; it is riven by division — racial and generational and political. It is

130

not civil, it is often profane; calls for civility are designed to protect the powerful by casting them as victims. It is a mass fury: occasionally so frenzied that it makes people nervous. Were it any other way, nothing would ever change.

This is the revolutionary mission, what the idealized vision of what this country might be was born of: the righteous fury of the unrepresented. We are taught it — *give me liberty or give me death, live free or die, don't tread on me* — as patriotic catechism, but only when it has been expressed by white men has it sounded or been transmitted to us as admirable, reasonable, as the crucial catalytic ingredient to political change. That's because white men were always and have remained the rational norm, the intellectual ideal, their dissatisfactions easily understood as being grounded in reason, not in the unstable emotional muck of femininity.

Those founders, so determined that no one would tread on them, were furiously codifying liberty for themselves, built on the oppression of others — enslaved people, women. Those who were oppressed made the opportunities for the oppressors greater, just as the colonies had enriched the British Empire. What our founders established was not a true representative democracy, but rather one in which a minority ruled, based on a myth of wide and just representation, and in which that minority benefitted from the labor of and reduced competition from a subjugated majority. In order to maintain minority rule, the majority's resistance must be repressed, its anger discouraged.

What happened in the second decade of the twenty-first century is that women began to rage publicly in ways that made them audible to one another; we began to hear one another and understand that we were not as isolated in our rage as we had been led to believe. Whether it was about police violence, or the election of a megalomaniac, or the defeat of Hillary Clinton, or about gun violence, or about low wages, or about abortion, women began yelling, and the effect was — is — seismic.

"People are starting to get angrier and remember our history, remember our roots," Jenny Craig, a teacher in West Virginia, striking for higher wages, told *New York Times* columnist Michelle Goldberg of the drive to stage a successful walkout in a state where striking is illegal.[56]

The teacher strikes, which spread from West Virginia to Arizona and Oklahoma, were taking place in the same weeks of

2018, one year into a Trump presidency, when a group of high school students, the young women and men who'd survived the mass shooting in Parkland, Florida, began their own campaign to end gun violence. The most incandescently furious of the group was perhaps the Cuban-American teenager Emma González, who wiped away her tears and bellowed into a microphone, "The people in the government who were voted into power are lying to us. . . . Politicians who sit in their gilded House and Senate seats funded by the NRA telling us nothing could have been done to prevent this; *we call B.S.*"[57]

In her public oratory, González recalled no one so much as Rose Schneiderman, the twenty-eight-year-old labor organizer who, one week after the 1911 Triangle Shirtwaist Factory fire killed 146 workers, almost all of them women, stood at a memorial service for the dead at the Metropolitan Opera House and angrily declared:

"This is not the first time girls have been burned alive in the city. Every week I must learn of the untimely death of one of my sister workers. Every year thousands of us are maimed. The life of men and women is so cheap and property is so sacred . . . But every time the workers come out in the only

133

way they know, to protest against conditions which are unbearable, the strong hand of the law is allowed to press down heavily upon us. Public officials have only words of warning to us — warning that we must be intensely peaceable . . . I can't talk fellowship to you who are gathered here. Too much blood has been spilled. I know from my experience it is up to the working people to save themselves. The only way they can save themselves is by a strong working-class movement."[58]

Many in the press, and likely in government, scoffed at González's speech in a country in which the National Rifle Association's power has held such immutable sway, a nation in which, in the years since the killing of twenty-six at Sandy Hook Elementary school, gun restrictions have only been made looser by state legislatures around the country. But those same assured and cynical pundits might remember that Schneiderman — alongside Frances Perkins, who witnessed the Triangle fire and was so enraged by it that she changed the course of her career to address labor issues — wound up drafting some of the very workplace safety requirements that are still in place today.

We must train ourselves to even be able to

see and hear anger from women and understand it not only as rational, but as politically weighty. It is, in fact, an anger on behalf of the nation's suppressed majority and therefore especially frightening and combustible because of the threat it poses to the minority. We are primed to hear the anger of men as stirring, downright American, as our national lullaby, and primed to hear the sound of women demanding freedom as the screech of nails on our national chalkboard. That's because women's freedom would in fact circumscribe white male dominion.

There will be, already is, a desire to treat this iteration of women's uprising as hysteria, a mob, a witch hunt, a passing phase, a childish tantrum, something irrational, something niche, something that can be averted or neutralized as soon as everyone just calms down. There will be assertions that the anger is not authentic but performed. There will be tremendous pressure to not take it seriously, to not listen too carefully to what the loud shrill voices are saying, insistence that women giving voice to their rage are sure to lose, or are simply working to provoke further discrimination and disregard. Women's anger will be — as it has long been — cast as ugly, unappealing, dangerous, something to be shut down or jeered. Nothing, we have long been assured, is more unattractive in a woman than anger, and those messages will be especially damaging — as they have always been — to nonwhite women. But these are all strategies that have long been used to get people, including women themselves, to look away from, disregard, and suppress one of the great drivers of social upheaval and political change in this country: their own fury.

PART II
MEDUSAS

My mother, when she was about to deliver me in El Paso, Texas, needed a cesarean section and they wouldn't admit her because she was black. It was a Catholic hospital. My grandmother, who was half Irish — because my great-grandmother, who was a domestic worker, had been raped by her white employer — looked white, so she had to convince the people in the admitting office that my mother was her daughter. They finally let her in and they left my mother on a gurney in the hall, unattended, and she was delirious. She *needed* a C-section. Finally a doctor noticed her, drove her into the operating room, and it was too late for a C-section. She almost died; they had to pull me out using forceps and I barely made it. She almost didn't live and I almost didn't get here. So you think I'm not mad? Please. I don't like talking about this stuff a lot. But I guess anger has been just a part of my life since the day I was born. It's part of what's motivated me to deal with racism, sexism, lack of access to health care for women — for my whole life — *that's* why I fight.

— Congresswoman Barbara Lee

CHAPTER ONE:
HOLD YOUR TEMPER/
HOLD YOUR TONGUE

Congresswoman Barbara Lee was mad.

It was the summer of 2017, and the very liberal Democrat representing Oakland, California, had recently produced one of the only true — and surprising — bipartisan victories of the long, miserable congressional term, one she'd been working toward for over a decade.

Lee, the *only* member of Congress to have voted against the Authorization for the Use of Military Force (AUMF) in 2001, three days after the September 11 terrorist attacks, had been campaigning practically ever since to have that authorization — which had granted the president the ability to go to war without congressional approval and had been used to justify at least thirty-seven military interventions in fourteen nations — repealed. Lee had, in June, finally rallied Republican support for the AUMF repeal, with a window of eight months to revise and

141

replace it. Over the objections of House Speaker Paul Ryan, Lee's amendment to a Defense Department spending bill had passed by a voice vote out of the Appropriations Committee with support from both Democrats and Republicans.[1] *Politico* had called the Appropriations vote "the rarest of congressional spectacles: an earnest debate in which minds were changed, followed by a vote no one could have predicted." In other words, in a very dark year, the vote to repeal the AUMF had been a singular example of functional democracy; when it passed the Appropriations Committee with overwhelming support, other lawmakers in the chamber had actually applauded.[2]

And then, three weeks later, Paul Ryan stripped Lee's amendment from the defense bill before it could come to a full House vote. The repeal was removed in the middle of the night, with no vote and no explanation.

"It evaporated," Lee said to me a few weeks after her repeal had been vaporized. "It's like they whited it out and rewrote something in. This is sleazy. This is sleaze all the way."

A shocked Lee appeared before the Rules Committee, where she calmly described her objections to the process by which the

142

repeal had been stripped to the committee chairman, Texas Republican Pete Sessions, who responded to her politely stated points with cheerful condescension. "I was so mad at Pete Sessions," Lee recalled. "But I tried to control my anger."

Lee recalls her inner calibrations, during the back-and-forth with Sessions: "I've got to not let them think that I'm not responsible, and that I don't know what I'm talking about. I've got to be logical and coherent, I can't let my emotions come out because otherwise they'll say *'There is this angry black woman again. She's always angry about something; here she goes again.'* "

Lee remained measured. She repeatedly expressed her disbelief and dismay at how and why the amendment had been removed at the discretion of a couple of individual lawmakers, despite its having passed the Appropriations Committee with broad support from both parties. She remained stone-faced as Sessions, a white man from Texas who's served in the House for about the same amount of time that she has, explained to her that this was just how things worked.

At the very end of the interaction, Lee finally allowed some of her frustrations to show, telling Sessions, "I am very shocked at this process and how this went down, and

143

I hope that in the future . . . in the spirit of bipartisanship and regular order and our democratic processes that this not be done very often, because this is really *raw.*" She quoted him numbers, noting that it had only happened two other times in the past year; he put his head in his hands, in a show of exhaustion. Lee pressed on: "I just hope people understand that democracy is very important and the Democratic process is important and members should not be undermined by three or four or five individuals if they have worked together, and put something together and gotten it in a bill, bipartisan, and then it's ripped out . . . It is perplexing that this could happen in the middle of the night."[3]

Her colleagues watching from her California district, she said, had cheered at the insistence with which she'd kept pointing out the injustice that had just been enacted. "They said, 'You kept coming back at him, wearing him down.' So it may have worked, because if I had gone off like he expected me to go off, then I may not have been able to wear him down." Lee's appearance was, indeed, a study in strategic containment, just as she knew it must be. While she was confronting a male colleague — and describing other male colleagues, who had

144

tricked, attempted to deceive, and were now condescending to her — she was, above all, courteous.

Those in her own party noticed, and, as she would tell me later, congratulated her for it. "Everyone told me how gracious I was, and how they could tell I was really getting ready to go off on him, but I was restrained. They could see my anger, but they were so proud of me because I handled it right," she said.

Their response, Lee said, enraged her even more than the committee's dirty play had.

"They expected me to be the angry black woman, okay? They were applauding me for not being the angry black woman, and I wanted to cuss them out. Because that was the implication: *you were so cool, you were so restrained, you handled it so well, and toward the end you were a little emotional but you were great.* And I'm [thinking] 'Doggonit, you guys don't even know what you are saying!' "

What they were saying was that it hadn't even occurred to them how limited Lee — an esteemed colleague who had every reason to be livid that the amendment she'd been trying to pass for fifteen years had been improperly removed by her political opponents — had been in her ability to fight

145

against those who wronged her professionally. They were suggesting to her, by congratulating her on not having shown her anger, that anger would have been the improper recourse, when in fact it would have been a wholly reasonable response to improper professional behavior by her colleagues. They were telegraphing to her that they had never considered the kinds of racial and gendered pressures put on women, and especially on black women, to bottle up their resentments and their frustrations, no matter how justified they might be.

The fact that Lee had understood that she *couldn't* get openly mad, that she had known that an expression of wholly valid, justified, rational rage would have worked to weaken her position, is a symptom of the same kinds of skewed power dynamics that permit white men to hold so much sway in government — to be the chairmen and the speakers in numbers so much greater than any other demographic.

The result of the hosannas for not having expressed her anger, Lee said, was that she just got angrier — at her colleagues, her opponents, and because the AUMF *still* wasn't repealed. "I was totally hurt and, yes, livid." But, Lee said, she will try again. "And again

146

and again and again until it is done. I am not going to let anyone stop me."

Barbara Lee was born in Texas, to a mother who was always upfront about her anger. "She didn't take any prisoners. She was really upfront about inappropriate speech and behavior. She didn't mince her words; she wouldn't take any mess," said Lee. Lee recalled a story her mother had relayed about how as a college student, she and a friend had wanted to join Alpha Kappa Alpha, the nation's first black sorority. Back then, AKA admitted only light-skinned women; that wasn't a problem for Lee's mother, the granddaughter of a domestic worker who'd been raped and had children by her Irish employer. "So my grandmother looked like she was white, and my mother was very fair with green eyes," said Lee. But the sorority turned down her mother's best friend Juanita, whose skin was darker. "My mother got furious," said Lee. "She said 'To hell with this; I'm not joining,' " and called on the civil rights activist and educator Mary McLeod Bethune to come down to Texas Southern University and help students organize in protest. "That's how my mother was," Lee said. "She was constantly pushing."

When Lee herself was a high school student in San Fernando, California, she wanted to be a cheerleader, but the school had never had a black cheerleader, in part because of the way the selection process was conducted, privately. "I was mad," recalled Lee of her teenage self, "because I knew all these white girls had had the opportunity to be cheerleaders, and I knew I couldn't. So I went to the NAACP out of anger and asked them if they could help me and they said yeah." Lee and her classmates staged protests to change the rules, ensuring that girls could try out in front of the student body. Lee became the first black cheerleader at San Fernando High, and was soon joined on the squad by an Asian American student. "That was anger," she said. "I was *really* angry. I voiced my anger. But I was strategic, and I got what I wanted, not just for me but for everybody else, for all these girls of color who wanted to be cheerleaders."

In her early twenties, Lee was a student at Mills College in California; she was by then a single mother of two sons, on welfare and Medicaid. "I was angry at the system of oppression and racism because I saw it, I lived it every day, and who wouldn't be angry? I was being dissed by social workers and jerked around by guys and all that stuff." She became the head of the campus Black

Student Union, and started doing community work with the Black Panther Party. "I wanted to make whatever intervention I could to make things better for other people." But her interventions did not include electoral politics; she had no interest of working within the American political system. "I mean, I was saying it was rigged back then," Lee said of electoral politics. Lee's lack of belief in the system was imperiling her grades; as a government major, she was required to do field work for a campaign, but she was not even registered to vote in early 1972.

That's when Shirley Chisholm came to speak at Mills College. Chisholm, in the midst of her presidential campaign, spoke to students in fluent Spanish; she talked about health care, poverty, women's rights, racial justice, and immigrants' rights. Lee couldn't believe it. She approached Chisholm afterward and suggested that she'd like to work on her campaign in the California primary, confessing that she'd previously not had anything to do with electoral politics. Chisholm, Lee recalled, "Shook her finger at me. 'Little girl!' — I was twenty-five! I had two little kids, they were probably with me! — But anyway, she said 'Little girl! If you really believe in what you stand for, then you'll register to vote, get involved with politics, and try to make change. Because we need you.' "

Lee wound up organizing Chisholm's Northern California campaign with other Bay Area college students, attending the Democratic National Convention in Miami as a Chisholm delegate. After Chisholm's campaign, and a stint working for Black Panther cofounder Bobby Seale's 1973 mayoral race, Lee worked for a decade for Congressman Ron Dellums, who had been one of Chisholm's supporters in the Congressional Black Caucus; she was then elected to the California State Assembly and the California State Senate. Lee would eventually win Dellums's seat after his retirement from Congress. She has served Oakland as a congresswoman for twenty years.

And in that capacity, she told me, "I've learned how to . . . I won't even say *finesse* it, but how to handle life without going ballistic every time I feel like I'm treated unjustly, or other people are treated unjustly."

For women in public life, especially those engaged in a fight for more equal opportunities for more kinds of people, the message has long been clear: their anger and

150

desire to challenge the system — ironically, perhaps the thing that motivated their engagement in social change and political life to begin with — will be used against them.

BRING IN THE BRANK

The furious female is, we are told to this day, in innumerable ways, both subtle and stark, a perversion of both nature and our social norms. She is ugly, emotional, out of control, sick, unhappy, unpleasant to be around, unpersuasive, irrational, crazy, infantile. Above all, she must not be heard.

The brank — also known as a scold's bridle, or a witch's bridle — was a sixteenth-century torture device used to muzzle a defiant or cranky woman, her head and jaw clamped into a metal cage. Some of the bridles, which were made of iron, included tongue depressors that would be inserted into the woman's mouth; some of those had spikes on the bottom to pierce the tongues of the insubordinate. The Tower of London features an internally spiked metal neck collar dating from 1588, labeled a "collar for torture," but described in guidebooks as a device to be "put around the necks of scolding or wayward wives."[4]

We may not be literally collared anymore,

but the men who tell us to smile on the street so we'll be prettier (reminding us simultaneously to stifle negative thoughts *and* that our purpose is to decorate their world) are echoed around us on national stages. During the 2016 primaries, MSNBC host Joe Scarborough chided Hillary Clinton, after a winning night, "Smile. You just had a big night."[5] In 2018, White House press secretary Sarah Huckabee Sanders said during a CNN appearance, about Nancy Pelosi's grim visage during Donald Trump's first State of the Union address, "I think she should smile a lot more often; I think the country would be better for it. She seems to embody . . . bitterness."[6]

The notion of bitterness, a word and descriptor that suggests cramped, uptight sourness — something that no one wants to express — crops up all the time around angry women. But bitterness tends to be an aspersion cast only at those with most to be bitter about, something that James Baldwin described decades ago with regard to black anger. "People finally say to you, in an attempt to dismiss the social reality, 'But you're so bitter.' Well, I may or may not be bitter, but if I were, I would have good reasons for it, chief among them that American blindness, or cowardice, which allows us to pretend that life presents no reasons for . . . being bitter."

The old view of disruptive women as Medusa — who was punished by Minerva after having been raped in Minerva's temple, cursed with a head full of snakes and the ability to turn men into stone just by looking at them, and who was finally effectively disarmed, via beheading, by Perseus — was not lost on Susan B. Anthony, who observed in 1893 to the *Chicago Tribune* that women were asked to echo the sentiments of the men who ran the major newspapers, "and if they do not do that, their heads are cut off."[7] In the same period, one preacher described the figure of the woman reformer, jostling into male spaces with her arguments for enfranchisement and temperance, as "a monstrosity of nature, a subverter of society . . . the head of Medusa, a bird of ill omen, a hideous specter, a travesty of all that is sacred and divine."[8] As the British historian Mary Beard has chronicled, critics have often used the same frame for Hillary Clinton, producing endless memes of snakes emerging from her scalp[9]; one Breitbart writer claimed that statues of the candidate hadn't been erected since "anyone who saw them would turn instantly to stone."[10]

But the labeling of the powerful political

153

woman as monstrous doesn't stop at Medusa; it's in the endless barrage of Republican campaign mailers featuring Pelosi as cackling witch or ghoulish villain. As the journalist Peter Beinart reported in 2018, "within days of Pelosi's ascension to House minority leader, in 2003 . . . the Republican Party featured her visage — 'garish and twisted,' in the words of a magazine article at the time — in an ad against a Democrat running for Congress in Louisiana." Pelosi is always shown with her mouth open, unrestrained by any brank or bridle. The impulse to depict the most powerful woman in Congress as threatening or unstable, and to direct her ideological foes to do what they can to shut her mouth, almost certainly can be traced directly to fear of her efficacy. She has been one of the most successful legislative strategists of the modern era, shepherding her often fractious caucus through the passage of healthcare reform and stimulus spending during the Obama administration. All this in contrast to the Republican men who've occupied the same spot and exhibited only the most flaccid leadership abilities: from Paul Ryan to John Boehner to Dennis Hastert.

Powerful women — especially those whose talents are inarguably more impressive than that of their male peers — are often perceived as monstrous or perverse, unwell or unwholesome in their challenge to male authority. "Madness," a term used to designate mental illness, is also a description of anger, and for women, the two seem to be understood as related.

THE MADWOMAN IN THE STATE HOUSE

The aspersion that a woman who is angry is also *unstable* is cast every day in popular political discourse, so often we probably don't understand how completely we absorb the connection. In 2017, Senator Kirsten Gillibrand aggressively questioned Marine Corps Commandant Robert Neller about a failure of the military to address a pervasive pattern of sexual harassment in its ranks. That night, Fox News anchor Tucker Carlson went on national television and announced, "Senator Kirsten Gillibrand of New York came positively unglued," describing her as "barking" at the commandant.

When Maxine Waters refused to yield in her questioning of Treasury Secretary Steven Mnuchin, announcing that she was "reclaiming [her] time," the website RealClearPolitics described it as a "meltdown"[11]; at right-wing sites TheBlaze and

155

Breitbart, Waters is regularly described as "unhinged."[12] Trump-supporting black pastor Darrell Scott has referred to Waters as a "crazy aunt . . . rambling and babbling incessantly over every little thing."[13]

The idea that women's anger is fundamentally illegitimate, because they have nothing *real,* no big things to be rationally angry about, is part of what undergirds the claim that furious women are mentally ill. But it can also cause women to *feel* crazy. "Our anger gets dismissed and devalued and gaslighted," Black Lives Matter cofounder Alicia Garza told me, speaking specifically about black women. "We are angry because people are telling us what is happening to us right in front of our faces is not in fact happening, and that is crazy to me."

Whether angry women are driven crazy, or whether their anger is confused for mental illness, the claim about them in a society that treats mental illness as a delegitimizing aberration becomes the same: they are received as emotionally precarious, irrational, untrustworthy, marginal, and unattractive.

Do a Google image search on any of the powerful women in politics or public life, especially those who threaten white male power — by pressing for reforms in the

156

military, the criminal justice system, the banking industry, or by running to beat powerful men — and you'll turn up scores of photos of Waters and Pelosi and Senators Kamala Harris and Elizabeth Warren with their mouths open, unrestrained: mid-yell, spittle-flecked, the very act of making a loud noise a sign of their ugly and unnatural personalities. The best way to discredit these women, to make them look unattractive, is to capture an image of them screaming; the act of a woman opening her mouth with volume and assured force, often in complaint, is coded in our minds as ugly.

"I struggle to think of women who lost their tempers in public and didn't face ridicule, temporary ruin, or both," wrote the feminist essayist Lindy West in 2017, citing public outcry against and condemnation of singers Sinead O'Connor, the Dixie Chicks, and Solange Knowles, as well as Juli Briskman, a government contractor who was fired after she was photographed giving Trump's presidential motorcade the finger.[14] When Caitlin Marriott, a twenty-one-year-old congressional intern, shouted, "Mr. President . . . fuck you!" at Donald Trump as he entered the Capitol in the summer of 2018, she was suspended for a week and had her credentials removed, though notably

157

her boss, New Hampshire senator Maggie Hassan, told the press that Marriott's behavior "shouldn't be equated with the president's destructive and divisive actions, like ripping health care away from people . . . like separating children from their parents. . . . And this young woman immediately accepted responsibility for her actions and is facing consequences for them. The president is doing neither."[15]

Perhaps the negativity around the yelling woman goes back to the disproportionate labor they perform as caretakers of the young, women's raised voices an unhappy reminder of reprimands, tones that make men feel like children again, under the punitive thumbs of their mothers, grandmothers, older sisters, nannies, and teachers who nurtured and educated them. "We're raised by women," said Gloria Steinem, "so we experience female power when we're younger. And men, especially, when they see a powerful woman as an adult, feel regressed to childhood and strike out at her."[16]

But the way in which adult female censure may return us to a youthful, domestic sphere — the only one in which women have been granted a kind of unchallenged power — speaks to the thing that women's

158

full-throated challenge does: it turns things upside down, reminds us of a time and place where women had authority, but when it's happening in politics, or in workplaces, or in activism, or elsewhere in the public sphere, it's an aberration, contextually inappropriate. In this way, women's angry voices, raised in challenge to power structures, vibrate with the threat of insurgency.

When Senator Kamala Harris, a former prosecutor, aggressively questioned Attorney General Jeff Sessions in 2017, Harris was instructed to stop interrupting Sessions by his friend, Arizona Senator John McCain. During that exchange, Sessions said aloud that Senator Harris's interrogation was making him "nervous." After the contentious exchange, former Trump advisor Jason Miller described the Attorney General as having had "vinegar and fire in his belly"; by contrast, in his view, Harris displayed "hysteria" in her interrogation of Sessions.

This coding doesn't just come from men: an angry woman can make other *women* very nervous too. After one furious postelection rant from Elizabeth Warren, MSNBC anchor Mika Brzezinski warned viewers, "there's an anger there that was shrill . . . unmeasured and almost unhinged." Even in the *New York Times,* Warren — whose great

159

gift is her ability to tell clear stories about the American economy that convey the frustrations and resentments of Americans who've been cheated or left behind as financial institutions have gotten more powerful — has been labeled a "scold," a word that seems well paired with another descriptor the paper has applied to her: "imperious."

What these women seem to represent is a kind of disarray. And here there is a deep historical reverberation: In early twentieth-century propaganda film strips about suffragists, women demanding enfranchisement are shown leaving their babies at home with their incapable husbands.[17] Nature has been thrown awry; the women's fury at their exclusion from civic participation has provoked disorder in the home. Women's ire in any political context remains coded as chaotic, while men's is comprehensible, understood as rational and often admirable.

This is probably why, as I was reporting for this book, nearly every woman I spoke to — especially in the months immediately following the inauguration of Donald Trump — described her anger as a thing of the past. "I *was* angry," an interviewee would say, "but I'm not angry anymore; I've taken my anger and turned it into action." Anger had to have been felt in the past tense in order to be something that many women I spoke to could describe to me with authority or confidence, let alone enthusiasm. About ten minutes into every interview I did in which a woman had assured me that she'd cast off her anger, I'd find her cursing and raising her voice, yelling about how livid she was: at Donald Trump, or her father, or her friends, or more broadly, at the nation and its injustices. These women were angry; *of course* they were angry. But they were conditioned to deny it from the start.

RECOGNIZING FURY

Gloria Steinem described to me the lifelong process of learning to feel, recognize, acknowledge, and express anger in real time. Steinem was raised in Toledo, Ohio, in a family in which her mother had given up a career as a journalist to raise children, and then suffered a mental illness that left her daughters as her caretakers. But Steinem was resistant to anger. "Coming from the Midwest, we have to be on LSD to know when we're angry," she said. For a while, she said, she "transplanted [her] anger, which is not uncommon for women to do, into other things." She could be angry at anyone who treated an animal badly, or

161

another person, but not angry on her own behalf.

When she was in her thirties and a working journalist herself, established as a glamorous denizen of the early 1970s New York media scene, Steinem made waves by posing as a Bunny at the New York Playboy Club and then writing about the experience; she'd also covered the antiwar and black power movements, and she'd been sent to cover a hearing on abortion. As Steinem recalled, "I'm sure that [anger is] what I felt at the first abortion hearing, the moment when I suddenly realized that *yes,* I had had an abortion, and so had one in three other women [but that it was illegal]. I'm sure what I felt was anger: *How is this okay? This is completely irrational!* I was fueled by anger." That fuel propelled her into the women's movement. Still, she said, for many years, "I could finally tell people on a Thursday that I'd been angry on Monday. I couldn't tell them in real time." Still, she said, with half a century as a feminist organizer and women's leader under her belt, as a woman who understands that "anger is great fuel for political activism; it's wonderful and I value it, I treasure it" — still, she said, to this day, she can express anger in real time "only occasionally."

If it is so difficult for Gloria Fucking Steinem to confidently let loose with fury, is it any wonder that in many places when I speak to students, young women ask me how *they* might express their own ire? They are scared, they tell me — in high schools, and on college campuses — to be publicly open about their rage, because they are afraid it will be alienating to their friends, to their peers, to men. They fear it will make them sound deranged or aggressive. They're not deranged and they're not aggressive; they're just angry. But how can they say that they're mad without drawing condemnation and raised eyebrows? How can they be confident and unapologetic in their rage? Won't they scare people off? They ask me what my secret is: How did I figure out how to get up on the stages at their schools and speak angrily?

What can I tell them? That when I was thirty-two and visiting a beach community with a friend, I told a glamorous older woman to whom I'd been introduced that I wrote about feminism, and that she looked me up and down and asked coolly, "How do men feel about your work?" as if this were the most crucial question about its consequence. When I told her that the man I was dating seemed interested in it, she raised an eyebrow and, disconcertingly, ran a finger along my leg, perhaps checking to see if it was hairless. "We'll see how that lasts." I don't want to recall to them that when I first started to write about politics and culture from a feminist perspective — and nearly always with careful humor and lightness intended to obscure my fury — about half of the responses I received were from readers anxious to tell me how furious I sounded, as if the assertion that I was angry was its own self-contained insult. Others suggested that the rage they presumed I must be feeling originated with the fact that I was ugly and that no man wanted me, while others were sure that if I could only land a man, he might be able to help me. Perhaps I should not mention to them that I was once told that a male friend — a good friend, a man I trust and care about — had said privately to another man, who had in turn told me, "Rebecca is so warm and so funny, you'd never connect the person she is with the angry stuff she writes."

But! I long to say to that friend, though he has no idea that his remarks were reported to me: the warm and funny me is the *same* as the writer who's furious about inequality; the woman who has been both

164

happily single and happily partnered, who is in love with a man who loves her, who has fun and feels joy and cares about her work and her friends and who vacations and drinks and eats and cooks and has kids she adores: she's also very angry.

But perhaps the belief that anger is somehow at odds with the otherwise affable feminine personality has to do with the fact that women have been so well conditioned to tamp down the rage, to disguise it or compartmentalize it, that the revelation that it's bubbling underneath feels surprising and discombobulating — even worrying — to others.

IT'S BAD FOR YOU

There is a persistent conviction that to be angry is *bad* for women. In early 2018, my dentist estimated to me that three-quarters of the women who'd come to see him since Trump's election were livid, information I quickly understood as a hopeful sign. But he shook his head sadly. "It's bad for them," he said. "They grind their teeth."

My dentist was not alone in his concern; plenty of activist, feminist women have shared his worries about rage's detrimental health effects. In the same days of 2018 that flood waters were covering Houston and

Donald Trump was once again threatening to repeal DACA and had pardoned racist sheriff Joe Arpaio and rolled back Obama administration provisions that forced companies to turn over their pay statistics, I received in my inbox a newsletter from goop, Gwyneth Paltrow's health and wellness brand, advising me on how to manage my anger. Though the newsletter assured me that according to psychotherapists, anger is "essential to our development" and acts as "a fuel that propels you through different life stages," the Q and A with the experts told a different story, warning goop's overwhelmingly female readership that feeling anger was an easy way out in personal relationships ("We'd rather get angry than admit our deep feelings of vulnerability") and also admonished that in politics, "So many politicians . . . are blinded by their own rage, leading to more mistakes. The mark of a true leader is that they can . . . make a mistake or people can disagree with them and they aren't taken over by anger. They may feel angry, but they don't act it out."[18]

So stigmatized is anger — viewed as somehow unclean, unhealthy — that even women whose politics have in part been driven by rage at injustice often renounce it and warn against its ill effects. The civil rights activist Septima Poinsette Clark, daughter of a formerly enslaved man, who grew up with reduced educational and economic opportunity and became a prolific educator and the founder of "citizenship schools" to increase black adult literacy and provide African Americans with tools they needed — and were often denied — to increase their chances at civic participation, famously said, "I never felt that getting angry would do you any good other than hurt your own digestion, keep you from eating, which I liked to do."

But women tamp it all down so effectively that I didn't realize until recently — as the rage began to overflow — how many other women, speaking about feminism around the country, get the same kinds of questions asked of them by young women as I do. The writer Roxane Gay has described how "at many events where I am speaking about feminism, young women ask how they can comport themselves so they aren't perceived as angry while they practice their feminism. They ask this question as if anger is an unreasonable emotion when considering the inequalities, challenges, violence, and oppression women the world over face."

Women yearn for permission, and simultaneously hunger for someone to express any curiosity at all about what they might be feeling.

"We get told all the time that our anger is disruptive, that it is a distraction, that it is not helpful, and that in fact it is divisive and moving us backwards," said Alicia Garza. "Yet nobody ever seems to question: *why are you so fucking mad?*"

"You are the first person who's ever asked me explicitly about anger," said Aditi Juneja, a twenty-seven-year-old lawyer and activist who cocreated an activism guide called *The Resistance Manual* in the wake of the 2016 election. "People ask me about self-care, about inclusion; no one ever asks me if I'm pissed off." But Juneja said she knows why. "If you ask women if they're angry, everyone will say no."

Juneja said she'd been thinking a lot about "who's even allowed to be pissed off and how they're allowed to express it" since the election. She said that she stopped watching Trump speeches or news about him almost a month before he was elected, because the experience of watching him, yet not seeing any of the rage he inspired in her reflected in the news media's coverage of him, was leaving her crippled by vertiginous self-doubt. "I felt like I was hearing him say

168

things that didn't make sense or that contradicted what he'd just said, but no one else was hearing this." The political media was covering him and the things he said as legitimate. "And I was questioning myself."

At some point in 2017, Juneja mentioned to her father that she'd stopped watching coverage of Trump because it had made her feel so confused and her father replied, "Well, I wasn't confused; I knew exactly who he was." Juneja said that she looked at her father with perplexity before realizing: "Oh, congratulations, no one has socialized you to wonder if maybe *you're* the one who's wrong. No one ever told you that the way you feel about the world is not valid."

There's perhaps no neater example of how rage is an emotion that is permitted and encouraged in (some) men — and can be used to their advantage — while for women it is forbidden, invalidated, and treated as a path to self-defeat, than the 2016 presidential election.

Chapter Two:
The Circle of Entrapment:
The Heavy Price of Rage

Back in 2008, when Hillary Clinton first ran for president, there was plenty of commentary about her voice and her aggressive, ambitious demeanor, which often got confused with each other. Her tone was understood on many levels to sound inherently villainous: whether it was when she laughed — routinely referred to in the press as her "cackle" — or when she spoke loudly, it was heard to match what was largely believed to be her unnerving ambition. Back then, *Washington Post* reporter Joel Achenbach fantasized about the good old days of the brank's bridle, writing that Clinton "needs a radio-controlled shock collar so that aides can zap her when she starts to get screechy."[19]

In 2008, the reaction to Clinton was in part about the sheer novelty of hearing a woman's voice register on a presidential campaign trail, and her volume and pitch stood out especially against that of her opponent Barack Obama, who, for reasons relating to his own historic identity and firstness, could not afford to raise *his* voice in anger, and whose calm tone and oratorical gifts proved a stark contrast to Clinton's. During Obama's administration, Clinton would continue to be caricatured as threatening and angry, with the *Washington Post*'s Dana Milbank and Chris Cillizza joking that if she'd ever attended a beer summit with the president, she'd be served "Mad Bitch" brew.[20]

The 2016 election was a different ball game. From the start, the theme of the presidential race *was* anger: Bernie Sanders was angry. Donald Trump was angry. And they talked about it directly. In 2016, after Republican South Carolina governor Nikki Haley advised voters not to listen to "the angriest voices," including Donald Trump's, on immigration, Trump told CNN, "She's right. I am angry. . . . As far as I'm concerned, anger is okay. Anger and energy is what this country needs."[21] Ten days later, Sanders took a similar approach, responding to Bill Clinton's description of him as angry. "You know what? It's true. I am angry. And the American people are angry." Four days later, Clinton herself got into the act. "A lot of people are not only worried and frustrated," she said. "They're angry. . . . I'm angry too."

But somehow Clinton couldn't persuade people that she was furious in the same way, perhaps in part because she couldn't quite get the tone of her voice right. A *Washington Post* write-up that included coverage of that speech opened with a description of how Clinton's voice "thundered through a bowling alley . . . then turned soft and thoughtful." The rest of the piece included two descriptions of Clinton as "shouting" and ended with a quote from one of Clinton's supporters who opined, "Bernie Sanders has an ability to connect in a charismatic way. It's that magnetism that she's not inherently able to transmit."

How could a candidate whose assertive expressions of anger were understood only as performative, imitative, and inauthentic *also* be heard by so many people, at the very same time, as constantly yelling at them?

After her first debate with Sanders, the *New York Times* evaluated the Vermont senator — whose everyday communication style involves finger-pointing, raised tones, and vigorous head-shaking — as having "kept his cool," while claiming that Clinton "appear[ed] tense and even angry at

172

times"[22] and wondered if her "ferocity" wasn't "risky, given that many voters . . . already have an unfavorable opinion of her." Watergate journalist Bob Woodward opined that Clinton's challenges originated with her "style and delivery . . . she shouts. There is something unrelaxed about the way she's communicating." On his radio show, after playing a clip of Clinton talking loudly — yes, angrily! — about standing up to the gun lobby, Sean Hannity asked, "What is likable about that? . . . Angry, bitter, screaming?"

And it wasn't just the right-wing or mainstrean press. It was the left as well. "Is she a presidential candidate or is she trying to star in the *Scream* reboot?" asked John Iadarola of the left-wing news network *The Young Turks,* arguing that what "needs to be borne in mind . . . is something can be historically true, a form of discrimination or stereotyping like women are shrill and they're nags and men have said that historically way too much . . . but that doesn't mean it's impossible for a woman . . . to speak loudly when she doesn't need to."[23] In other words, just because it's sexist doesn't mean it's not true.

It was a perfect, and perfectly maddening, circle of entrapment: a candidate who yelled

173

too much, but who didn't express anger enough, and when she tried to express anger better, was presumed to be faking it.

"She was exactly the wrong candidate for this angry, populist moment," wrote liberal journalist Thomas Frank in his election postmortem, noting that Clinton was "an insider when the country was screaming for an outsider." Frank could see the anger of people who were screaming, and understood the moment as a furious one. Yet what Frank saw in *Clinton,* working to her detriment, was a "shrill self-righteousness, shouted from a position of high social status, that turns people away."[24] Given that her opponents were also multiple-home-owning powerful white people, one an almost three-decade veteran of Congress and one a billionaire real estate tycoon, it's hard to imagine that it was the high social status and not something qualitatively different about her shouting that struck Frank as the *really* shrill turn-off.

The irony was that while there was plenty of reasonable debate about Clinton's friendliness with banks and history of centrist compromise, her economic agenda was directly targeted at many of the populations that were angriest, *including* coal miners and those white working-class communities in

174

the throes of the opioid epidemic. Clinton had policies on subsidized childcare and creating more economic stability for caregivers, on addressing racial and economic inequality around reproductive autonomy via abolishment of the Hyde Amendment. But she was widely understood to be bad at talking about these issues in a persuasive way, and part of that badness surely did stem from her own oratorical shortcomings. But those shortcomings might well have been exacerbated by all the ways that Clinton — and lots of public-speaking women who came before her — had been discouraged from talking loudly or too aggressively, leaving her nervous and hesitant about getting too passionate, too enflamed, too screechy or shrill or emotional or any of the other ways America hears women's voices raised in feeling. She had to walk a very thin communicative tightrope, often sounding boring and robotic, wholly unable to viscerally convey her interest in the frustrations of voters.

That the forceful expression of fury might not just be okay from (white) men but might in fact actually work to their benefit, while at the same time working *against* their female peers and competitors, is backed up by some emerging research.

The psychology professor Lisa Feldman Barrett has described in the *New York Times* a study in which her research team showed people photographs of men and women making facial expressions. They found that their subjects were more likely to assume that whatever was causing a woman's emotion was something internal, whereas whatever was provoking a man's response was something external, or as she put it, "She's a bitch, but he's just having a bad day."[25] It's a problem that John Neffinger, a political advisor who's been coaching candidates for years, and who wrote a series of memos to Clinton during the race, trying to help her balance the ways in which she expressed herself, has been wrestling with. He and fellow researchers have reviewed studies on two general criteria in how the public evaluates candidates: strength and warmth. Going in, he explained, male candidates are presumed to have strength — a category imaginatively tied to skill, authority, capability, and economic power — and female candidates are intrinsically assumed to possess warmth — which in political terms is meant to convey affinity, fun, friendliness, and also the sense that a candidate really cares about the people they want to represent.

176

"When somebody manages to project a lot of strength and a lot of warmth, we say they're charismatic and magnetic, we want to be *with* that person, we want to *be* that person," said Neffinger. Those who read as having more strength than warmth are viewed as "fearsome" and those with more warmth than strength as "adorable." The question of how these qualities are valued in politicians is as old as Machiavelli's argument that it is better to be feared than loved, though best to be both. According to Neffinger, "It's really hard to find candidates who combine the two." Male candidates *can* theoretically squeak by as fearsome, especially in times of national crisis, when authoritarian male figures are generously viewed as protectors: think Rudy Giuliani after 9/11, or famously ill-tempered John McCain, revered as a war hero. They can't be wholly adorable, precisely because that means they've been feminized and are therefore taken less seriously.

For women, both poles are toxic: to be fearsome is to be vilified and unpalatable, unnatural and monstrous. To be adorable is to be unserious and incompetent. The strategic problem for women is that the work to balance both poles is delicate and precarious: As it turns out, for men, a little

177

warmth goes a long way. For women, a little strength goes way too far.

Bernie Sanders, a disheveled grump whose style was to yell righteously but repetitively at his audiences about inequality, was able to exude charm simply by smiling at a small bird that landed on his podium during a speech. But when a woman, said Neffinger, "asserts herself in some fashion having to do with strength, she quickly slides out of the warmth category. She becomes perceived as a threat to the social order. Guys can be a little nice, without throwing out their strength. But women cannot add a little strength without losing warmth."

Those were the dynamics facing Hillary Clinton as she competed against two men who were trading on their strength — their anger — as a major selling point to the American public. To compete with them in this vein would be to invite further, compounding anxiety about the ways in which she was already upsetting the order of things simply by running against these men for the highest office in the land. And no one on her team was naive about what kind of impact these conditions had on her range of expression.

As her lead speechwriter Dan Schwerin told me in 2017, "There's a reason why male candidates can shout and are called passionate, and if a woman candidate raises her voice to whip up a crowd, she's screeching and yelling." Because his boss understood this, Schwerin said, "she's controlled, she doesn't rant and rave, she's careful. And then that's read as inauthentic; it means that she doesn't understand how upset people are, or the pain people are in, because she's not angry the way those guys are angry. So she must be okay with the status quo because she's not angry."

Clinton herself addressed her frustration with this seemingly unsolvable equation in her campaign memoir *What Happened,* barely able to contain her simmering disdain for the impossibility of the dynamics facing her as a candidate. "I've tried to adjust," she wrote. "After hearing repeatedly that some people didn't like my voice, I enlisted the help of a linguistic expert," who told her to focus on deep breathing and positivity. Clinton is drily smoldering as she explains how she was pushed to such *unnatural* lengths to maintain the illusion of a naturally cheery femininity: "That way, when the crowd got energized and started shouting — as crowds at rallies tend to do — I could resist doing the normal thing, which is to shout back." Clinton told the

179

linguistic expert that she'd try her best to comply. "But out of curiosity, can you give me an example of a woman in public life who has pulled this off successfully — who has met the energy of a crowd while keeping her voice soft and low?"

The linguistic expert could not.

MICHELLE OBAMA, THE "ANGRY BLACK WOMAN"

If Hillary Clinton had a hard time figuring out how to express complex emotions, including frustration, without being understood as threatening, her path was a walk in the park compared to that of Michelle Obama.

Michelle Robinson had grown up on Chicago's South Side, the daughter of a stay-at-home mother and a city employee. She graduated from Princeton and Harvard Law School, and met her future husband Barack Obama when she was assigned to professionally mentor him at the white-shoe Chicago law firm Sidley Austin. During the years in which the couple lived in Chicago, when Barack worked as a community organizer and law professor, and Michelle left the fancy firm to work for the city, and then for the University of Chicago, she was considered the star of the couple: the gregarious, charismatic, funny, dynamic one. Having grown up around Chicago's corrupt political machine, she was distrustful of politics and didn't want anything to do with them. But her husband did.

Then Barack Obama became the brightest star to streak across the American political landscape in a generation, and his wife fell under national scrutiny. Her impassioned speeches, her emotive candor, her clear and informed view of American history, including her grim take on politics and her sharp sense of humor, all began, perplexingly, to work against her.

As her husband became a sensation in the Senate, she was caught by a reporter rolling her eyes and commenting, "Maybe one day he will do something to warrant all this attention"; by the time he hit the presidential campaign trail two years later, she was still affectionately complaining about his failures to make the bed or put his socks in the laundry basket; she called him "snore-y and stinky" when he woke up in the morning, and described him, memorably, as "a gifted man, but in the end, he's just a man." This quickly earned her the attention of the *New York Times* columnist Maureen Dowd, who worried that people heard Michelle as "emasculating" for "casting her husband . . .

181

as an undisciplined child." Again, the critical voice of a woman was cast as maternal reproach.

This was the gentlest treatment Michelle Obama was to receive in the press during that presidential campaign.

After her husband began to win primaries and it seemed possible that he might win the Democratic nomination, Michelle gave a speech in which she said, "People in this country are ready for change and hungry for a different kind of politics. . . . For the first time in my adult life I am proud of my country because it feels like hope is finally making a comeback."

It was a positive, warm, forward-looking statement. But coming from the mouth of Michelle Obama, it was heard in some quarters as a resounding and unpatriotic affront. Conservative columnist Bill Kristol chided her for not having been grateful for America winning the Cold War, while at the *National Review,* Jim Geraghty wrote, "America hasn't been good to her? What, opportunities to go to Princeton, Harvard Law, working for top-shelf law firms and hospitals . . . that's not enough?" as if any sentiment short of fawning appreciation for the country in which she had worked hard and excelled was unthinkable.

The very act of mild critique — of a nation in which her great-great-great-grandmother had been enslaved, in which her husband was the first black man ever to come close to being nominated for the presidency, in which she was being asked to sacrifice her job and independent identity to try to move into the White House, a building constructed by slave labor — was enough to confirm a popular vision of Michelle as a worryingly angry black woman.

She appeared on the cover of the *National Review:* mouth open (of course), her eyes cutting menacingly toward the viewer, under the headline "Mrs. Grievance." The conservative columnist Michelle Malkin began referring to her as "Barack's Bitter Half." The black conservative columnist Mychal Massie wrote that Michelle "portrays herself as just another angry black harridan who spits in the face of the nation that made her rich, famous, and prestigious."

As the novelist Chimamanda Ngozi Adichie would write of Michelle, "Because she said what she thought, and because she smiled only when she felt like smiling, and not constantly and vacuously, America's cheapest caricature was cast on her: the Angry Black Woman. Women, in general, are not permitted anger — but for black American women, there is an added expectation of interminable gratitude, the closer to groveling the better, as though their citizenship is a phenomenon that they cannot take for granted."

Medusa-Michelle memes proliferated on the internet. The already incorrect description of Michelle as angry transformed into her being militant. Juan Williams, then an NPR commentator, called Michelle Obama "Stokely Carmichael in a designer dress," connecting her to the civil rights leader who had in the 1960s transitioned from nonviolent organizing to the more militant approach he described as "black power." In *Slate,* the former left journalist turned neocon Christopher Hitchens published a breathtakingly dishonest attempt to connect Michelle's undergraduate thesis at Princeton — which had been about the experience of being black at Princeton — to the black power movement, claiming inaccurately that twenty-one-year-old Michelle said she had been "much influenced" by Carmichael, who in turn Hitchens connected to Nation of Islam leader Louis Farrakhan. Fox News went further, asking if the fist bump, or dap, that Michelle had shared with her husband on the night he'd

184

clinched the Democratic nomination was in fact a "terrorist fist jab." A *New Yorker* cover parodied the panic over Michelle's perceived militancy — and memorialized the view of her angry black femininity — with a Barry Blitt cartoon portraying her in a 70s-style Afro, carrying a machine gun. The illustration was called *The Politics of Fear.*

By the time her husband was accepting the nomination in Denver, Michelle's public persona had been remade: she talked about clothes and pantyhose, not about politics or the nation, and not with any critical inflection about her spouse. At the convention, she was framed (accurately!) as a devoted wife and mother, a little girl who'd loved the Brady Bunch, but as nothing else. In her own speech, she carefully expressed her love of country and gratitude for the chances it had afforded her. Michelle had been effectively muzzled, any querulousness tamped down. She'd never actually expressed true anger on the trail, but the very act of having opened her mouth in a free and frank way had so quickly been heard as rancor that her opinions and her open mouth, and anything that could be heard as frustration or complaint, had had to go.

Before she left the White House, in an interview with Oprah Winfrey, Michelle would say of that period, of being cast as "that angry black woman," "Dag, you don't even *know* me, you know? . . . Where'd that come from?"[26] More than a year later, Michelle — speaking at a gathering of black women in Florida — would speak even more frankly to former White House advisor Valerie Jarrett of this process, explaining that early on, "I looked at one of my speeches and I saw that what was animation and passion to me, could easily be turned into sound bites of anger and aggression." At that point, she said, "I was like, *oh, this is a game.* It's a game. And what was I thinking? I thought this was real, but it was a game too. And I wasn't playing the game, I was just being passionate because I thought that's what people wanted . . . But they don't know what they really want. So I had to learn how to deliver" — and here, she pasted a big smile on her face, and offered a shake of her hair — "a *message.*"[27]

Writing at the start of her 1940 memoir, the civil rights and suffrage activist Mary Church Terrell described her story as one about "A colored woman living in a white world. It cannot possibly be like a story written by a white woman. A white woman has only one handicap to overcome — that of sex. I have two — both sex and race. I

186

belong to the only group in this country which has two such huge obstacles to surmount. Colored men have only one — that of race." Terrell's is what the Rutgers women and gender studies professor Brittney Cooper has called "one of the earliest articulations of the political stakes of intersectionality," a term that would be coined by Kimberlé Williams Crenshaw nearly five decades later to describe the interlocking sets of biases faced by women of color in America. This was more than simply a doubling of bias; for the racism faced by nonwhite women is amplified and altered by sexism, and the sexism they encounter is perverted and exacerbated by racial bias.

In practice, these dynamics have long meant that black women's expressions of frustration, resistance, or even mild critique have been refracted through an American lens that has enlarged them, rendering them as some defining feature of black femininity. One crucial result of the national mythos around black women's anger, said the writer Joelle Owusu in 2018, is that as a black woman, she is regularly "perceived as the aggressor in every situation . . . Even when you are being polite and respectful during an altercation, someone will always make a remark about a black woman's 'attitude' or 'aggression.' "[28]

The problematizing of anger in black women takes many forms. There's a reflexive defensiveness against it from white women and from men, a resistance to actually reckoning with the roots of black female dissatisfaction — whether that dissatisfaction is expressed gently or furiously or perhaps merely inferred — that gets conveyed via irrational allegations of spoilt ingratitude, negativity, or instability.

"We are told we are irrational, crazy, out-of-touch, entitled, disruptive, and not team players," writes Cooper in her exploration of black feminist anger, *Eloquent Rage.* "Angry Black women are looked upon as entities to be contained, as inconvenient citizens who keep on talking about their rights while refusing to do their duty and smile at everyone."

THE RIGHTEOUS FURY OF MAXINE WATERS

In October of 2017, Maxine Waters, speaking at an event to benefit the Ali Forney Center, which supports LGBTQ homeless youth, made remarks about how moved she'd been, hearing the story of the black, homeless, trans youth advocate after whom the center had been named, noting that "with this kind of inspiration, I will go and take Trump out tonight."

Waters, a leading and vocal proponent of impeachment, was quite clearly not referring to any sort of violent action, but in the following days, conservatives pounced on her sound bite. One right-wing pundit, Lawrence Jones, said on *Fox and Friends* that, "When you incite violence, that should be investigated," expressing his concern that Waters's remark would "[send] people out to assassinate Republicans" and when challenged, reiterated that "She could have said impeachment if she wanted impeachment; she talked about essentially assassinating the president."[29] Omar Navarro, Waters's political opponent in California, tweeted, "I'm calling for the arrest of Maxine Waters."[30]

The deranged attempt to cast Waters's remarks as a murder threat didn't remain on the Fox News fringes of political coverage; it was repeated in the mainstream press, with CNN anchor Chris Cuomo asking Waters on air about her comments in ways that cast her as militaristic from the start. Cuomo observed that the conflict between the president and his critics "has become an ugly war of words" with Waters "a named combatant in this battle." Playing

189

the clip of Waters's speech, Cuomo said, "those words have been interpreted as an attempt on the president's life." Waters called his assessment "absolutely ridiculous," noting that "nobody believes that a seventy-nine-year-old grandmother who is a congresswoman and who has been in Congress and politics for all these years [was] talking about doing any harm."[31]

But of course people *did* believe that, or were willing to, in part because rational political challenge to white male presidential authority, coming from a black woman, was such a disruption of the power structure. Cuomo's interrogation of Waters made clear that her words had violated natural assumptions about which kinds of people were permitted to deploy aggressive language, and toward whom, when he asked her if she believed that she should "have a more high level of decency in how you discuss those that you want to criticize, especially when it's the president of the United States?"

Waters understood the resonance of his analysis perfectly. "I think I have been extremely responsible in laying out the case in which this president should be impeached," she said, but "people are not accustomed to a woman, in particular an African-American woman, taking this kind

190

of leadership. How dare *me* challenge the president of the United States?"[32]

A cult of adoration sprang up around Waters during 2017 and 2018, and millions publicly appreciated her willingness to speak in lengthy and righteously aggressive tirades about Donald Trump, to snap back and stand up for herself. Memes of Waters staring censoriously over her glasses spread across social media. A clip of Waters, insisting during her questioning of Treasury Secretary Steve Mnuchin that she was "reclaiming [her] time," became a viral GIF and was remixed as a gospel song. The performer of that remix was a surprise guest during Waters's interview on the daytime talk show *The View,* provoking a dizzying moment during which the show's four white and one black cohosts, along with a predominantly white studio audience, danced along to a man singing words Maxine Waters had said during a tense congressional hearing.[33]

It was kind of great, but also kind of weird, the popular celebration of the woman who became known in some quarters as "Auntie Maxine," in reference to a black familial figure who expresses her regard and affection in part by taking no shit and doling out real talk. Waters was celebrated as "righteous, furious, uncowed" in a Buzzfeed piece in which Campaign Zero co-founder and Black Lives Matter activist Brittany Packnett described Waters as "the Auntie Boss: As real as your auntie and as powerful as only a black woman could be." The mass feting of Waters, a black woman who was quoted back in 1989 saying "I have a right to my anger, and I don't want anybody telling me I shouldn't be, that it's not nice to be, and that something's wrong with me because I get angry," was surely a balm in a nation that has rarely acknowledged black female rage as beautiful, patriotic, or inspirational.

Yet Waters wasn't just signaling righteous fury, she was also incurring the costs of that fury, costs that many of those deploying her side-eye GIFs and memes had never incurred through all the many years in which Waters had stood against the tide and been vilified for it.

It's true that Waters had been the subject of a long-running ethics investigation on charges that she helped a bank in which her husband held stock (she was cleared of wrongdoing and one of her top aides was reprimanded). But before and after that investigation, she was treated as a sideshow, and with often virulent racism by her political detractors. In 2012, after she'd torn into

Republican leaders Eric Cantor and John Boehner, calling them "demons," Fox News anchor Eric Bolling advised her, "Congresswoman, you saw what happened to Whitney Houston. . . . Step away from the crack pipe." In 2017, Bill O'Reilly responded to a clip of one of Waters's speeches excoriating Trump by claiming that he hadn't heard a word of it, having been too distracted by her "James Brown wig."[34]

But it's not just her political opponents who have fallen in line with the vilification of black female anger. In the summer of 2018, as fury on the left built, partly in response to the Trump administration's zero tolerance policy regarding refugee seekers at the Mexican border, their separation of at least three thousand young children from their parents, and the expansion of family internment camps meant to house asylum seekers indefinitely, angry protesters began interrupting the meals and movie nights of Trump administration officials; one restaurant owner in Virginia refused to serve Trump press secretary Sarah Huckabee Sanders. Maxine Waters was one of the only Democratic politicians to meet this rising tide of politically meaningful and valid rage with respect, acknowledgment, and encouragement.

In a speech in California, she urged those who were furious to "show up wherever we have to show up," suggesting that "if you see anybody from that Cabinet in a restaurant, in a department store, at a gasoline station, you get out and you create a crowd and you push back on them and you tell them they're not welcome anymore, anywhere." Waters was not advocating violence; she was calling for assembly and pushback. It was in line with her history as a representative of disempowered populations; she was hearing and channeling the exertions of the furiously oppressed against the oppressors.

But when Waters applied her view of the role of insurrectionist protest in 2018, members of her *own party* stepped in to censure her. Senate Minority Leader Chuck Schumer advised that "no one should call for the harassment of political opponents," chastising Waters's suggestion as "not American." (It was of course deeply American, a tradition stretching back to the Revolution.) Nancy Pelosi also chimed in, claiming, "Trump's daily lack of civility has provoked responses that are predictable but unacceptable." Horrifyingly, neither Democratic leader bothered to defend Waters against the implicit threat sent in a tweet by the president, where he called Waters "an

194

extraordinarily low IQ person" and falsely accused her of advocating "harm to [his] supporters," concluding with the grim warning, "Be careful what you wish for Max!"

To publicly rebuke a black woman's support for political protest but not the powerful white patriarch's thinly veiled call to violence against her was to play on the very same impulses that Trump and the white patriarchal party that supported him played on: racist and sexist anxiety about noncompliant women and nonwhites, and the drive to punish them. That her own colleagues would cast Waters as too much, as too combative and fearsome, while letting the threat made against her by the most powerful of white men go unremarked upon, was a goddamn travesty. Especially given the decades of work Waters had done to recognize and address the potentially consequential fury of underrepresented and disempowered populations on behalf of whom her party is supposed to advocate, and the way in which her exertions are a service to those yearning to have their fury heard and seen and acknowledged as valid.

Alicia Garza recalled to me how Waters had gained early prominence "fighting to make visible" the case of Eula Love, a poor

195

black woman shot and killed by police in her district after a dispute over a gas bill in 1979.[35] Describing the news coverage of the event, Garza said, "Maxine was certainly angry. And she was portrayed as absolutely batshit crazy. She was portrayed as not credible. And she kept going."

These days, Garza said, "everybody is all 'Auntie Maxine, you go girl!' But this has been her *career*. She has always used anger in the service of a higher purpose." Garza pointed out how black women's anger can get fetishized, yet never really taken to heart. "So we can love Maxine reclaiming her time, but do we love what she is saying about the conditions that black people are living in? We get to ignore that in a way by taking on this trope of the angry black woman as someone who is performing for us, as opposed to taking on the substance of what she's talking about."

It also matters that enthusiasm for Waters has ballooned in a period when her party wields no power: Republicans haven't had as big a majority in the House since the 1920s. Waters may talk directly about the desire to impeach a president — a desire she's channeling for millions of Americans — but she has no power to do so. It's far easier to admire the spitting fury of a woman when she poses absolutely no political threat, a phenomenon that is also observably true about the adoring memes around non-black women including Ruth Bader Ginsburg and Hillary Clinton When She's Not a Candidate, but that sheds light onto how the sometimes appreciative treatment of certain Angry Black Women in fact reflects their relative powerlessness.

Ginsburg, whose fiery dissents have become the stuff of internet legend, and who has become known on the internet as the Notorious RBG, is in the minority of the Supreme Court. The pleasures of celebrating her toughness stem in part from her actual physical stature: she is a short, thin, octogenarian who has twice had cancer; the whole punch line of admiration for her is in part rooted in the improbability of her threat; she's like a little doll of female anger who we can all cheer for, even as she is outvoted again and again and again. It's extremely difficult to imagine the same kind of tattoo-inspiring admiration for her angry opinions if those opinions were actually reshaping the law.

As for Clinton, she was perhaps never more lauded for her aggressiveness than in the years after having lost the Democratic primary to Barack Obama when she went

197

on to work for him as his secretary of state. In those years, she was the subject of social media love; a Tumblr called "Texts from Hillary" was built around an image of her looking like a badass in sunglasses, sending savage messages to other powerful people. But this was in an era when she was widely celebrated for having been a team player, subsidiary to her former political rival. As soon as she again became a candidate for president, the fact of her individual power and the threat it posed to her male competitors was recalled, and the mass affection for that tough and righteously censorious version of Hillary was extinguished almost instantly.

These provisos on a celebration of female fortitude — that they take place almost exclusively around women who do not pose an imminent threat to power — must be acknowledged when considering the ways in which black women's anger can get fetishized and celebrated. In some ways, the cultural caricature of neck-snapping, side-eye-casting black female censure becomes easily embraceable precisely *because* it is disconnected from real political, economic, or social power, because its relationship to the threat of actual disruption of white male authority can be understood as inherently comical. Black women's relative distance, from both white supremacy and patriarchal advantage, makes it easier, in some ways, to applaud their toughness, precisely because it is so far removed from being a true threat to white male domination.

And when it *does* threaten a white man? John Neffinger pointed to the treatment of Kamala Harris, whose sharp prosecutorial interrogations knocked Attorney General Jeff Sessions off his game in 2017, bringing the punitive force of white patriarchy on her head. "When Kamala took Jeff Sessions apart," he said, "it immediately became a Republican talking point, and they pushed the narrative that she was hysterical. Now, you watch that interaction and my god, she's the furthest thing from hysterical. But they knew that to discredit her, that's where they had to go, that that's how you undermine a cool customer and threateningly competent woman like Kamala Harris. You cast her as an Angry Black Woman."

As with Waters, some on Harris's side quickly took up the video as a meme, cheering her as a you-go-girl rebuke to Sessions's assumptions of white male authority. But the popularity of the Angry Black Women cartoon also leaves these women doing a lot of the work of expressing anger that white

199

women feel, but are discouraged, in different ways, from expressing themselves. This is crucial to an online social media phenomenon that has been dubbed "digital blackface," a practice whereby white and other nonblack users turn to GIFs of black people expressing the emotions they wish to convey.

For example, among the most popular means of conveying women's cutting feminist rage at men in digital shorthand is to post a GIF of the actress Angela Bassett taken from a scene in the 1995 film *Waiting to Exhale,* a scene in which Bassett's character, angry at her husband for leaving her for a white mistress, puts all his clothes and belongings in a car and sets it on fire. When people on the internet are anxious to express suspicion or the feeling of seeing through some bullshit, it's to the side-eye of black women — from actress Viola Davis to pop star Rihanna to civil rights hero Dorothy Height staring at Dr. Martin Luther King, Jr., during his 1963 "I Have a Dream" speech — that they often turn to do the work of expressing their anger for them.

"We're your sass, your nonchalance, your fury, your delight, your annoyance . . ." the writer Lauren Michele Jackson told journalist Amanda Hess, who argued that "on the internet, white people outsource their emotional labor to black people."[36] When so much social opprobrium is directed at women for expressing anger toward the white men to whom white women are likely to be more proximate, many white women rely on black women, expected to be angry as a default setting, to perform the emotion in their stead.

These are the dynamics that the black feminist Audre Lorde details in her famous 1981 address to the National Women's Studies Association, "The Uses of Anger," when she describes reading from her work, "A Poem for Women in Rage" and having a white woman approach her to ask, "Are you going to do anything with how we can deal directly with *our* anger? I feel it's so important." Lorde asks her how she uses her rage, and then has to turn away "from the blank look in her eyes." "I do not exist," Lorde writes, "to feel her anger for her."[37]

These relationships have long been in play politically. For generations, black women have been asked to do the work of opposing the rise of the right wing — as the most reliable Democratic voting bloc, as some of the most vocally furious women in Congress, as the backbone of organizing, activism, and political and civic engagement in the nation — even as the Democratic Party has invested little in them as candidates, and too little in policy that would better support and protect them. Meanwhile, during the Trump administration, the political media has regularly passed them over for serious political analysis, while filling newspapers with endless deep ethnographic dives into the lives and motivations of white working-class Trump supporters.

In a crucial 2017 special election for the Alabama senate seat, 98 percent — *98 percent* — of black women voters voted for Democrat Doug Jones over the openly racist accused sexual predator Roy Moore; almost 50 percent more black women than black men voted in that election; and 63 percent of white women voted for Moore. After Alabama, there were all kinds of social media messages and op-eds "thanking" black women for "saving America," a message that implicitly suggested that black women were themselves inherently adjacent to, or marginal within, America, even in the very moment at which their centrality to deciding its representation was purportedly being acknowledged. The credit that black women received in the wake of the Alabama election, wrote political consultant Angela Peoples in the *New York Times,* is "one small step in the right direction. But we don't need thanks — we need you to get out of the way and follow our lead."[38]

MEN AND ANGELS GIVE ME PATIENCE

In the face of all of this multifaceted judgment of their fury, how are women in public and political spheres supposed to strategize around the anger that they sometimes — often — feel?

"Men and angels give me patience," Elizabeth Cady Stanton wrote to Susan B. Anthony in 1852, frustrated about the impositions of motherhood and wifely duty on her ability to express her political anger through writing and speaking. "I am at the boiling point! If I do not find some day the use of my tongue on this question I shall die of an intellectual repression, a woman's rights convulsion."[39]

In 2017 came a million schemes for how to get women to express their anger in some appropriate way, something that might release them from it, but that still fell within the purview of acceptability. Magazines recommended exercise classes to women for whom "Scream ALL the expletives" was the first thing written on [their] to-do list today"[40]; Mama Gena, head of "The School of Womanly Arts," urged her devotees to

203

"FEEL loudly . . . RAGE like an angry lioness . . . HOWL like a bitch in heat . . . cry MORE . . . SCREAM your head off."[41]

For A Bad Time, Call, "a podcast dedicated to women's anger," launched, encouraging nonmale-identifying people to phone into a recorded line and vent their frustrations. The litanies were then stitched together into audible quilts of female ire: "I am just really, really tired of grown-ass men who have their own jobs and their own lives telling me what I should be doing with mine/I'm just so tired of women being made to feel like we're not enough in anything we do/I'm just so pissed off about having to be pissed off. It's almost the new normal to be pissed off literally all the time because bad shit is constantly happening to women." At the end of the podcast, one of the hosts reassures listeners and callers alike: "Your anger is real. Your rage is valid. And we want to hear it."

In the fall of 2016, I appeared on *Real Time with Bill Maher.* It was days after the second presidential debate, to which Donald Trump had invited the women who'd accused his opponent's husband of sexual misconduct, at which he'd loomed over Clinton, practically pawing the ground with undisguised loathing and resentment toward her. Clinton had gripped her microphone with white-knuckled control, had not confronted him nor acknowledged the bizarre malevolence of his approach; she had kept her voice steady and her manner professional. Maher was frustrated by this, suggesting to me during his panel discussion that she should "say it to his face; he's right there, say 'You're full of shit, you asshole!' "

Maher likely hadn't done the math on how risky it would have been for Clinton to have turned on Trump in anger — the ease with which any ire directed toward him would have been reframed as her having played the woman card for strategic effect, how promptly she'd have been understood as having cast herself as a victim of bullying in order to earn cheap sympathy, how she might have come off as castrating, unhinged; the satisfaction that might have been gained by her critics in having seen evidence that her opponent had gotten under her skin.

But the person who *had* done that math — in real time — was Hillary Clinton, who months later would describe that debate to me as one of the most difficult moments of the campaign, shivering with the visceral recollection of how Trump's demeanor had been "so personally invasive . . . following me, eyeing me." She said that she *did* consider, as a presidential debate was going on, whether she should turn on him and shout "Get away from me!" But she had figured that that would be playing into his hands: "He will gain points and I will lose points," she recalled thinking (she had thought right; she was widely acknowledged to have kicked the ever living shit out of Trump in that debate, even without actually kicking him). Acknowledging how tight her grip on her microphone was during the debate, Clinton told me it was an extension of the internal control she was mustering. "Think of all the times where you are either mentally or physically gripping yourself," she said. "[Willing yourself] not to respond, not to lash out, not to display the anger that you feel, because you know it will redound to your detriment. So you swallow it."

You swallow it. It's a choice made by millions of women throughout time: the decision that the best strategic approach is to take the anger you feel and stuff it way down deep. Because to let it out is going to do more damage to you than it's going to damage the person or forces you're angry at. As a woman in public life, "you can't be angry for yourself," said Clinton. "You just can't. You can be indignant, you can be annoyed, you can be frustrated, but you can't be angry."

When Barbara Lee described to me the efforts she has made, in multiple circumstances, to contain and channel her fury in ways that are productive and will not backfire on her, I asked her whether she guessed that men had any idea how much internal strategizing went on inside women's heads. She sighed. "No, they're not aware of anything, if you ask me," she said with a smile. "They can't see women differently from the way they think women are." Which is often contained, their simmering unease covered over by politesse. But, Lee maintained, the fact that men have no idea how mad women are beneath the surface "works to our advantage, because that's how we win."

Perhaps it is how we win the debates, but so far, it is not how we win the elections. And it can be maddening — in both the enraging and the crazy-making sense of the term — to come to grips with the fact that many men have no idea how rocky the terrain of anger is for women.

Chapter Three: Dress Up Your Anger

Understood plainly by many women to be an impediment to effective communication, anger is often dressed up in other guises to make it more attractive, more legitimate. These are some of them.

God's Go-Ahead

Among the most popular strategies used to justify women's rage in public spheres is to attribute it to someone else, emphasizing that whatever anger you're feeling is actually channeled from a more authoritative source. Like, for instance, God.

This was a point made to me about women in politics by Senator Kirsten Gillibrand, who said in 2018 that "women have to be angry on behalf of someone else in order to be taken seriously. So if you're Harriet Tubman, or Joan of Arc, you have God bringing you this passion." Gillibrand nudged me toward the eccentric case of Victoria Woodhull, the first woman ever to run for president of the United States. Woodhull, a Wall Street broker, clairvoyant, and a free love advocate, made outrageously bold assertions, once declaring, "We mean treason; we mean secession . . . We are plotting revolution; we will [overthrow] this bogus Republic and plant a government of righteousness in its stead." But she also believed herself to be a medium speaking on behalf of the long-dead Greek orator Demosthenes, or channeling Napoleon and Josephine.

In this, Woodhull was not so different from some of her more officially respectable suffragist peers, some of whom took advantage of the period's fever for spiritualism to give a valence of beyond-the-grave authority to their disruptive ideas. The table in Seneca Falls at which Elizabeth Cady Stanton would write the Declaration of Sentiments was one that had previously been used for séances.[42] And the nineteenth-century reformer and suffragist Frances Willard described how, in the midst of her travels on behalf of the temperance movement, she sat down to pray one Sunday morning in 1876: "Upon my knees alone . . . there was borne in upon my mind, as I believe from loftier regions, the declaration: 'You are to speak for a woman's ballot as a weapon of protection to her home and tempted loved ones from the tyranny of drink."[43]

In addition to getting God's go-ahead to push for voting rights as a means to curb drinking, as the historian Carolyn DeSwarte Gifford has noted, Willard "also received 'a complete line of argument and illustration' for her first speech on home protection, which she delivered later in the year at the Woman's Congress in Philadelphia." Indeed, Gifford writes, those women advocating for temperance via the vote — largely, it should be noted, as a means to protect women from physical abuse at the hands of drunken husbands — "had to be able to justify their political and suffrage activity religiously. It was absolutely essential for them to believe that their behavior sprang from an experience that convinced them that God wanted them, indeed called them, to vote."[44]

Willard's more radical peer in the temperance movement, Carrie Nation, would also cite God as working through her, not only to rage against the evils of alcohol, but also to physically destroy drinking establishments. As Nation would later recall, she was visited one day in 1900 "by a voice which seemed to me speaking in my heart, these

210

words, 'GO TO KIOWA,' and my hands were lifted and thrown down." The interpretation of this message from the divine, Nation felt, "was very plain, it was this: 'take something in your hands and throw at these places in Kiowa [Kansas] and smash them.' " It was plainly God's direction, Nation maintained, that she gather up large rocks and use them to destroy saloons in Kansas, until her husband joked to her that she should use hatchets instead, which she described as "the most sensible thing you have said since I married you." They divorced the next year. Nation, who took the hatchet suggestion to heart, and became famous for chopping up bars all over the west, would go on to describe herself as "a bulldog running along at the feet of Jesus, barking at what He doesn't like."

JUST A MOTHER AND A WIFE

Close behind calling on the divine as a justification for rage — at least rage that has taken the form of social, political, or economic challenge — has been the practice of invoking maternal morality, mothering instincts, and wifely responsibility as the motivator for political agitation.

Mary Harris Jones was a dressmaker and a teacher who became a labor organizer and

211

an early member of the Industrial Workers of the World after her family died of yellow fever and her dress shop burned in the Great Chicago Fire of 1871. Jones opposed women's suffrage, believing it was a diversion of the upper classes, and arguing that "you don't need the vote to raise hell." She herself raised a lot of hell, and is responsible for the labor movement's famous call to action, "Pray for the dead and fight like hell for the living"; she also dressed in the clothes of an old woman, referred to the miners and other workers on whose behalf she fiercely battled "her boys," and in her fifties became known as "Mother." A US senator once condemned Mother Jones as the "grandmother of all agitators," to which she replied, "I hope to live long enough to be the great-grandmother of all agitators."

Twenty-five years her junior was Ella Reeve Bloor, a trade union organizer and socialist agitator who was a founding member of the American Communist Labor Party. Bloor helped Upton Sinclair gather data for his exploration of urban poverty *The Jungle;* she was a great proponent of women's rights and suffrage; she helped to organize farm workers in Iowa in the 1930s — including an action in which dairy farmers protested low wages by dumping milk off delivery trucks. She was arrested thirty-six times and dubbed by *Life* magazine "the grand old woman of the U.S. Communist Party."[45] And she was known as "Mother Bloor." The historian Mary Triece has described both Mothers Jones and Bloor, while different in their particular politics, as having "enacted a persona of militant motherhood that proved successful in organizing entire families in struggles against corrupt bosses and company-owned towns across the country."[46]

In 1930, Fannie Peck was fed up with the limited professional opportunities available to the swelling population of African Americans who'd moved into northern cities as part of the Great Migration. She gathered a group of fifty women in the basement of the Bethel AME Church in Detroit, and together they strategized the boycotting of businesses that did not hire black employees or that charged exorbitant prices, particularly targeting the meatpacking industry; some accounts claimed that the group burned down a huge packinghouse. By 1935, there were more than ten thousand women members of what Peck had dubbed "Housewives Leagues" in cities across the country, and thousands of members marched through Chicago, shutting down the whole meatpacking industry. The historian Stephen Tuck has argued that Peck "was a canny strategist" in that — despite being a successful mass organizer — she adopted "the nonthreatening posture of a group of housewives."[47]

You can see the evidence of exactly this sort of nonthreatening posture — or perhaps the way it is taken on, cannily, in response to the diminution and underestimation of motherhood — in the 1992 Senate campaign of Patty Murray from Washington. In 1980, Murray was a stay-at-home mom of two who became enraged after her state cut preschool funding. She put her kids in the car and drove to the state capitol to register her fury. "I was going around the hall and finding who I could talk to," Murray recalled to Jay Newton-Small, "and one state legislator said, 'That's a nice story, but you're just a mom in tennis shoes.' " Murray, further enflamed, went home and called the other moms in tennis shoes. "And they called the moms they knew — all were mad — and we were back at the state legislature." The women staged an uprising, ultimately succeeding in having the education cuts reversed, and Murray embarked on a career in electoral politics, further motivated by her fury over the treatment of Anita Hill in

1991 to run for the Senate in 1992. She was among the historic group of four women to win seats that year; her campaign's tag line was "Just a mom in tennis shoes."

Murray's self-minimizing reputation has worked to continue to disguise the anger that first prompted her entry into electoral politics. "[Patty's] not emotional," Republican House Speaker Paul Ryan once said of Murray. "Some of these folks walk out of the room, and they huff and they puff. She's not like that."

During the eighty-year suffrage battle, a concerted effort was made by feminists in the press to rehabilitate the image of legendarily prickly Susan B. Anthony as a kind of familial goddess, despite the fact that she had very intentionally chosen not to marry or bear children, and had shown nothing but disdain for the institution of marriage entered into by her colleagues, including Ida B. Wells, whom she endlessly belittled for having wed. But just a few years before Anthony's 1906 death, as the movement to enfranchise women ground on, *Pearson's Magazine* published a profile called "Miss Anthony At Home" in which the writer Ida Husted Harper marveled, "What a housekeeper is Susan B. Anthony, domestic in

215

every fiber of her body!" Harper referred to the aged suffragist and labor leader as "Aunt Susan," and enthused, "like a lovely grandmother . . . [she] never has suggested ways for repairing the damages of society with one-half the skill she employed in teaching her nieces her wonderful method of darning rents in garments and household linens." As historian Sara Hunter Graham writes of the process of taming Anthony's reputation through domesticating and maternalizing her, it "helped to replace the stereotypical image of a masculinized fanatic with a nonthreatening feminine heroine imbued with domestic virtues."[48]

And damned if it didn't work. When Anthony died, the press would report warmly on mourners at her grave; the progressive organizer and politician Eugene V. Debs described her as "a moral heroine, an apostle of progress, a herald of the coming day." Graham argues that the remaking of Anthony meant that in this stage — the final haul — of the suffrage movement, "gone was the taint of extremism that suffragists believed had haunted the movement for decades; the parlor meeting had adopted 'Aunt Susan' as its patron saint, and suffragism had come of age."

But while the maternalizing of female

216

political participation permits it to exist without grave social penalty, it can simultaneously obscure the anger that so often drives that participation — and insurrection.

Perhaps the most viscerally catalytic moment in the nascent civil rights movement was the murder of Emmett Till, a fourteen-year-old African-American child from Chicago, who was beaten to death and left in a river after having been accused of making a pass at a white woman while visiting an uncle in Mississippi in 1955. After his body was finally found, authorities tried to bury him in Mississippi without allowing his mother, Mamie, who was back in Chicago, to even look at him. "I don't know what authority [they] had to bury my son but [they] took that authority," Mamie Till recalled in a 2005 documentary. She insisted on having the casket delivered back to Chicago. Once there, the Chicago funeral director told her he had been prohibited from opening the box containing her son's body. Till recalled saying to the funeral director "Do you have a hammer? . . . [Because] if you can't open the box, I can, and I'm going in the box."

The box was opened, and interviewed fifty years after the fact, Mamie Till was still driven to describe in detail what she saw as she gazed at her son's dead body: "I saw his tongue had been choked out and was lying down on his chin. I saw that his eye was out and was lying about midway to his cheek. I looked at this eye and it was gone. I looked at the bridge of his nose and it looked like someone had taken a meat chopper and chopped it. And I looked at his teeth because I took so much pride in his teeth . . . and I only saw two . . . They'd been just knocked out, and I was looking at his ears . . . and I didn't see the ear. . . . That's when I discovered a hole about here and I could see daylight on the other side . . . And I also discovered that they had taken an axe and they had gone straight down across his head and his face and the back of his head were separate."

Mamie Till recalled looking at the funeral director and saying "Oh yes, we're gonna open the casket." When he looked back and asked if he should try to fix Emmett's features, she replied, "No, let the people see what I've seen."[49]

The people saw. More than fifty thousand of them saw Emmett's body — identifiable only because of a ring he wore — in person. They saw because Mamie Till, grieving the brutal murder of her child, insisted on having an open-casket funeral to which the public was invited. They saw because Mamie Till wanted the photos of his bloated, mutilated face to be published nationally in *Jet* magazine.

Mamie Till is credited as a transformative figure, but is most often pictured as a grieving mother being held up at her son's coffin, weeping at his gravesite, supported and barely able to stand, her mouth open not in fury but in keening loss. What we are never trained to consider is that alongside her sorrow and suffering was a burning rage. Lamentation and sadness do not drive a woman to fight for her son's body, to vow to smash open his casket, to commit the crimes done to his body and face to eternal memory, to *make damn sure* that the world has to look at the same image of racist brutality that has been visited on your family and your life.

Anger does that. In the case of Mamie Till, anger lit a match under a burgeoning social struggle that would help to partially remake the United States and lessen (though not in any way obliterate) many of the legal and political obstacles to racial parity.

And we never think — have never been asked to think — of *her anger* as that righteous spark.

SIMPLE ERASURE

Of course, there is also the reality that when women do explode with rage, seven if the effect is to catalyze a social movement, their anger will never be recorded, never noted, never recalled or understood as nation-reshaping. The fact that we can often only register the fury of white men as heroic is so established that it would verge on the comical if it weren't so deeply tragic.

Lots of people were gathered inside a bar in lower Manhattan in the early morning hours of June 28, 1969. In the years since, there have been angry disputes over who was inside, who was outside, who said what or threw what and at what time. But what is established is that the Stonewall Inn, a dingy establishment that lacked running water, was the rare gay bar in New York City that permitted dancing, and that it had become a mecca not only for gay white men, but also for drag queens, transvestites, some lesbians, sex workers, and homeless youth. It was a bar for the particularly marginalized, in a city and an era that already marginalized homosexuality in any form. Police raids on gay establishments were a regular occurrence, and cops often forced cross-dressing patrons to go to the bathrooms and reveal their genitalia to them; at the time, impersonating a member of another gender was illegal in New York City, dressing in less than three pieces of gender-appropriate clothing was considered grounds for arrest.

Historians and participants may still disagree about exactly what happened in 1969, but in most recollections of the night, transvestites, drag queens — people who would now be called trans — as well as a handful of lesbians were probably at the center of events. Marsha P. Johnson, an African-American trans drag performer, was celebrating at the bar. A butch lesbian named Stormé DeLarverie was there; Sylvia Rivera, a trans gay rights activist, was outside on the street.

When the cops raided the Stonewall Inn that night, patrons were not in the mood to comply. Because they resisted, the raid took a long time, and onlookers and friends began to gather in large numbers outside. By some accounts, Johnson was among the first to resist inside the bar, throwing a shot glass and shouting "I got my civil rights"; many agree that it was DeLarverie who pushed back hard at cops, cursing and angrily complaining about her handcuffs being too tight as she was led out of the bar. When cops put her in a police car, DeLarverie is reported to have shouted at the staring, sympathetic crowd, "Why don't you guys do something?" It's at this point that Rivera, perhaps, threw a bottle at police, and others threw pennies, and the crowd outside rushed toward the paddy wagon containing those who'd already been arrested. Soon bricks, bottles, and glasses were flying and the crowd outside had launched an attack on the officers still in the bar, throwing rocks through its windows, pulling a parking meter from the street and using it as a battering ram. As Rivera would recall later in life, the resistant fury that overtook the crowd and patrons of Stonewall felt like this: "You've been treating us like shit all these years? Uh-huh. Now it's our turn!" She would also recall it as "one of the greatest moments in my life."[50]

The so-called Stonewall Riots would last for days and mark the start of the gay liberation movement. Johnson and Rivera would go on to found and be active in the Gay Liberation Front, and together found STAR, the Street Transvestite Action Revolutionaries, dedicated to supporting homeless drag queens and trans people of color. DeLarverie was described in her *New York*

Times obituary as, in her post-Stonewall years, having walked the streets of lower Manhattan, "like a gay superhero . . . She was not to be messed with by any stretch of the imagination."[51]

DeLarverie would also later insist that the events of those nights be spoken about with care, and is reported to have framed them consciously as righteous political action. "It was a rebellion, it was an uprising, it was a civil rights disobedience," she reportedly told a symposium of Stonewall veterans. "It wasn't no damn riot."[52]

But the angry women and gender nonconformists who were likely at the heart of that rebellion were very often erased from its retelling, and from the popular view of the gay rights movement, a movement so often embodied by the wealthy straight white men who were its most public figures. When, in 2015, Hollywood released its big film about the movement, *Stonewall,* focusing on the events at the Stonewall Inn, it did not star trans women, drag queens, lesbians, or nonwhite gender nonconformists as its heroes. Rather it was a fictionalized story of a young white cisgender man from the Midwest, the figure who could most comfortably be cast as the first to hurl a brick through a window and yell, "Gay power!"

Choosing to Hold Our Tongues

During the flood of #metoo stories about sexual harassment and gendered inequity, flowing particularly out of Hollywood, a reporter asked the actress Uma Thurman about her feelings on the movement. "I've learned that when I've spoken in anger," Thurman replied, "I usually regret the way I express myself. So I've been waiting to feel less angry. And when I'm ready, I'll say what I have to say."[53]

Thurman's forbearance drove feminist Lindy West wild with frustration. "Not only are women expected to weather sexual violence, intimate partner violence, workplace discrimination, institutional subordination, the expectation of free domestic labor, the blame for our own victimization, and all the subtler, invisible cuts that undermine us daily," wrote West. "We are not even allowed to be angry about it."

Sometimes, there is a strategy behind the suppression of rage; in Thurman's case, she was waiting to tell her story in full, as she later did to *New York Times* journalist Maureen Dowd.

Cecile Richards, the longtime president of Planned Parenthood, described in her memoir, *Make Trouble,* how, as she was entering the House of Representatives in

2015 to be grilled for five hours by Republicans over a set of doctored videos that inaccurately claimed to show members of her organization selling baby parts, a friend had texted her to stay strong, reminding her "to carry the rage of women through the centuries with you this morning!" The message bolstered Richards, yet her tactic while being interrogated by her ideological foes was to *contain* all that rage. Her refusal to show her ire, she said, worked to drive her inquisitors bonkers, which in turn put their spluttering, punitive frustration on display in front of a television audience.

When, in public conversation with Richards, I pointed out to her that this strategy perfectly mirrored that of nonviolent civil rights organizing in the Gandhian tradition — the idea that peaceful protest on the part of the oppressed would provoke aggressive and discrediting rage on the part of the oppressors, hopefully in full view of television cameras — she said that she hadn't considered it a strategy going into the hearings. "It was just my instinct," she said. Remaining cool, keeping that anger simmering, and watching her interrogators explode in response was part of an unconscious plan.

It can be effective, but is also part of the dynamic that leads us to ignore — to never

225

even see — the catalytic power of women's rage, simply because if it is kept beneath the surface, even strategically, we never have to acknowledge its existence. It was the teachings of nonviolent protest techniques that led Rosa Parks — in the same year that Mamie Till forced the world to see what lynching looked like — to not give up her seat on a Montgomery bus in 1955.

Parks is widely remembered and celebrated as a civil rights heroine, but she is also memorialized as stoic, pitied for having been exhausted, appreciated for her very refusal to show anger.

In fact, Parks was a lifelong furious fighter against sexual and racial violence, a defender of black men wrongly accused of sexual misconduct by white women, and an elected NAACP secretary who investigated the rape claims of black women against white men, including the brutal 1944 gang rape of the sharecropper Recy Taylor in Abbeville, Alabama. In her later life, Parks became interested in the black power movement, and expressed admiration for Malcolm X. Much of Parks's antirape activism wasn't unearthed for the general public until Danielle McGuire's 2010 book *At the Dark End of the Street,* and the intensity of her political investments were obscured

226

beneath the sanitized, rage-free caricature of her propagated by the press and by the leaders of the very movement she helped to kick-start. But women within the civil rights movement, including activists Pauli Murray and Anna Arnold Hedgeman, were angry at movement leaders who minimized Parks's role as an active, dynamic, driven political agitator, and many have strained since to offer a fuller and more complete picture of her.

"Dr. Martin Luther King, [Jr.] is the name most people associate with the Montgomery bus boycott," observed Angela Davis in *A Place of Rage*. "Of course Rosa Parks's name is known because she refused to sit in the back of the bus, but most often she is portrayed as someone who was not politically involved, who simply one day got tired of sitting in the back of the bus and refused to move. . . . Well of course she probably did get tired of sitting in the back of the bus. But that wasn't the reason why she refused to move to the back of the bus. That was a political act on her part."

And of course, keeping anger tempered and controlled isn't always a positive, strategic approach; sometimes it's about flat-out repression, the stuffing down of rage, the terror of revealing or even permitting ourselves to *feel* anger, precipitated by a culture that tells us it is bad for us physically and mentally, that it perverts and distorts us, rendering us ugly and marginal.

In her memoir of the election, Hillary Clinton describes the anxiety she felt about her own rage, explaining that she prayed "to stay hopeful and openhearted rather than becoming cynical and bitter . . . so that the rest of my life wouldn't be spent like Miss Havisham . . . rattling around my house obsessing over what might have been." Many of us recognize this impulse; none of us *wants* to be driven by unwaning anger for the rest of our lives; but Clinton wrote this less than a year after her loss; she had every rational reason in the world to feel rage, and yet she was so terrified that it would poison and dement her that she asked God to help her stop it up.

June Jordan speculated in *A Place of Rage* that "one of the reasons why you see such an affliction of drugs on black communities and low-income communities throughout the United States today is because rage has lost its respectability since the 1960s. The thing that you had in the civil rights revolution was an absolute upfront embrace of rage . . . when you don't rage against the evils and the enemies against you what you

228

do is you turn in against yourself and you begin to despair and give up . . . and that leads to this kind of plague proportion of drugs."

Others, from Sigmund Freud to Gloria Steinem and the fictional therapist Jennifer Melfi from *The Sopranos,* have warned that anger turned inward leads to depression, perhaps making it no coincidence that one of the most common ways for women to express their anger is through tears.

THE TEARS OF WRATH

Maybe we cry when we're furious in part because we feel a kind of grief at all the things we want to say or yell that we know we can't. Maybe we're just sad about the very same things that we're angry about.

The writer Meghan O'Rourke, who has studied grief in the wake of her mother's death from cancer, wrote of friends who suggested that they needed to sit Shiva in the week after the 2016 election, noting that "we are experiencing not just the pain of political defeat but the grief of mourning something that feels irrevocably lost." What we were grieving, O'Rourke argued, was "for the nation we could have been, a nation some of us feel we *are:* a nation that elected a female president and rejected the

229

rhetoric of nativism and fear that Donald Trump so casually embraced."[54]

But maybe it's also the instinct that it will go better for us tactically — especially if we are white — if we emote through tears, which are associated with women's vulnerability, rather than through rage, which is associated with our threat. Crying affirms us as female, and if you're a woman (again, especially a white woman), comporting yourself in traditionally female ways is rewarded, while lashing out is punished. There have been studies showing that when women who accuse men of domestic violence get angry while testifying, judges are likely to go easier on the accused; but if they show grief while on the stand, and thus comport with a view of vulnerable and nonabrasive femininity, the sentence is likely to be heavier.[55]

As the writer Leslie Jamison wrote about the pride she used to take in claiming she was "sad" rather than "angry": "Sadness seemed more refined and also more selfless — as if you were holding the pain inside yourself, rather than making someone else deal with its blunt-force trauma."[56]

A 2000 review of studies compiled by psychology professor Ann Kring found that while men and women self-report instances

230

of anger at similar rates, women report feeling more shame about them. Kring also found men more likely to express anger through physical or verbal assault, while women, in Jamison's words, "are more likely to cry when they get angry, as if their bodies are forcibly returning them to the appearance of the emotion — sadness — with which they are most commonly associated."[57]

Whatever the connection, there's been a lot of crying in politics, and very little of it has stemmed from women feeling sad.

Back in 1876, when five suffragists, including Susan B. Anthony, disrupted an official celebration of the nation's centennial, they handed out their own declaration of women's rights and read a speech about the injustice of women's disenfranchisement, one that began by framing their political resistance as having been undertaken in grief: "While the Nation is buoyant with patriotism, and all hearts are attuned to praise, it is with sorrow we come to strike the one discordant note."[58]

And Congresswoman Barbara Lee recalled to me a century later how Congresswoman Shirley Chisholm, "cried behind closed doors when she was hurt. You know how pain leads to anger." In public, Lee recalled,

Chisholm would be "so cool, her voice and demeanor tough and strong and *boom, boom, boom.* But get her behind closed doors? She'd let her guard down and acknowledge her pain." Lee recalled Chisholm's propensity for tears as a product of her being "very sensitive, very hurt, and very angry."

"Remember," Lee told me, "she was the only black woman with all these men, white and black. You come into an environment that is really the deck stacked against you: you're black and you're a woman. I remember she'd say, 'Barbara, these rules weren't made for you or me.' " Lee remembered Chisholm as equally sensitive to the slights of the Congressional Black Caucus and her white colleagues in the women's movement. "Shirley was very clear that the white feminist movement did not understand the nature of racism and what black women and black people have to deal with. And she was equally angry at a lot of the African-American leadership, because she didn't think they understood how women were being treated." And so, while Lee emphasized that Chisholm "never let anyone break her down in public," in private, she cried.

And she was never the only one. In 1972, at the convention to which Chisholm brought her delegates, at which Flo Kennedy and her group of agitators screamed at newscasters to keep their hands off, George McGovern had persuaded many feminists to support him (over Chisholm and others). But McGovern would double-cross them, instructing his delegates not to support a plank that would legalize abortion and violating an explicit promise to the women by permitting an antiabortion activist to speak from the floor. The journalist (and later screenwriter) Nora Ephron covered the messy convention for *Esquire:* At four o'clock in the morning, Ephron wrote, Gloria Steinem "in tears, was confronting McGovern campaign manager Gary Hart: 'You promised us you would not take the low road, you bastards.' "

The next day, Ephron trailed Steinem out of a hotel where she'd gone to confront McGovern directly, but hadn't succeeded. "If you're a woman, all they can think about your relationship with a politician is that you're either sleeping with him or advising him about clothes," Steinem seethed to Ephron, walking away from the hotel and starting to cry again. "It's just that they won't take us seriously," Steinem told Ephron through tears. "And I'm just tired of being screwed, and being screwed by my friends. By George McGovern, whom I raised half the money for in his first campaign, wrote his speeches . . . he just doesn't understand. We went to see him at one point about abortion, and the question of welfare came up. 'Why are you concerned about welfare?' he said. He didn't understand it was a woman's issue. They won't take us seriously. We're just walking wombs. And the television coverage . . . . saying that now that the women are here, next thing there'll be a caucus of left-handed Lithuanians."[59]

Steinem's tirade, as recorded forever by Ephron, is righteous diatribe, months and years of fury spilling over, and she can't get it out without weeping.

"We cry when we get angry," Steinem said to me forty-five years later, recalling the conversation, and still shaking her head with some apparent regret that she wept, and that Ephron had caught her at it. "I don't think that's uncommon, do you? That women cry when we get angry?" That Steinem would look for reassurance on this point is stunning in itself: of course women cry when they get angry. But she continued, "I was greatly helped by a woman who was an executive someplace, who said she also cried when she got angry, but developed a technique which meant that when she got angry and started to cry, she'd say to the person she was talking to, 'You may think I am sad because I am crying. No. I am angry.' And then she just kept going. And I thought that was brilliant."

The unpleasant revelation accompanying the realization that tears are one of the most frequent outlets for our wrath is that they are permitted in part because they are fundamentally misunderstood. One of my sharpest memories from an early job, in a male-dominated office, where I too once found myself weeping with inexpressible rage, was being grabbed by the scruff of my neck by an older woman — a chilly, hard-ass manager of whom I'd always been slightly terrified — who dragged me into a stairwell. "Never let them see you crying," she told me. "They don't know you're furious. They think you're sad and will be pleased because they got to you."

Congresswoman Patricia Schroeder from Colorado was working as the chair of Gary Hart's presidential campaign in 1987 when the married Hart was caught in an extramarital affair aboard a boat called *Monkey Business*. Schroeder, angry with Hart and deeply frustrated by the situation, thought, "Well, I've been going out and doing appearances for him, engaging in some debates." She decided that with her candidate out of the race, there was no reason that she shouldn't explore the idea of running for president herself.

"It was not a well-thought-out decision," she said to me with a laugh thirty years later. "There were already seven other candidates in the race and the last thing they needed was another one. Somebody called it *Snow White and the Seven Dwarves.*" She understood that because she was a late entry, she was behind on fund-raising, and vowed that she wouldn't enter the race unless she raised two million dollars, but it was an arduous battle. Studying the fund-raising documentation, she'd find that some of her supporters who gave a thousand dollars to men would then give her only $250. "I'd read this and think: do they think I get a discount?" Schroeder recalled that as the fall of 1987 came into view, a *Time* magazine poll had ranked her third in the Democratic field, "but when you looked at the polls, and how many people said they'd never vote for a woman, and then realized that a lot of people lied when they said yes, they would, I figured *no way this is going to happen; I'm gonna be third forever and third won't get me there.*"

She decided to announce that she would

236

not launch a formal campaign. And when she made her speech, she was so overcome by a series of emotions — gratitude for the people who'd supported and fought for her throughout a long hot summer, frustration with the system that made it so difficult to raise money and to target voters rather than delegates, and anger at the sexism — that she got choked up."[60]

"You would have thought I'd had a nervous breakdown," recalled Schroeder of how the press reacted to her. "You'd have thought Kleenex was my corporate sponsor. I remember thinking, *What are they gonna put on my tombstone? 'She cried'?*" For a while Schroeder kept what she called "a crying file," a little list of all the male politicians who'd wept publicly that year. "Reagan would tear up every time he saw a flag," she remembered. Her file included records; New Hampshire governor John Sununu, who cried as he was stepping down as governor of New Hampshire, and George H. W. Bush, who was a steady weeper. But the reaction to tears from those men was wholly different from what Schroeder got in response to her congestion.

Saturday Night Live mocked Schroeder in a skit in which Nora Dunn, as Schroeder,

237

repeatedly burst into tears while moderating a debate. Later, the *New York Times* would describe her as having dissolved "in a flood of tears."[61] An editorial in one Vermont paper read, "What a devastating indictment of this girl's character." One *Washington Post* columnist wrote about how older women like Schroeder were setting the cause of young women back a century, calling it "crazy, reckless, for one of Congress's few women . . . to give ammunition to those who saw women as sugary little girls rather than serious people to be taken seriously."

Schroeder found this last argument the most galling. Recalling a man who *had* suffered politically after he wept in public, Edmund Muskie, whose tears effectively ended his bid for the presidency back in that crucial year, 1972, she still wondered, thirty years later, "Why don't I remember anyone saying that he set *men* back?"

There is another dimension to the choice that many women make to cry: the fact that this emblem of helpless suffering provokes a sympathetic and protective response, mostly when the tears are being shed by white women. The protection those tears are understood to invite has often been used as the justification for racial violence. "White

238

women's tears" have derailed important conversations about race, provoking sympathy for and connection with *some* kinds of women, but not others. "Not all tears matter," observed the writer Shay Stewart-Bouley in 2018. "Rarely do the tears of a nonwhite woman carry any value. . . . The damsel in distress is never black."[62]

When I described to Alicia Garza some of the stories I'd been hearing during my reporting for this book, she said that they make *her* feel sad. "What is underneath my anger is a deep sadness," she said. "It actually breaks my heart to hear that a woman as visionary as Shirley Chisholm used to cry. It breaks my heart to hear that a woman as courageous as Barbara Lee has to keep her voice from shaking. It bothers me to no end that Maxine Waters gets portrayed as a crazy person, with no shade to people that are crazy, but she's not. And I know that feeling, and I often feel like *I'm* crazy. I often feel like there's something wrong with me and if I wasn't really intentional about building a community of people around me that get me one hundred percent, I would probably not be in this movement. And that makes me sad."

239

A Spoonful of Humor Makes the Medicine Go Down

The close cousin of sadness is laughter, and another common — and widely misunderstood — means of expressing socially acceptable wrath has come through comedy.

Pat Schroeder used to channel her congressional frustrations into witty, sharp-tongued retorts that didn't always fall merrily on the ears of her colleagues. Some of her witticisms became famous, like her dubbing Ronald Reagan "the Teflon president." After the millionth time she was asked whether she would run for president "as a woman," she began to snap back "What choice do I have?" As a member of the Committee on Armed Services, Schroeder once cracked to Pentagon officials that if they were women they'd always be pregnant because they never said "no." A *New York Times* story noting that Shroeder had been sworn into Congress with diapers in her purse also included reference to her most famous comeback, her response to being asked how she could be both a mother and a congresswoman: "I have a brain and a uterus, and I use both."[63]

"That was obviously sharp and I shouldn't have said it," Schroeder said to me in 2017, and has long noted — including in that same *Times* story — that "I don't think anyone likes a smart aleck."[64] o me, she said retrospectively, that a lot of her sharp humor was nderstood as aggression. She remembered being referred to by colleagues as "the wicked witch — or bitch — of the West." Schroeder recalled the unfairness of it all, noting that often her barbs came in her own defense against sexist diminishment. "If a guy says something in his own defense," she said, "he's standing his ground. If you say it, you're just being petty or being thin-skinned. Women are just supposed to put up with it, suck it up, and move on."

The irony is that Schroeder was consciously using her wit and her cheery feminized persona — she famously drew smiling faces in the "P" in her signature and giggled a lot — to ease anxieties about her political ambitions, her willingness to censure her opponents, and her often-confrontational style. When she was the most senior woman in Congress in 1990, the *New York Times* described Schroeder's "shrewd, even lethal political savvy," noting that "over the years she has helped bump not one, but two, chairmen off the House Armed Services Committee." But she often cited advice from her father: "Never frown at your

241

enemies. Smile — it scares the hell out of them."

Among the commands the antifeminist crusader Phyllis Schlafly issued her foot soldiers during her campaign against ratification of the Equal Rights Amendment in the 1970s was that they should always, always smile; one of Schlafly's best-known books was titled *The Power of the Positive Woman.*[65] But grinning positivity may disguise ambitious intent only in women fighting on the side of white patriarchy. After all, Schlafly defeated the ERA, and was rarely pressed too hard on the disingenuousness of her message: as a powerful political woman who traveled the country, she was regularly telling other women that their calling was to stay at home. Meanwhile, despite all the smiley faces drawn by the left-leaning feminist Schroeder, her critics still saw in *her,* according to the *Times,* "a 'hard' look, a grin that is really a grimace, a nasal-voiced delivery through clenched jaws and eyes that disappear behind a squint. . . . The reality is that Schroeder is a driven politician who smiles too hard" and whose penchant for one-liners "belies and often undercuts [her] seriousness."[66]

But even if it doesn't always work to fully obscure ambition and aggression, humor can certainly make it go down a little easier. Despite a reputation for humorlessness — earned, ironically enough, by objections to dirty jokes and the injunction *against* telling all women to smile as if they were decorative objects — many of the second-wave feminists were in fact pretty hilarious. Chief among them, Flo Kennedy.

"The classic Flo line," recalled Steinem, her regular speaking partner, "was when some guy in the back got up and asked us 'Are you lesbians?' and she responded 'Are you my alternative?' " Kennedy, said Steinem, "could always say something that made people laugh. But it always had a point. I mean, she was not letting anybody off the hook by making people laugh."

Sometimes humor is the best way to stick the shiv in, to express the vivid fury that, for any number of reasons, can't emerge straight, but can be more plausibly laid out as parody of what a marginalized angry person would say were her anger permitted space and respect.

During the Obama presidency, comedians Jordan Peele and Keegan-Michael Key had come up with a character named Luther, who served as the "anger translator" for the preternaturally even-tempered commander in chief — the black president who could

243

never be mad. During the 2016 campaign, the best retailing of Hillary's imagined anger came on the internet, on the website Medium, via a pair of pieces filed under the byline @shitHRCcantsay, absolutely ripping apart the way that Clinton had been treated: "I've been preparing my whole fucking life for this job. So stop making me dab on Ellen and just give me a fucking chance already," read one. The fantasy Hillary of this parody was all the things women are not supposed to be and therefore what the real Hillary could *never* be: self-confident, braggadocious, condescending, and livid at the petty stupidity she had to wade through in order to comport with America's standards of femininity. And it provided such relief to read.[67]

The release was even more necessary when the parody account produced a post, five days after Clinton's loss, cutting through the pitiless finger-pointing at Clinton's sole culpability. In the parody, Clinton turned the blame on everyone *but* herself with a defensive self-righteousness that was as satisfying in parody form as it would have been disqualifying in real life, precisely *because* it was a torrent of vivid wrath that no actual woman could ever unleash on the public and survive:

I'd like to extend a hearty fuck you to the national news media. This is for spending more time talking about my emails than all policy issues combined. . . . This is for constantly saying I "am flawed" or "have flaws" . . . motherfucker, name one!!! My fucking charity that gives HIV meds to poor people? Are you for real with this shit? And the Monday morning quarterbacks right now? You're gonna criticize my campaign?? Bitch, I won the popular vote and I was running against America! Last toast: undecided voters . . . honey, if you were undecided after the Mexican rapist speech it means one thing: You needed me to be perfect. . . . You know, back in 1965, I ran for class president of my high school and lost to a boy who told me, "You are really stupid if you think a girl can be elected president." Well, I put in fifty years of tireless, grueling work, and now, at long last, that little boy has been vindicated.[68]

Comedy gives cover to the unspeakable, and for women, that can be the anger that needs to boil over sometimes — not just in righteousness but also in ugliness and self-pity. Why the hell shouldn't Hillary's supporters, the ones who'd actually been committed to her winning the presidency — and who'd

245

been the object of angry tirades from all sides — get to engage in some mean, vulgar, angry release of their own?

Plenty of women who went into the business of comedy understood it to be an outlet for their fury, or perhaps that their anger was the predicate for their profession. "The minute you're not angry about things, the minute you're not upset about things, what are you talking about?" Joan Rivers asked in the 2010 documentary *A Piece of Work*. "I'm furious about everything. . . . But if I didn't have the anger . . . I wouldn't be a comedian. Anger fuels the comedy."

Phoebe Robinson, a comedian from an entirely different generation, has written in her memoir, *You Can't Touch My Hair,* of the way that comedy helped her to channel her pain and temper the public's view of her dissatisfactions. "If I expressed my hurt in a clever, joking manner, no one can take offense then, right?" Robinson, half of the comedy podcast partnership *2 Dope Queens,* wrote, "No one can call you an angry black woman if we're all laughing, right?"[69]

Humor can be such a good way to hide anger at racist, sexist degradation and to challenge white male authority sideways — without risking as much direct blowback —

246

that it perhaps shouldn't be a surprise that the comedian Tina Fey wrote jokes about Harvey Weinstein's sexual predation — lines about being pinned under Weinstein, and turning down sex with him — that aired on her show *30 Rock* in 2012, years before his behavior could be reported straight. In 2013, during the Oscars, the white male comedian Seth MacFarlane also made a Weinstein joke — about the lead actress nominees no longer having to pretend to be attracted to the producer. After 2017 reporting revealed the extent of Weinstein's predation, MacFarlane explained that a friend of his, an actress who'd been harassed by Weinstein, had confided in him, prompting his joke. "Make no mistake," he said at the time, his one-liner had come "from a place of loathing and anger."[70]

After years of stories about women who claimed to have been sexually assaulted by the comedian Bill Cosby prompted no repercussions, the comedian Hannibal Buress, angry at how Cosby lectured African Americans to "pull their pants up," began retorting during his stand-up act, "Yeah, but you rape women, Bill Cosby. So turn the crazy down a couple notches." It was only after Buress's joke got picked up by the media that the multiple allegations against Cosby finally began to take hold.

Comedy doesn't just offer an affable disguise for fury. It can also absorb and defuse it. When her TBS show launched, comedian Samantha Bee set up a special "rape-threat line" in response to the kind of online abuse that she took as a female comedian. Callers heard this message: "No one is here to take your call, but your offer of nonconsensual sex is important to us, so please select from the following menu: to tell me I'm a dumb bitch that needs to be raped, press 1; to tell me you're going to violate every hole in my idiot libtard body, press 2 . . ."

"It's not a joke for everyone," Bee told me drily in 2016. "This is as dark as satire can probably be. It's also about the condition of being a woman in this business."

Bee's weekly show would turn out to be one of the major outlets for angry feminist humor throughout the election and the years that followed, her opening monologues often simply extended rants, the laughs stemming not even always from *jokes* but from the giddy pleasure of hearing bad people correctly excoriated. The raw venting of spleen became its own humor, the punch line being that this was the most rational response, but one that couldn't be voiced — or wouldn't be taken seriously — outside the confines of a comedic monologue.

During the 2018 week that Paul Ryan announced his retirement from the House of Representatives, my husband and I had sat slack-jawed in front of very serious cable news programs, on which many experts told us gravely that Ryan — the Wisconsin congressman who'd been serving as Republican House Speaker since 2015, and who had spent years on the leading edge of the virulent strain of conservatism that had landed us with President Trump — was in fact just a well-meaning tax geek, his resignation a signal that Ryan's brand of responsible, moderate conservatism was out of favor in Trump's administration. We had been incandescent with anger: this retroactive beatification of Ryan, a man who'd been fantasizing about stripping poor people of health-care benefits through Medicaid since he'd been standing around a keg in college, a guy who'd stayed in the administration long enough to push through a tax break for the very rich, a legislator who'd spent his whole career maintaining his total opposition to abortion rights, even in cases of rape and incest . . . it was irrational, untrue, divorced from reality. But on the straight news, the idea that Ryan was a man fueled by personal moral convictions was everywhere.

Days later, we settled in to watch *Full Frontal with Samantha Bee* and found Bee, fuming. "Paul Ryan is a bad person," she said in her opening monologue. "He's not a statesman, he's a wing-nut." Predicting that Ryan would someday run for president, Bee continued, "He's counting on us forgetting how fuckin' horrible he is, but we will not forget. Paul Ryan, your legacy is making poor people pay for rich people's massive tax cuts, fighting to take health care away from millions, trying to gut social programs, defending the Muslim ban, enabling a constitutional crisis and somehow convincing everyone that torching Democratic norms and the social safety net is *moderate*." My husband and I cheered. There was practically no pretense that there was even a joke here. It was just the furious truth, laid bare so unapologetically that it elicits a laugh.

Not everyone sees Bee's approach to angry expression as useful. After Bee dedicated an October 2016 monologue to the *Access Hollywood* tape — during which she called Trump and Billy Bush "two leering dildos" and claimed that "every woman I know has had some entitled testosterone monster grab her like a human bowling ball" — the *Atlantic* writer Megan Garber worried that Bee's response to Trump's predatory incivility had offered "anger that didn't attempt to temper itself under the guise of 'satire.' Anger that seethed . . . anger that trusted in itself as its own end." Garber felt that that while Bee's "anger at Trump may be . . . righteous, it's an open question how productive it is . . . Anger is one way of making sense of things. Very rarely, however, is it a terribly good one."[71]

Garber's anxiety about Bee's profane ire may have stemmed from the understanding that when comedy actually challenges power too sharply, power will condemn the comedy. That dynamic couldn't have been made clearer than it was during the 2018 White House Correspondents' Dinner, at which the comedian Michelle Wolf performed a venomously funny skewering of the Trump administration and the press corps that had gathered for its annual self-celebration. Wolf's foul-mouthed excoriation of the press employed a comedic distancing device, getting the audience to chime in on a riff about Donald Trump's lack of wealth, with a chorus of *How broke is he?* and answering with a bunch of anodyne one-liners before going in for the kill with the final punch line that was not a joke at all: *How broke is he?* "He had to borrow money from the Russians, and now he's compromised and susceptible to blackmail and possibly responsible for the collapse of the republic . . . Yay. It's a fun game."[72] Wolf went hard after Trump's press secretary, Sarah Huckabee Sanders, comparing her to Aunt Lydia from *The Handmaid's Tale,* a reference to a woman who works to uphold a violent patriarchal political regime, suggesting that Sanders "burns facts" in order to get a good eye-makeup effect, and wondered how to refer to her, asking, "What's Uncle Tom, but for white women who disappoint other white women? Oh, I know: Aunt Coulter."

It was brutal, and Wolf was no more sparing toward the press, riffing, "I think what no one in this room wants to admit is that Trump has helped all of you. . . . He's helped you sell your papers and your books and your TV. You helped create this monster, and now you're profiting off him. And if you're gonna profit off Trump, you should at least give him some money because he doesn't have any."

Wolf's ire was direct and unmistakable; she concluded the speech — in a room that had turned cold — with a double-angry

252

sign-off, reminding guests at the high-end, civilized, bipartisan party of grittier realities, experienced by Dreamers and by residents of the Michigan city where a government choice to save money had led to toxic levels of lead in the drinking water: "All right, like an immigrant who was brought here by his parents and didn't do anything wrong, I gotta get the fuck out of here. Good night. Flint still doesn't have clean water!"

As Masha Gessen wrote for the *New Yorker,* the monologue "burst the bubbles of civility and performance, and of the separation of media and comedy. It plunged the attendees into the reality that is, in the Trump era, the stuff of comedy. Through her obscene humor, Wolf exposed the obscenity of the fictions — and the fundamental unfunniness of it all."[73]

Right-wingers predictably hit back, but so did members of the political press corps. *Morning Joe*'s Mika Brzezinski tweeted in defense of Sanders, "Watching a wife and mother be humiliated on national television for her looks is deplorable,"[74] while the *New York Times*' Maggie Haberman tweeted that the fact that Sanders "sat and absorbed intense criticism of her physical appearance" — despite the fact that Wolf had not

253

in fact criticized her appearance — "her job performance and so forth, instead of walking out, on national television, was impressive."[75] CNN's Chris Cillizza also marveled at Sanders's ability to withstand the attack, arguing that "being funny is one thing. Bullying people because you can is another. And Wolf's treatment of Sanders was bullying . . . [bullying is] wrong. Always." Recall that Cillizza was the reporter who in 2009 made a joke about Hillary Clinton being a "mad bitch" and has published a list of his favorite Donald Trump insults — including near the top his racist references to Elizabeth Warren as "Pocahontas" — referring to the then-candidate Trump as "the Michael Jordan of name-calling."

Through unflinchingly angry comedy, Wolf had framed the argument she was making about the press and Trump henchwoman's complicity in the rise of an abusive, cruel, and authoritarian political regime as a neat trap. The objects of her monologue reacted to it in a way that proved her point, about their drive to protect and cover for power, very precisely.

FUCK IT

Getting an equally mixed reaction from the public is women's use of profanity as a

254

cathartic and communicative tool to express their ire. I had been startled — though pleased; I love profanity — when, during the 2016 Democratic National Convention, I'd been interviewing Congresswoman Gwen Moore from Milwaukee; she'd been describing the economic obstacles she'd faced all her life as a single black mother, and offered what she called a "one-finger salute" to anyone planning to vote third party in November. She'd then looked at me steadily and confessed, "I'm scared shitless." I'd rarely heard elected officials, especially *female* elected officials, curse on the record to a reporter, but it was refreshingly direct. After all, I knew *exactly* what she meant.

By 2017, plenty of other women in Washington were cursing. Both Kamala Harris and Kirsten Gillibrand, U.S. senators, had turned to public vulgarity in their attempts to convey the intensity of their antipathy to the Trump administration and the party that had enabled it and was standing by it.

While discussing the GOP's plan to repeal and replace Obamacare at an event in San Francisco, Harris had mocked a congressman who'd said, "Nobody dies because they don't have access to health care." "What the fuck is that?" Harris asked onstage.

255

Some months later, profiled in the *New York Times,* Harris was only slightly more careful. "I was told one should not say" — here the reporter left a blank, but enough description to let readers know the word was "motherfucker" — "in these kinds of interviews . . . So I'm not going to say it."[76] After Gillibrand was freely profane in conversation with me during the same health-care fights of 2017, noting at one point that as senators, "if we're not helping people, we should go the fuck home," I got plenty of responses from readers who felt that her use of expletives was imitative of the president. She had in fact used profanity throughout her 2014 memoir, and acknowledged within it her particular weakness for bad words, but the Trump era was permitting her to deploy them from the stump, and she didn't stop. In July of 2017, Gillibrand asked a crowd, "Has [Trump] kept his promises?" and then responded, "No, fuck no!" In response, she was, naturally, labeled "unhinged" in right-wing publications.

It turns out that the women immersed in the legislative hell of the Trump administration might have been turning to obscenities as an analgesic. The psychology professor Richard Stephens told the *New York Times*

256

of a study he'd done, in which he'd asked subjects to submerge their hands in ice water for as long as they could, repeating a word that was either a profanity or a neutral term. Those who swore were able to keep their hands in the ice water for fifty percent longer and reported that the pain had felt less intense. Cursing, the *Times* summed up, can "offer catharsis . . . [and] might help you tolerate the pain better." Other studies are underway, trying to determine if, in addition to numbing our discomfort, cursing might also increase our strength, a possibility that would inform and complicate an understanding of why so many protesters — feeling impotent in the face of a Trump administration — might choose to decorate their marching signs with expletives.

Like anger itself, cursing has been discouraged in women, as it is considered unladylike and masculinizing. But in fact it's useful precisely because it is an outlet for all that pent-up anger. "Cursing is coping, or venting, and it helps us deal with stress," the professor Timothy Jay told the *New York Times*. Profanity, he said, permits us to "express our emotions, especially anger and frustration, towards others symbolically," rather than physically or violently.[77]

Unlike direct voicing of anger or displea-

257

sure from women, foul language has more readily become a calling card of coolness, good humor, a sign of integration with the men. It can be funny, humanizing. And also, in moments of true explosive rage, it can be instinctive, almost animal.

The former NPR ombudsman Alicia Shepard has recalled a meeting of a trade group at which she asked for clarification from the executive director, an older white man. When he replied "It's on the website, dear," she reflexively responded, "Don't call me dear, fuckface." "I don't even know where I got the word 'fuckface,' " Shepard told the media organization Poynter in 2017. "It was years of being called sweetie and dear . . . that came bubbling to the surface and caused an outburst."[78]

"There are some people who are really offended by profanity," Gloria Steinem told me. "But I find the art is to put the "fuck" in the middle of the word, not to say it by itself." Steinem said she learned this trick from the musical *Hair,* in which a song lyric to "Abie Baby," about Abraham Lincoln, refers to the sixteenth president as "the Emanci-mother-fucking-pator of the Slaves." Steinem loved it, and uses oaths to break up, draw emphasis to, and otherwise play with the words she's using. "So I say fan-fucking-tastic or fan-fucking-ridiculous or something."

But there's also perhaps a lesson in how curse words came to carry such outsized weight. According to the researchers cited in the *New York Times,* "profane words are powerful only because we make them powerful. Without their being censored [so-called bad words] would just be average terms."[79] It is the suppression and censure of profanity that gives it its potency, something that those who remain invested in repressing women's fury might do well to remember.

GETTING VOLCANIC

When every other method — suppression, almighty justification, tears, jokes, and four-letter words — has failed, some women in politics have simply decided to throw their cards in the air and get openly mad. Without apology or pause. When, in 2014, Congress failed to pass the Paycheck Fairness Act, which would have added protections to the Equal Pay Act and better ensured equal pay for women, especially women of color, Maryland senator Barbara Mikulski gave a speech on the Senate floor.

"I'll tell you what I'm tired of hearing: that somehow or another we're too emo-

259

tional when we talk," Mikulski thundered. "Well, I am emotional . . . It brings tears to my eyes, to know how women every single day are working so hard and are getting paid less. It makes me emotional to hear that. Then when I hear all of these phony reasons, some are mean and some are meaningless, I do get emotional. I get angry. I get outraged. I get volcanic."

There are plenty of instances in which the expression of their fury — raw and remorseless — has been effective rhetorically, even if, as in Mikulski's case, it did not produce a desired legislative or legal or political or repercussive effect.

People often consider Gloria Steinem — white, cisgender, traditionally feminine and foxy — as the great communicator of feminist rage. During her decades in the spotlight, the media regularly, and hungrily, positioned her as perhaps the *only* feminist that America was interested in hearing from. But on the road, she said, where she spoke regularly with Flo Kennedy — the unapologetic purveyor of frank fury — "I always had to speak first because if I went after Flo, it was such an anticlimax. There was no question, I had to go first."

There is perhaps no better example of undisguised anger working as a rhetorical super-power than Flo Kennedy. Kennedy's life was a study in unapologetic and furious resistance to injustice. As a young woman in Kansas City, Missouri, she had participated in a boycott of a nearby Coca-Cola bottling company that did not hire African-American truck drivers. When she was denied entry to Columbia law school — not because she was black but because she was a woman, administrators told her — she threatened a discrimination suit and was admitted, as one of eight women, and the only African American, in her class. As a lawyer, she represented members of the Black Panther Party on charges of conspiracy to commit bombings, sued the Catholic Church, and in 1969 organized feminist legal objection to New York State's abortion ban, which was overturned in 1970. In 1973, when students at Harvard were agitating to get the gender ratio at the school to 50–50, Kennedy waded in, calling Harvard Yard "the asshole of the world" and orchestrating a legendary "pee-in" protest there, in response to the school's paucity of women's bathrooms.[80] Kennedy was in the cast of the 1983 feminist movie *Born in Flames,* about revolutionary women who band together in a renegade women's army to battle gender and racial oppression.

261

She was described by *People* magazine as having "the biggest, loudest, and, indisputably, the rudest mouth on the battleground where feminist activists and radical politics join in mostly common cause."

When they were on the speaking circuit as partners, Steinem recalled being admonished by Kennedy for being too school-marmish, too afraid to yell and get viscerally emotional, and instead relying too heavily on annotated backup in her speeches. "In the beginning I remember her taking me aside, because I was into facts and figures — I felt I had to prove that we were discriminated against. And Flo hauled me off and said, 'Honey, when you are lying in a ditch with a truck on your ankle, you do not send someone to the library to find out how much the truck weighs. You get it off!' "

But even if Kennedy was rhetorically indefatigable in her anger, her dynamism wasn't always embraced by those in the movement. Steinem recalled inviting Kennedy to speak in Washington at a big women's organizing meeting. "Tons of people were coming from all over, in complete disorganization, and I invited Flo," Steinem recalled. "I remember Betty Friedan calling me up, furious, saying, 'You cannot invite her, you cannot have her there. She will mau-mau us' " (a racist term taken from the Kenyan rebellion, meant to indicate hostile attack). Steinem ignored Friedan. Kennedy came and spoke at the meeting, "and of course it was fine." More than fine. Along with Kennedy's rage burned an "incredible generosity" and good humor, Steinem recalled. In all the hand-wringing over the perils of feeling too much rage, or the idea that to be angry is to be prickly, inhospitable, aggressive, what's often missed is that the exhalation of anger can accompany, and perhaps prompt, joy, goodwill, warmth, and kindness.

"Flo was very accepting of the idea that people are activists in a lot of different ways and that's okay," Steinem remembered. But Kennedy's willingness to unleash anger — the impulse that is so derided in some women — was also a habit that inspired (if occasionally terrified) so many others.

"A big reason it's very important for women in public life to be able to express anger on behalf of all of us who feel it [is] so that we can have a champion," said Steinem, recalling another friend and contemporary, the throaty, tough-talking fireplug of a congresswoman Bella Abzug. At the 1977 Women's Conference in Houston, at which

Maxine Waters, then a thirty-nine-year-old state assemblywoman, was waiting to talk to Abzug, Steinem recalled, "Bella was yelling at me, screaming at me something like 'You've ruined everything!' " Steinem remembered noticing Waters watching her altercation with Abzug. "I could see that Maxine was appalled. So I took Maxine aside and said, 'This is just the way we talk to each other in New York. Don't worry about it.' "

But however startling her asperity, Steinem continued, "Bella could be our champion. I mean, she pushed some people away, but the people *loved* her for getting angry. Flo too. Flo could be our champion."

Kennedy's close friend, the former New York Supreme Court judge Emily Jane Goodman, said at the time of Kennedy's death in 2000 that Kennedy "showed a whole generation of us the right way to live our lives." The exuberance of Kennedy's rage was contagious. Here was a model of righteous female fury that people wanted to be near. As Kennedy wrote in her memoir, "I'm just a loudmouthed, middle-aged colored lady with a fused spine and three feet of intestines missing, and a lot of people think I'm crazy. Maybe you do too, but I never stop to wonder why I'm not like other people. The mystery to me is why more people aren't like me."

265

Chapter Four:
How Minority Rules

Among the trickiest and most central dynamics between angry women is the degree to which they have often been angry at one another, and often for very good reasons, chief among them, the racial, economic, and sexual inequities that have contributed to making solidarity between women so elusive, so difficult, and often so painful.

In January 2017, twelve days before millions of women would gather in Washington, DC, and in cities around the world in furious mass protest, the *New York Times* ran a front-page story about the anticipated demonstration. It was headlined "Women's March Opens a Raw Dialogue on Race" and detailed the internal conflicts between women planning to march — or not march — later in the month.

"Many thousands of women are expected to converge on the nation's capital," read the first paragraph. "Jennifer Willis no

266

longer plans to be one of them." Willis, the story explained, was a fifty-year-old wedding minister from South Carolina who had planned to take her daughters to Washington but would no longer be doing so because "she read a post on the Facebook page for the march that made her feel unwelcome because she is white."

The 1,600-word piece went on to examine the racial anxieties cropping up around the march, whose aims were not simply about addressing gendered inequality, but criminal justice reform, the Middle East conflict, the mistreatment of native populations, environmental racism, and a broader approach to reproductive justice beyond just abortion rights. It was a thrilling, if risky, pushing forward of a conversation, using the moment of mass dissatisfaction as an opportunity to expand the scope of a feminist conversation and call it to account for its previous inequities and omissions.

The *Times* coverage — written by the Pulitzer Prize–winning journalist Farah Stockman, who quoted organizer Linda Sarsour as explaining that the contentiousness was by design, that "this was an opportunity to take the conversation to the deep places" — nonetheless zeroed in, via its headline and choice of emphasis, on what it framed as the fragility of the imagined coalition. It described the white South Carolina woman it began with as having been "stung by the tone" of a post by a black activist from Brooklyn, who'd urged "white allies" to do less talking and more listening and reminded white women who were newly awakened to political rage that many other women — women of color — had never had the luxury of *not* being mad. It was this post that had caused Jennifer Willis to cancel her trip, telling the *Times,* "We're supposed to be allies in equal pay, marriage, adoption. Why is it now about [how] 'white women don't understand black women'?"

The *Times* story wondered whether "debates over race . . . reflect deeper questions about the future of progressivism in the age of Trump. Should the march highlight what divides women, or what unites them?"

The irony was that the story itself was making that choice: electing to headline divisions between activists, rather than the possibilities that hundreds of thousands of women and men might move past those divisions and come together in what would turn out to be the biggest single-day protest in America's history.

The next year, in 2018, as women geared up for a reunion protest — one that would turn out to be bigger, in some American cities, than it had been the year before — the *Times* again ran a front-page story in anticipation. "One Year After Women's March, More Activism but Less Unity."

To point out that an undue amount of attention is regularly paid to the internal conflicts within feminism is not to diminish the seriousness and centrality of those conflicts: they are real, and understanding whence they stem is crucial to understanding the very mechanisms of bias, oppression, and inequality that the women's movement theoretically aims to dismantle.

DISPUTE IS THE MIDDLE NAME OF ACTIVISM

In the popular imagination, feminism has since its inception been on the verge of collapse, thanks to the intensity of its very real internal conflicts: divisions over race, class, sexuality, and generational difference, not to mention the flare-ups of personal jealousies and combative power plays. These rifts have often been serious and damaging. But they have not set the women's movement apart from any other social justice movement, from the civil rights or Black Power or immigration or gay rights or the New Left or socialist movements, all of which

269

have at times been riven by generational, racial, gendered, and class divides, by homophobia, strategic differences, and personal feuds. To some degree, this is the nature of mass activism.

The natural fractiousness of any large political movement or campaign is so universal that it was one of the key elements of America's revolutionary rhetoric. The nation's first political cartoon, attributed to Benjamin Franklin, is of the colonies represented as a segmented snake; it accompanied his editorial about the importance of bringing together the "disunited state" into a unified force; the cartoon exhorted colonists to "Join, or Die." There is also a famous revolutionary-era story about a snowball fight that broke out between militia members from different colonies — men from rural and urban areas, men who dressed differently from one another, some of whom were black, some southern, some northern — as they were amassing an army against the British in Harvard Yard. The snowball fight turned so violent that General George Washington had had to step in and break it up. I was taught this story young, as one that exemplified the best of the United States in its revolutionary moment of birth: an ability to bring diverse people together toward a greater civic, political, and national goal.

As Linda Sarsour told me in 2017 about the reports of internal dissent in the lead-up to the women's march, "The idea that we were supposed to immediately and seamlessly bring strangers together in a kumbaya march team, when we're from different backgrounds, have different experiences, religious backgrounds, are from inner cities and suburbs, is crazy." She was exactly right; that expectation looks positively foolish in light of the nation's own founding history, which we're taught as an example of overcoming differences to form a united and victorious revolutionary front.

Yet very few movements — from the amassing of America's first rebel forces through its civil rights campaigns — have had their squabbles regularly presented as the most notable thing about them, often in advance of, or in place of, acknowledgment of their unifying aims and their improbable achievements. The highlighting of dissent over accomplishment is a way to undermine a movement, and it has everything to do with the structural reality of the lengthy campaign for gender equality.

The women's movement is a movement not of an oppressed minority, but of a subjugated majority. Majorities, by the very nature of their scale, are bound to include groups with varying — and warring — priorities and goals. By dint of size, a majority has the power over a minority — unless its foundations are eroded. The cheapest way to weaken and undermine a mass movement is to use its differences to divide it, and thus maintain power over it.

But there have been periods in which alliances have formed among women, and between divergent groups, on behalf of marginalized Americans who can see their struggles as interlocked. In the 1830s, for example, seeds of what would later become nation-shaping movements to diminish the grip of white male capitalist power began to germinate together.

Young girls who worked in the Lowell Mills in New England staged their first walkouts, the antecedent for what would become the labor movement; at the same time they were forming one of the country's first women's anti-slavery societies, a recognition of the ways in which oppressions and injustices were linked.[81] In 1833, the American Anti-Slavery Society was founded by William Lloyd Garrison, with Frederick Douglass as an active member; in 1835, Garrison would publish a letter written by

272

Angelina Grimké, the daughter of a southern plantation owner, in his abolitionist newspaper, *The Liberator.* Grimké and her sister Sarah would go on to be leading abolitionists, sympathetic also to the fight for women's rights, and among the first women in America, along with Maria Stewart, to give speeches to mixed audiences of men and women. It was in the early 1830s that Stewart, the daughter of free blacks from Connecticut, became the first American woman to address mixed-race audiences, and the first black woman to give public lectures on both abolition and women's rights. In 1837, black and white American women came together for the first of three conferences on ending slavery. The second of those three conventions, held in Philadelphia, posed such a threat that the hall in which it was to be held was burned to the ground. At the World Anti-Slavery Convention in London in 1840, women attendees — including Elizabeth Cady Stanton and Lucretia Mott — were barred from speaking, but many met one another for the first time, and together started to put down the roots of the suffrage movement.

In 1848, Frederick Douglass attended the convention at Seneca Falls at which Stanton would draft the Declaration of Sentiments.

Of Stanton, Douglass would later say, "She saw more clearly than most of us that the vital point to be made prominent, and the one that included all others, was the ballot, and she bravely said the word." Douglass would also later claim that "There are few facts in my humble history to which I look back with more satisfaction than to the fact . . . that I was sufficiently enlightened at that early day, and when only a few years from slavery, to support [her] resolution for woman suffrage."

It seemed there was a possibility that the young nation's majority, people on whose subjugation and labor the country's economy and political power were being built, might come together, coalescing around what they understood to be their linked conditions, ready to do battle against the white patriarchal minority power that oppressed them. The fight would be for abolition, for women's suffrage, for reform of exploitative capitalism.

THE BALLOT BOX DIVIDE

But a minority power has ways of preserving itself against attack by an allied majority, and in the wake of the Civil War and emancipation of the slaves, when the vote was granted by the American government to black men, but not to women of any color, this extension of patriarchal power managed to sever the cooperative forces. Some of those who were most committed to both abolition and slavery sided with the granting of black men the vote over women; Frederick Douglass believed black men to be in greater need, due to the violent treatment they faced, and because white women already enjoyed proximal political power via their white husbands.

But other activists saw the move to grant citizenship and the vote to black men as a way to *strengthen* systemic sexism by defining citizenship for the first time — as masculine. "The sons of pilgrims" in Congress, Stanton wrote, were simply "trying to get the irrepressible 'male citizen' into our immortal constitution."[82] And the formerly enslaved abolitionist and suffragist Sojourner Truth is reported to have said, "There is a great stir about colored men getting their rights, but not a word about the colored women. And if colored men get their rights, and colored women not theirs, the colored men will be masters over the women, and it will be just as bad as it was before."

Some white suffragists, including Stanton and Susan B. Anthony, livid at having put aside their emphasis on women's enfranchisement to focus on abolition through the Civil War, and angry at their abolitionist allies for what they understood as political abandonment — were so mad at having to stand back as their allies moved a step forward, that they struck out fiercely, revealing their own deep racism.

Stanton began giving speeches in which she spoke freely of her disdain for the black men she was affronted would now be able to cast votes while white women like herself would not. After years of working toward woman suffrage and abolition, she wrote in 1865, "It becomes a serious question whether we [white women] had better stand aside and see 'Sambo' walk into the kingdom first." Activist forces were further splintered by the strategic pitting of women's suffrage against black male suffrage, including on state ballot referenda, such as one in Kansas in 1867, and via racist arguments that enfranchising white women, who, it was presumed (not incorrectly) would vote like their white husbands, would negate the new power of black voters, and thus keep power in white hands.

Overriding the pleas of her fellow suffragists, Susan B. Anthony accepted the offer of George Francis Train, a so-called Copperhead Democrat who had opposed abolition, to fund a women's suffrage publication called *The Revolution.* Anthony and Stanton toured Kansas with Train, denouncing the Republican Party (which was on the side of black male suffrage) and standing by his side as he made, in the words of historian Andrea Moore Kerr, "demagogic pronouncements about the dangers of black suffrage."[83]

Train was using the competing factions as grist for his own racist political platform, pitting the prospects of white women against those of African Americans, both rhetorically — arguing that if African Americans were permitted citizenship and the franchise "we shall see some white woman in a case of Negro rape being tried by twelve Negro jurymen" — and strategically, by offering Anthony the support and economic resources she was desperate for but not getting from her former allies. As Anthony explained at the time about her association with Train: "All there is about him is that he has made it possible for us to establish a paper. If the Devil himself had come up and said ladies I will help you establish a paper I should have said 'Amen!' " In this paper, Anthony and Stanton pushed an ever more racist line of argument, Kerr writes, "mak-

277

ing frequent references to the 'barbarism,' 'brute force,' and 'tyranny' of black men."[84]

In 1869, during the months after the Fifteenth Amendment had been passed by Congress and activists were working to get it ratified by the states, there was an ugly showdown at the annual gathering of the American Equal Rights Association. Though Train had by then backed away from *The Revolution,* Anthony and Stanton were still agitating against ratification, while their fellow suffragist and staunch supporter of the Fifteenth Amendment, Lucy Stone, was trying to herd the rest of the suffragist and abolitionist allies into line in support of the Amendment — and of an imagined *Sixteenth* Amendment that would bring women the vote.

"It is still true today over almost this entire country that no black man or woman finds the same sort of recognition either in public or in private that the white man or woman finds," Stone had said in a speech, as she worked desperately to allay fears that all of the suffrage movement was opposed to African-American men getting the vote. Stone correctly feared that if Stanton and Anthony's racist arguments against the Fifteenth Amendment worked to doom its ratification, it would be suffragists who'd be blamed. "It is not true that our movement is opposed to the Negro," Stone would write anxiously to fellow suffragists. "But it will be very easy to make it so, to the mutual harm of both causes. . . . I feel dreadfully hurt by this new load we have to carry, and there is no need of it."[85]

The Fifteenth Amendment would, of course, be ratified. And the fantasized Sixteenth Amendment, which Stone had imagined would give women the vote, would not come to fruition . . . at least not for another fifty years, until it was, in fact, the Nineteenth Amendment. The racial tensions that had riven the women's movement did not lessen, and suffragists would split into two separate organizations: one headed by Anthony and Stanton, another by Stone. The groups would not be reconciled for another twenty years, and the split would delay the progress of the suffrage movement by decades.

Even the eventual passage and ratification of the Nineteenth Amendment in 1920 — widely understood as the moment at which "American women" got the right to vote — represented forward motion principally for *white* women, since black women in the Jim Crow South remained stopped at the polls by taxes, literacy tests, and the threat of

279

lynching. The long-fought victory for women was in fact a victory only for *some* women, creating resentments that lasted well beyond the additional forty-five years it took to pass the Voting Rights Act of 1965.

To campaign on behalf of just over half the population is by definition an unwieldy enterprise, one that tries to represent fundamentally conflicting interests, divergent perspectives, and people from varied backgrounds who have lots of good reasons to distrust, resent, and disagree with one another. The immensity and diversity of the women's movement has always been used against it by those who fear its potential power. As Gloria Steinem told me two days before the first Women's March, "Because it's a majority movement, it is subject to the same divide-and-conquer tactics that colonial powers used on countries — turning races, classes, and generations against each other" and using as its particular cudgel "the myth that women can't get along and are our own worst enemies."

And so, in moments at which it seemed that women might in fact come together in massive and meaningful numbers to voice their anger — as they did in 2017 and again in 2018, from Hawaii to Houston, and from Poland to Antarctica — it was wholly un-

280

surprising that the frame offered to the public for this unsettling and potentially disruptive event would be one of internal tension, rather than of the will to overcome it and gather together in temporary but furious solidarity.

But importantly, the *magnification* of internecine resentments to diminish the power of insurgent movements isn't the only tool available to the powerful against the marginal: the powerful minorities also have the power to *create* the inequities that provoke those resentments to begin with.

White patriarchal minority rule was established by America's founders when they encoded slavery into our founding documents and built our electoral apparatus around its protection. It was strengthened when they granted white men the franchise and violently guarded that exclusivity for almost a century, ensuring that it was only they who created and controlled the courts, the businesses, the economic systems, who wrote the legislation and created the customs and set the norms on which the country was built. The mechanisms of white male minority rule have been varied: from the denial of equal pay protections to the criminalization of reproductive autonomy and the denial of full health-care options to

281

women, and especially to poor and nonwhite women. From racist housing policy to social safety nets and government-subsidized benefits that have accrued predominantly or exclusively to white Americans, from the enforcement of marital law that left women unable to exert financial or legal independence to the failures of protection against rape, lynching, assault, harassment, and discrimination.

White men have had a nearly exclusive grip on political, economic, social, and sexual power in the United States, despite being only around a third of its population. The way that a minority power protects itself from the potential uprising of a majority is to discourage unification of that majority. And the best way to discourage unification is to split the majority against itself, by offering benefits and protections of power to some, while denying them to others.

WHAT'S THE MATTER WITH WHITE WOMEN

And so, some American women have been offered the advantages of white supremacy, advantages that turn on other women's disadvantages. But even white women's privileges to some degree have turned on all women's patriarchal subjugation, and the dependency dynamics that patriarchy creates: Women were historically legally barred from property ownership, educational and professional opportunity, the chance to build their own credit or the ability to control their own reproduction; some of these challenges remain, as does wage inequality that means, simply, that women earn less money than men; these conditions have rendered them dependent on men. And women's dependence on men has in turn made it in many women's interests to support policies and parties that protect the economic and political status of the men on whom they depend.

This dynamic applies most specifically to white women, who — as wives, daughters, mothers, sisters, neighbors, employees, colleagues, and friends of white men — have been offered a kind of proximal power: greater access, via their relation to powerful white men, to wealth, jobs, educational opportunities, housing, and health-care options. For white women, this dependency on white men incentivizes a dedication to and protection of white male power, because these women's advantages are linked so closely to white men having the power to in turn dole out to them.

But the particular form of their subjugation and ensuing dependency also works to divide them from nonwhite women, to whom none of the advantages or protections of this economic or social or political supremacy accrue, and discourages potential alliances between white and nonwhite women who might otherwise rise up together to challenge white male power. This is what Hillary Clinton was trying to describe, in the months after the election, when she, often ham-handedly, spoke of the women, "principally . . . white women," who faced "tremendous pressure from fathers and husbands and boyfriends and male employers not to vote 'for the girl.' "[86]

Many of Clinton's critics, on the right and the left, seized on this analysis as a fundamentally antifeminist one, in which Clinton was ascribing to women a lily-livered lack of intellectual and political self-direction.

But her error was in using the language of individualized relationships and choices (which, not for nothing, probably applied in some cases) when what she was in fact aiming to describe were the architectural, systemic incentives that work to secure white women's fealty to and investment in the protection of white male power. She was describing how white patriarchy persists in part by making white women dependent on white men, and then ensuring that those women enjoy benefits in exchange for their support of those men's continued dominance, at the purposeful expense of identification with, connection to, and support of other women — whether those other women are political candidates or simply other marginalized people who would benefit from the diminishment of white male control.

This partially explains the huge partisan divide between married and never-married women, especially white women. Those white women who are or have been most directly connected by marriage to white men are far more likely to vote Republican than their never-married peers. According to a paper published by political scientists Dara Strolovitch, Janelle S. Wong, and Andrew Proctor, who reviewed the 2016 Cooperative Congressional Election study numbers on voting patterns, a majority 59 percent of never-married white women voted for Hillary Clinton, compared to the almost reverse majority of married white women, 57 percent, who voted for Donald Trump. Sixty percent of white widows voted for Trump; 56 percent of white women who were separated from husbands voted for Trump; and 49 percent of white divorced women voted for him. In other words, the study concluded, "The more distant" white women are "from the benefits of and investments in traditional heterosexual marriage, the less likely they are to support Republican presidential candidates," i.e., candidates of the party more likely to support traditional white heteropatriarchy.

It has long been true that some of the most energetic opponents of women's political advancement have been . . . women. Back in the nineteenth century, anti-suffrage campaigns were led by women, and of course the campaign that defeated the ERA in 1982 was led by a woman, Phyllis Schlafly. This dynamic repeated itself in focus groups leading up to the 2016 election.

Jessica Morales, a left-wing activist who worked for the Clinton campaign, remembered those groups. "In every focus group for two years basically, always white women, some college-educated, but most not, would say things [to us] like, 'I'm not sure if my husband likes her. He's gotta like her for me to vote for her.' 'It doesn't really matter to me that she's the first woman president.' 'Is it really that historic?' A thing that people don't realize is that we knew that non-college-educated white women were the problem." Morales believed that these women were the crux. "It's them basically deciding to be on our side and not be Phyllis Schlafly. And the answer is that of course we lost because these women have never chosen our side, ever. Never, ever, ever."

YOU, TOO, CAN BE A PATRIARCH

But racial advantages are not the only thing the white patriarchy is willing to dole out to divide people. There is also patriarchy itself, the benefits of which have been offered up to men of all races. Though nonwhite voters overwhelmingly chose Clinton over Trump, in all racial categories, more men than women voted for Trump. Only 4 percent of black women voted for Donald Trump, but 13 percent of black men did. According to forecaster Harry Enten, that number inched slightly higher, to 15 percent, for black men who made over $100,000 a year.[87] Black men may enjoy, and work to perpetuate, advantages that accrue to their gender, even as they are oppressed because of their race.

The student activist and civil rights leader Diane Nash has recalled how when she was working to found the Student Nonviolent Coordinating Committee, "there was a huge problem of good old boys getting together, and I was the only female in the group that was setting up SNCC originally. . . . Later on, in the Southern Christian Leadership Conference, black ministers dominated it. There was a great deal of misogyny there . . . it was expected that leadership would be male."[88]

Civil rights leaders including Nash, Rosa Parks, Gloria Richardson, Dorothy Height, and Anna Arnold Hedgeman, who'd been charged with drawing thirty thousand white Protestants to attend the 1963 March on Washington, bristled during some of Martin Luther King, Jr.'s speech that day, frustrated that they'd been discouraged from giving speeches themselves, that they'd been instructed to march with the male leaders' wives, behind the men. Height would later recall, "I've never seen a more immovable force. We could not get women's participation taken seriously." What she learned, she'd go on to say, was that if black women "did not demand our rights, we were not going to get them." And Hedgeman would later admonish, crisply, "The male would be better advised to spend less time mourning the loss of his superiority and more time working in partnership with women."

As Brittney Cooper has regularly observed, it's the fact that black women have been offered neither patriarchal nor racial

288

advantage in exchange for support that has enabled their steady and unremitting leadership of the resistance to white patriarchal power in America. "White women and black men both want what white men have — white women want to have corporate power and black men want to be patriarchs. Black women a) know we're never going to get that and b) don't want that. We don't want to wield corporate power and we don't want to oppress people. That's why I look to black women as the political future."

Black women have long been the backbone of our political and progressive past: the strategists and protesters and organizers and volunteers, the women who've gotten out the vote and licked the envelopes, pioneered the thinking that led to the revolutions. Yet they've been only barely represented in leadership of the political parties they've bolstered, their policy priorities have often gone unaddressed and unrecognized; their participation has long been taken for granted. And when white women have caught up to where black women have been for a long time, the work of the black women has often been appropriated, ignored, and uncredited by those with greater economic, cultural, and racial advantage.

In the 1930s, the black Philadelphia

lawyer Sadie Alexander wrote extensively about how women's work outside the home had salutary benefits for black women and their families. But it wasn't until 1963, when Betty Friedan published *The Feminine Mystique,* that the argument was understood as revolutionary. Of course, the suburban white women woken by Friedan desperately *needed* to be woken; Friedan's address of their isolation and suffocation within the homes of the white men in whom the government had invested so much power and authority would become politically revolutionary precisely because of the mass power of that anesthetized population. Yet her book made no acknowledgment of black women or their very relevant circumstances: that racism and its economic disadvantages meant that the majority of black women in America had *always* had to work for wages, had never en masse experienced "the problem that has no name." The asphyxiating ennui of stay-at-home subservience mostly plagued a generation of white women who'd been nudged out of the colleges and off the factory floors into which they'd only recently won entry, and into early married middle-class homes via the very same mechanisms — housing loans and the GI Bill and new highways — that had cut black families off from the resources that might boost them into a middle class. *The Feminine Mystique* was aimed squarely and exclusively at white women. Yet Friedan was long hailed as "the mother of the movement."

But when black women push back against the white women who come in and take up a disproportionate amount of space, when their own complaints about race complicate a white women's movement, it is too often black women who are framed as the ones being divisive. This dynamic was reflected in the coverage of the Women's March conflicts, in which black women letting white women know that they had not invented political resistance to white patriarchy were viewed as somehow inhospitable.

Part of the problem stems from understanding whiteness as simply normative, central — any challenge to it is disruptive in the same way that challenges to patriarchy are disruptive, insofar as they discomfit the more powerful group. But that echo is lost on too many white women, who have a hard time absorbing the ways that even as they have been marginalized by men, so they themselves have often marginalized nonwhite women.

Alicia Garza described her experience of reading Hillary Clinton's righteously angry memoir about the 2016 election and being "befuddled" by it. "Yes, women's anger is not considered to be valid or legitimate," said Garza. "So in one way she has every fucking right to be mad as shit about the way in which the patriarchy has impacted her aspirations and goals, and even though I disagree with her on a lot of things, she deserves to be seen in her humanity and in her dignity." But, she went on, "I am livid when I read these excerpts. Because, yes, you get to be in all of your anger. But what I felt very viscerally from her anger was that it wasn't just [directed] at the men who kept her down, it was also very much [directed] at the people" — including Black Lives Matter activists and criminal justice reformers — "who challenged her around things she absolutely should have been challenged around."

Saira Rao, a lawyer and editor who lives in Colorado and became so angry in the wake of 2016 that she decided to run for office against her incumbent Democratic congresswoman, Diana DeGette, said that anytime she brings up race or white privilege among her friends, "this particular group of white women fly off the handle." She said she has had a friend, "a white woman, a liberal feminist, tell me 'the problem with you is it's always about race.' " Rao said, "I think the reason white women are the way they are is because the system is working for them and because they're comfortable in their Lululemon and comfortable putting aside their law degrees. So they want us to shut the fuck up because the system is working for them."

These are the dynamics that Audre Lorde works to describe in "The Uses of Anger," when she recalls "the most vocal white woman" responding to a week-long forum on black and white women, " 'I think I've gotten a lot. I feel black women really understand me a lot better now; they have a better idea of where I'm coming from.' " This, Lorde points out, is an example of the assumption that "understanding her" — the white woman — "lay at the core of the racist problem."

Women of color, and specifically black women, are the demographic most likely to see their struggles as intertwined both with other women's and with black men's, and to work alongside white women and black men — often pioneering the thinking and doing the labor of organization — central to movements for liberation and equality. Which makes it a terrific injustice that the movements to liberate women and African

293

Americans have so often been understood as having been led by white women and black men. They are understood this way because white supremacy and patriarchy permit white women and black men greater access to money, and more proximity to the media that covers social movements and the politicians who respond to them, than black women have.

So it should be no wonder that when white women decided to participate in a protest against Donald Trump, after an election in which white women's willingness to protect white male power by electing an openly racist and misogynistic incompetent with authoritarian tendencies had been laid bare, black women would be anxious to explain that the white women newly awakened to rage were just that: newly awakened, and might have something to learn.

The post-2016 moment offers a chance for white women to be awakened to the many reasons that they should be angry. But crucially — *urgently* — the opportunity is not simply to be angry on their own behalf, but also at the injustices faced by other women, women who experience those injustices in part thanks to the very mechanisms that protect and enrich those white women. And in order for a new white wokeness to be integrated effectively into a contemporary movement, it must not take it over; there must be acknowledgment that white women are late to the party.

WHAT'S WRONG WITH MESSY?

"I have started to tell people when I do talks that there has been no movement ever in history that hasn't been messy or that hasn't had issues internally," said Alicia Garza. "That is a characteristic of human behavior and human relationships. The question for us is: are we prepared to try and be the first movement in history that learns how to work through that anger? To not get rid of it, not suppress it, but learn how to get through it together for the sake of what is on the other side? And I think that is what our core challenge is in this moment."

"Contentious dialogue is by design," Linda Sarsour told me before the Women's March. "As women of color who came into this effort, we came in not only to mobilize and organize, but also to educate, to argue that we can't talk about women's rights, about reproductive rights, about equal pay, without also talking about race and class." Organizers, Sarsour said, "are actually okay with people being offended. We are hoping the conversation continues and that we can

295

move into a different place and focus on the way we're coming together *nonetheless.*"

There is indeed an argument that the women's movement has survived over centuries not in spite of but *because of* its cacophony: because those who have pushed the movement from the inside, forcing it to grow and change and be better — even when they haven't always agreed on what better meant — have helped it to meet the shifting forms and expressions of inequity from era to era.

And whatever the tensions in advance of the Women's March, it *did* turn out to be the largest single-day demonstration in United States history. Millions of women, many of them white, many of them new to activism, drove and walked and took trains and planes to come together under banners and alongside women who'd long been fighting for black lives and indigenous rights and better health care and fairer wages and not just for reproductive rights but for reproductive justice that takes into account racial and economic inequities. An iconic photo from that march showed a sign reading "I'll see you nice white ladies at the next #BlackLivesMatter march, right?" A lot of white women have seen that sign, and at least some of them have been reckoning with its troubling, and accurate, premise.

In the summer of 2017, after white supremacists marched in Boston as a follow-up to their torchlight brigade in Charlottesville, a massive counterprotest was held — in Boston, a city with a deep, old strain of racist white supremacy. That march was dominated by a fair number of those nice white ladies. When the Women's March held its 2017 convention in Detroit, the session called "Confronting White Womanhood," billed as being "designed for white women committed to being part of an intersectional feminist movement to unpack the ways white women uphold and benefit from white supremacy," had a line out the door. It was so oversubscribed that they had to hold it twice, and on the second day, they had to move it to a space that could hold five hundred.[89]

In 2018, it was a white actress, Ashley Judd, who first used the word "intersectionality" — in reference to Kimberlé Crenshaw's theory of intersecting forms of bias and how they shape the differing experiences and perspectives of oppression — on an Oscar stage. In the summer of 2018, when six hundred women took over the central lobby of the Senate's Hart office building, wrapping themselves in foil blankets and sitting on the floor, arms locked protesting immigration policy, the majority of them looked to be white; most of them were arrested. The next week, after Nancy Pelosi rebuked Maxine Waters for encouraging angry protest and failed to defend her against the implicit threat made against her by Donald Trump, some white women wrote an open letter. "When you attack a Black woman for speaking out about injustice, and when you call for 'civility' in the face of blatant racism," it read in part, "you invoke a long history of white supremacist power . . . To our great discredit, white women continue to act far too often in ways that support white supremacy, even when it is to our detriment . . . when you chide Representative Waters for bravely and passionately speaking up for the most marginalized, you're on the wrong side of history." Within a week, more than six thousand women had signed the letter.

It seems possible that we are witnessing a large-scale civic and social education. That in the wake of Trump's election millions of previously somnambulant Americans have been provoked, in their shock and panic, to evolution. Some of them decided to learn: about local and state elections, about the way that government works, about policy, and about what it means that racism, sexism, and economic inequality are *systemic;* some began to see how these issues are linked in ways that go beyond academic jargon.

Kat Calvin, whose organization, Spread the Vote, aims to help voters get their voter IDs in states with restrictive laws, has noted with surprise that while black women turn out in higher numbers to vote, "the women who make up resistance volunteers and run resistance organizations are actually an incredibly diverse mix. It's been amazing to see. I'm a black woman who runs a resistance organization and I'm pretty shocked every day." A majority of her organization's volunteers, Calvin said, "are white women who are going to homeless shelters every week, driving people they have never met and wouldn't normally speak to all over town, and [they] are really putting their hearts into it. It's kind of amazing."[90]

"Look, grandmothers were knitting something called a pussy hat," marveled Jessica Morales of the Women's March. "And they cherish it like it's a keepsake. And when you went on social media there was the Native Women's Caucus, who looked dope as hell, and they were singing next to the domestic workers, who had their red shirts on, and

English is their second language and they all make about $11,000 a year, and they're standing next to this rich-ass lady who has a sign about her vagina. And you think, you know: *America!*"

"There was something about the Women's March that shook me to my core," says Alicia Garza. "Because this regime change is unlike anything we've ever seen in my lifetime. Not even in the lifetime of my parents. And that to me seemed more important than anything else." Garza acknowledged that many of her peers feel differently, that their communities' suffering has been steady and is not materially worse now. But she feels the key difference is that the democracy is dismantling *itself.* "So the notion that we shouldn't try to figure out how to build a movement that is bigger than the people who already agree with us seems like a death warrant," she said.

But, she hastened to add, "That does *not* mean that you don't continue to hold people accountable. It is not my job to make white women less racist; that is the job of other white women. And I will absolutely hold white women accountable every step of the way. But at the same time, when somebody says 'I want to learn,' I want to figure it out."

As Morales says, "I like to play chess, not checkers. The checkers part of me is like, 'Look at all these white ladies. . . . Where were you?' But honestly, I don't want to be a part of a movement that demands that you flagellate yourself to prove you're real." And so, she said, she's trying to cultivate a different approach: "Welcome. We really need you, because even if every person of color woke the fuck up and was like *La raza!* that's only 38 percent of America. And y'all control the banks, the businesses, you're the head of all the entertainment companies. So let's go, we need you."

This isn't, of course, satisfactory or reparatory. Asking nonwhite activists to grade newly hatched white protesters on a forgiving curve is itself unfair. But it's also part of the project if we want to move forward, and in fact leverage that proximal power enjoyed by white women — who can draw media attention, who have more access to political power, without whom we lose elections to disastrous effect — and use that power as a cudgel against the minority of white men who have had everyone in their grip.

Garza said that she's been thinking a lot about Lorde's "Uses of Anger." "Lorde projects a vision," she said. "What if we could be in anger with accountability? Yeah

301

girl, you get to be mad as shit that all of those things happened, but also where are the places in which you were liable for the anger of others? It's a both approach and not an either-or."

"For black women and white women to face one another's angers without denial or immobility or silence or guilt is in itself a heretical and generative idea," wrote Lorde, arguing that the honest expression of anger between women of different races is necessary if coalition building is ever going to happen. "It implies peers meeting upon a common basis to examine difference[s], and to alter those distortions which history has created around our difference. For it is those distortions which separate us. And we must ask ourselves: Who profits from all this?" The angers between women, Lorde argued, "can transform difference[s] through insight into power. For anger between peers births change, not destruction, and the discomfort and sense of loss it often causes is not fatal, but a sign of growth."

Garza's still wrestling with it. "For me, my anger at white women for excluding women of color, and black women specifically, for generations is still very palpable. That hasn't changed. What has changed is that I understand that the coalition that is going to save us has to be much bigger than what it is. I want people to get free. I'm mad as hell about a whole bunch of things, every single day I'm mad inside, seething right beneath the surface. But I want to be free more than I want to be mad. And I want to work with people who *also* want to be free more than they want to be mad, because maybe we will actually get to something that makes sense."

EPITAPH

On the day that Frederick Douglass died in 1895, he had spent the morning with Susan B. Anthony at a meeting of suffragists. In fact, he'd had such a good time that he had been in the midst of telling his wife about the meeting when he'd fallen to his knees, hands clasped, and his wife had simply believed that his pose was one of narrative enthusiasm, not realizing that he was in fact dying.

"It is a singular fact," the *New York Times* reported in Douglass's obituary, "that the very last hours of his life were given in attention to one of the principles to which he has devoted his energies since his escape from slavery. . . . Mr. Douglass was a regularly enrolled member of the National

303

Woman Suffrage Association, and had always attended its conventions." The obituary noted that his companion at the suffrage meeting that day was "Miss Anthony, his lifelong friend," and that when "Miss Susan B. Anthony heard of Mr. Douglass's death, at the evening session of the council, she was very much affected. Miss Anthony has a wonderful control over her feelings, but tonight, she could not conceal her emotion."[91]

The racism that had riven the women's movement had by no means abated, nor would it anytime soon; twenty years later, one of the next generation's white suffrage leaders, Alice Paul, would try unsuccessfully to force her elder, the black suffragist and anti-lynching leader Ida B. Wells, not to walk with her state's delegation in the enormous 1913 suffrage march on Washington, DC, but instead to march with the rest of the black women suffragists where they'd been told to position themselves: behind all the white women. And the year that he died Anthony had asked Douglass not to appear at a suffrage convention in the South, because she was trying to strategically win white women to the cause. But neither did women of any race have the vote, nearly six decades after the first meetings of the black and white women joining to push for abolition, more than forty years after Douglass had joined Stanton at Seneca Falls.

Frederick Douglass was seventy-eight at his death; Susan B. Anthony would die eleven years later at eighty-six. Elizabeth Cady Stanton, who had turned to such baldly racist rhetoric in her anger at the inclusion of black men in the franchise before she herself had won the vote, was seventy-nine at the time of Douglass's death and would live another seven years. Near the end of his life, Douglass would observe of their linked battles, "We should all see the folly and madness of attempting to accomplish with a part what could only be done with the united strength of the whole."[92]

None of the three, of course, would live to see the passage and ratification of the Ninteenth Amendment, much less conceive of the Voting Rights Act. In fact, only *one* woman who attended the Seneca Falls convention would survive long enough to cast a ballot after the ratification of the Nineteenth Amendment. These struggles, and the internal dissent they engender, have the power to last longer than any of us, even those who have given lifetimes to the fights, both external and internal. But every once

305

in a while, in the long, conjoined fight for liberation and equality, there is a rare opportunity to unite — if never in perfect alignment — the whole.

PART III
SEASON OF THE WITCH

I've been thinking a lot about the ways that women are required to perform our emotions during this moment, and in particular how much thought and effort we put into mitigating the risk of being seen as angry. These performances have belied the reality that if you consider yourself fully human as a woman, and fully endowed with dignity, then anger is a very reasonable response to sexual harassment, assault, or other gendered violence. This is another thing I've been thinking about: How anger has both limited me and led me astray, and also been a wonderful motivator. Anger leads me to seek answers, to seek change.

— Moira Donegan, via Twitter

CHAPTER ONE:
GETTING AWAY WITH IT

HARVEY

For several months, in the late summer and early fall of 1789, after the storming of the Bastille and the food shortages that had come in its wake, some of the men agitating for political change in France had spoken of staging a protest at the royal palace at Versailles. There had been talk of a mass demonstration of starving Parisians outside the opulent home of King Louis the XVI and his family; it had not yet come to fruition.

But on the morning of October 5, a Parisian woman, driven to a seething fury by the scarcity and high price of bread at the city's markets, began to bang a marching drum. Other women quickly joined her and began to walk through the Paris streets. As the crowd of women grew, some of them brought along their knives; some forced a church to begin tolling its bells to draw attention to their growing protest. They gathered outside the Hôtel de Ville, Paris's city hall, demanding both food and weapons.

From there, the mob, by then reaching perhaps ten thousand, headed to Versailles, dragging cannons they had seized. After an overnight standoff, the crowd would grow to more than fifty thousand and return to Paris the next afternoon, the king and his family with them.

Two hundred and twenty-eight years later, on October 5, 2017 — also nearly a year to the day of the release of the *Access Hollywood* tape that had not succeeded in delegitimizing the man who was now our sitting president — the *New York Times* published a story by Jodi Kantor and Megan Twohey headlined "Harvey Weinstein Paid off Sexual Harassment Accusers for Decades." It chronicled multiple allegations of sexual predation and harassment made by women — including some famous actresses — against Weinstein, a powerful movie producer.

It was a story that I had been waiting, hoping, and, to the degree that I'd been able, agitating to read for almost twenty years. Frankly, I had never believed that I would ever see it in print.

312

One of my earliest jobs out of college had been back in 1999 when I was an editorial assistant at a magazine that Harvey Weinstein's company Miramax had financed. As a young secretary at the magazine, adjacent to his then company, I knew of his brutal bullying of employees, had begun to hear hushed rumors of hotel rooms, nudity, and then of whispered payoffs; I'd also heard plenty of gossip about which actresses in which movies — the beneficiaries of which book deals or writing contracts — had slept with Harvey in order to get them. Back then it had been gossip, and also unthinkable that anyone would have or could have gotten *angry* about it, to any effect at all. Harvey was the key to the resurgence of New York's film culture; he opened doors to stardom, to Oscars, to edgy writers and directors; he even financed feminist movies directed by Jane Campion.

My next job, which I'd begun in my mid-twenties, had been as a reporter at a weekly New York newspaper, where part of my beat was covering the film business in the city. In the weeks before the 2000 presidential election, I had been working on my first deeply reported story, about *O*, a star-studded but violent reimagining of *Othello* that Miramax's Dimension Films division had been

313

refusing to release, perhaps out of deference to the cringy clean-media message of the Al Gore–Joe Lieberman campaign, which Weinstein was publicly supporting; already there was talk of Weinstein's ambitions in Democratic politics.

Since Weinstein had failed to respond to my calls for comment, I had been sent by my editor, on Election Eve 2000, to cover a book party he was hosting, along with a more senior male colleague whom I happened to be dating at the time. I asked Weinstein to comment for my story; he didn't like my question. There was an altercation; he began shouting at me, pushing me hard with his finger against my shoulder; he called me a "cunt" and a "bitch" and declared that he was glad he was the "fucking sheriff of this fucking lawless piece-of-shit town." When my colleague intervened, first trying to calm Weinstein and then trying to extract an apology from him, Weinstein went nuclear, pushing my colleague down a set of steps, knocking him over with such force that his tape recorder hit a female party guest in the head, knocking her out. Then, screaming to the crowd about how my colleague had "hit a woman," Weinstein had dragged him onto Sixth Avenue in Manhattan and put him in a headlock.

Such was the power of Harvey Weinstein in 2000 — when you're a star, you can do anything — that despite the dozens of camera flashes that had gone off on that sidewalk that night, capturing the sight of a famous and physically gargantuan film executive trying to pound in the head of a young newspaper reporter, I never once saw a photo. None were published. Harvey was famous for having the power to spin — to suppress — anything.

The next day, Election Day, the *New York Post* reported on the event and cast it as "a couple of pushy reporters" who had "pushed [Weinstein] to the breaking point." The *New York Times* reported that Harvey and my colleague had "had words" and that I had started the whole thing by "question-[ing] Mr. Weinstein about an article that had nothing to do with . . . the party"; Weinstein, according to a Miramax official quoted by the *Times,* had "realized it really wasn't appropriate and was upset."

Here it was: power at work. Weinstein's physical aggression, the act of beating up a journalist, transformed into an exchange of "words," while the actual *words* in question — my questions of a powerful man, questions lodged as part of my *job,* my work as

315

a reporter — were described in the newspaper of record as "inappropriate" and "upsetting." Though he had done the physical pushing, we — the less powerful human beings he had pushed — could be comfortably described in the press he controlled as "pushy."

In the months and years that had followed my own run-in with Weinstein, I began to hear from other reporters who'd gotten wind of other kinds of power abuses: the whispered dalliances I'd heard about in my earlier job were rumored to be worse than what I'd understood — did I know anything? Could I, as someone who'd been a firsthand witness to his verbal and physical aggressions, help them track down evidence of his sexual misbehaviors? I talked to every reporter who ever came to me for help with these attempted stories — and there were many, some of them legendary investigative journalists; I shared what I had heard, the rumors and gossip; I collected numbers and shared email addresses of anyone I thought could help them tell a full story about Harvey.

But mostly from these other journalists, I learned more than I offered. I heard about the stories *they'd* heard, yes — about the ubiquity of his behavior, about an ever clearer view of this man as a monster, perhaps a rapist. But far more than that, I learned about what felt like the complete, Sisyphean impossibility of ever bringing this information to light. Because all of these journalists, some working for *years* to report the story of Harvey Weinstein, traveling the globe to track down leads, fearing weirdly (as I had, after my incident with him) that their phones were tapped and that they were being followed (it seems it was all true): they never got the story.

The danger and impossibility of challenging a powerful man was made all too clear. I remembered what it was like to have the full force of this mountainous man screaming vulgarities at me, his spit hitting my face; of watching him haul my friend into the street and try to hurt him. Among the reasons that I never really entertained the idea of reporting the story myself was that I had been shown *so clearly* that I could not have won against that kind of power — both physical strength and the ability to manipulate the power of systems and institutions to cover up its abuses.

There was the suffocating force of cultural expectation itself, long since calibrated around patriarchal abuses, making it hard for any woman to trust that anyone would believe she had been wronged. We *knew* that rape and even sexual harassment were wrong, of course: this was years after Anita Hill. But the normalized notion of a casting couch, the nostalgic view of legendarily brutal studio bosses like Louis B. Mayer and of desperately ambitious actresses willing to do anything for a part: these had been worked into our romantic, imaginative DNA, and that romance, the easy way we integrated the exchanges made between men who had power and women who needed a piece of it as just part of how things worked, provided insulation to those men.

Then, there were less sentimentalized protections in place: Weinstein had employees sign elaborate nondisclosure agreements; he gave consulting jobs and book contracts to journalists who might otherwise expose his behavior; he gave money to powerful people in politics, building enough goodwill with them to provide a layer of protection, a kind of deafness to the ugly rumors that might circulate among *less* powerful people. For decades, the reporters who *did* try to tell the story butted up against a wall of sheer power that was leveraged against those who'd otherwise want to challenge him: the ambitious actors, vulner-

318

able assistants, all the executives and subordinates whose careers, salaries, and reputations were in Harvey's hands.

And then all of a sudden, the power was imbalanced. The revelation of Weinstein's abuse — sexual submission fetishized, yes, but also simply submission and humiliation, the transformation of power into a weapon of degradation via massages and masturbation and daily diminution — was laid bare.

After the *Times* piece came one from Ronan Farrow at the *New Yorker,* reporting on long-suspected allegations that Weinstein was not simply a harasser but a rapist. Then came more. And more. And more. Women, and a few men, poured into magazines and newspapers and onto television to tell their own stories, about Harvey and about so many others: actor Kevin Spacey and television journalist Charlie Rose and magazine editor Leon Wieseltier and political pundit Mark Halperin and morning show host Matt Lauer and chef Mario Batali and comedian Louis C.K. and restaurateur John Besh and professors and Ford factory plant managers and progressive activists and fast food managers and senators and congressmen. The stories were told by farmworkers and flight attendants and hotel workers and union organizers and police officers and by

319

women in Silicon Valley and Sweden and China and France.

The rage had been building, had leaked out earlier in the mini-uprisings, the insistence that other men whose behaviors had been open secrets — from comedian Bill Cosby to Fox News machers Bill O'Reilly and Roger Ailes — be finally made to pay a price for their behavior toward women. But something had shifted. Perhaps it was the election of Donald Trump, the fact that he stood in as the ultimate, inflated embodiment of white patriarchal power abuse who had faced no repercussion for his behavior, or maybe it was having seen women gather as armies to bring down Cosby and Ailes and to protest Trump's inauguration and the Muslim ban and efforts to repeal health care. Then again perhaps it was simply the impossibility of containing the fury any longer, after we'd had this view of its injustice, its breadth and depth.

The reporters and the storytellers had finally banged the marching drum, bringing thousands onto the streets and ringing the bells, in 2017, insistent on making a historic charge and extracting the kings from their grotesquely guarded palaces.

The anger window was open. For decades, for centuries, it had been closed. Something bad happened to you, you shoved it down, you maybe told someone but probably didn't get much satisfaction — emotional or practical — from the confession. Maybe you even got blowback. No one really cared, and certainly no one was going to do anything about it.

But in the four months that followed the reporting on one movie mogul's sexual predation, a Harvey-sized hole was blown in the American news cycle, and there was suddenly space and air for women to talk — to yell and scream and rage.

Fixing on a hashtag — #metoo — that had been pioneered by the activist Tarana Burke in 2006 as a movement designed to reveal the ubiquity of sexual violence done to women and girls, but was taken up more broadly as an internet campaign in the fall of 2017, women spilled so much that had been bottled up for so long: they told stories of bosses and colleagues and teachers and mentors who had grabbed them or coerced them or insulted them or belittled them. There was a huge range of tales — everything from violent assaults to unwanted kisses to quid-pro-quo offers of professional advancement in exchange for sex, to more minor offenses, like groped butts and grazed boobs, unwanted come-ons and lewd late-night messaging from colleagues.

What united the stories was the way that they made the storytellers feel, what the events had led them to understand: that in public spheres, they had been regarded, treated, evaluated differently; that they had been used or degraded, had not been taken seriously professionally by powerful men. Many of the women who told their stories (there were men who told theirs too, but the majority were women) felt that the treatment they'd experienced had damaged their careers, dulled their prospects, muffled their ambitions, and kept them from the kinds of achievements in the public sphere that the powerful men of whom they complained had reached.

Some of those who spoke did so to friends or family members or to other colleagues, many for the first time. Some women lodged complaints, years later, with HR departments. Some spoke to reporters, providing corroborating evidence, contemporaneous witnesses, photographs and diaries for documentation; they showed their nondisclosure agreements and settled lawsuit filings; they produced the friends and husbands they'd told at the time, though many, many of them had told *no one.*

Then there were others who simply took the things that had always been private, quiet — the whispers, nudges, and meaningful stares that had served as warnings — and made them public and loud, with no mediation; they wrote their stories on social media, in tweets and Facebook posts that could be sent around the world in seconds. Some women in the media compiled a shared document, anonymously detailing their encounters with "shitty men" in their industry, men they named. It was dangerous and irresponsible and a sign of exactly how desperate, how utterly, profoundly furious they were, and how out of fucks they were about letting the world know.

There were other bizarre and creative acts of revolt: when the feminist writer Nicole Cliffe got wind of the fact that the antifeminist polemicist Katie Roiphe was planning to leak the name of the original compiler of the Shitty Media Men list in *Harper's Magazine,* she announced that she would match the fees writers would have otherwise been paid for publishing their pieces in that issue, in exchange for pulling them from the magazine in protest. Cliffe was open about the fact that she did not ask her husband before promising funds from their joint account — a move that recalled the second-wave feminist Alix Kates Shulman, who'd remembered writing a check from her joint checking account, her first without asking her husband's permission, in order to pay for members of the New York Radical Women's collective to get inside the 1968 Miss America pageant and drop a banner reading "Women's Liberation" at the moment the new winner was crowned.[1]

I wasn't sure I liked the Cliffe approach, or the Shitty Media Men list; they were destabilizing to my profession, to the norms of professional and ethical behavior I'd been raised to respect, and — I feared — to feminism itself. They seemed too much, too risky, too intense. I felt like I was in some space movie, on a ship getting rocked by fire as it moved forward at a speed I'd never traveled before. Would it hold? Would we survive? I think it was the first time that I had experienced anything like radicalism in my own sphere, and it felt unsafe. Exhilarating. Terrifying. Uncomfortable. Necessary and long overdue and as if it were either going to burn us all up or save us.

It was definitely not feminism as I'd known it in its contemporary rebirth — packaged into think pieces or nonprofits or

324

Eve Ensler plays or Beyoncé VMA performances. That stuff had certainly had its place and had done its crucial job, pulling feminism out of the suffocating murk of backlash. But this was different. This was 70s-style, organic, mass radical rage, exploding in unpredictable directions. It was loud, thanks to the human megaphone that is social media and the "whisper networks" that were now less about speaking sotto voce than about frantically typed texts and all-caps group chats.

Extremely powerful men lost their jobs — Harvey Weinstein lost his company; Charlie Rose was fired; Mario Batali was exiled from his restaurant empire; Matt Lauer was dismissed from the *Today* show; Senator Al Franken was asked to resign by his colleagues, many of them female. The list of men kept growing until there were too many too count, too many pieces to read. Never before, in my memory, had so many white male authority figures been censured, dismissed.

It was feral in its intensity, and even for those of us who were completely persuaded of how urgent and correct the process of reckoning was, it was not fun. Because the stories were so awful, many of them the sickening, chilling stuff of nightmares. But also because the conditions that had created this perfect storm of female rage — the pervasiveness of harassment and abuse; the election of a multiply accused predator who now controlled the courts and the agencies that were supposed to protect us from criminal and discriminatory acts — were so undeniably grim.

It was also harrowing because it was confusing, because the wrath might have been fierce, but it was not uncomplicated. In the shock of the house lights having been suddenly brought up — of being forced to stare at the ugly scaffolding on which so many of our professional lives had been built — we had scant chance to parse what exactly was enflaming us and who. It was the tormentors, obviously, but it was also our friends, our mentors, *ourselves*.

GETTING MAD AT MEN

Among the greatest challenges faced by the women's movement in all its iterations has been the structural difficulty of persuading women to express sustained, public anger toward their most direct oppressors: men.

This difficulty exists for many reasons, and takes us back to the fact that women, unlike many racial, ethnic, or religious groups in the United States, are not an oppressed minority, but rather a majority population, integral to homes, families, personal and professional networks in every geographic, religious, racial, and ethnic category. Here's what that means, practically: every man has a woman in his life, and every woman has a man in hers.

The intransigent bitch about sexism and misogyny is that even when women recognize, truly *feel* the weight of the numerous and varied ways in which they have been subjugated and offered less based on their gender, we must confront the fact that the bad guys are, in many cases, also our good guys: the men in our beds, our hearts, our families. They are our brothers and fathers and uncles and friends and lovers and husbands and roommates and sons.

We love them.

We also often *need* them: to be our colleagues and family members and boyfriends and buddies, to help us raise our kids, to bring home paychecks on which we subsist. Because they have so much more professional and economic power, men are very often our bosses, our mentors, the guys who gave us our breaks and who we continue to rely on to give us promotions, raises, assignments. Because white men have had such disproportionate political power, it is often

327

they on whom women — feminists, left activists — rely on a larger scale: as representatives, advocates, party leaders; to challenge them is to potentially imperil a whole political party, and with it, crucial protections, advocacy, an ideological agenda itself.

Of course it is precisely this reality — once again, this *dependence* — that has permitted powerful men to mistreat and discriminate against those with less power. It is also what has often kept women paralyzed — by fear, risk, love, loyalty — and reluctant to push back angrily against their own ill treatment, or in response to the ill-treatment of other women.

The potential for damage to relationships on which women depend is *real;* consequences may be both emotional and material. Women's challenge to male authority or power abuse can send a family into disarray, end a marriage, provoke a firing, either of a woman *or* of a man on whom other women — colleagues and family members — rely economically. Fear of these repercussions (alongside a long-ingrained and realistic fear of simple futility) are very often fierce enough to inoculate women against expressing, and perhaps in many cases even feeling, the outrage at men that they might otherwise make known.

It is so much more peaceful to not get mad, to not even *think* about the gross injustices that pepper our daily interactions with men: double standards, intellectual disregard, objectification, sexual harassment, pay inequity, differential domestic expectations and burdens, unequal representation, the banality of daily diminution. Often it is simply easier not to consider any of this, much less try to fight back against it, especially when fighting back means fighting men you'd prefer to keep thinking well of.

"Once you know something, you cannot unknow it," wrote Judith Levine of what it means to have felt feminist anger toward men in her 1992 book *My Enemy, My Love.* "You can't sign up for consciousness-razing groups . . . but neither does the new knowledge erase the feelings that preceded it. . . . [W]hat do you do if you also love the hated person, need him emotionally, or depend on him materially, if you feel compelled to placate him or fearful to disturb him? A powerful unspoken theme of post–World War II feminism — and women's lives since feminism — is the struggle with . . . the fury of recognized oppression."

During the onslaught of #metoo-inspired allegations, a few of the many women who were both supportive of the movement and close to the public men accused of harassment gave eloquent voice to the paradoxical pains they felt.

CBS This Morning host Gayle King said of her former coanchor Charlie Rose, a man who was accused, all told, by more than thirty women of harassment, of exposing and forcing himself on younger colleagues, "I've enjoyed a friendship and a partnership with Charlie for the past five years. I have held him in such high regard and I am really struggling, because what do you say when someone that you deeply care about has done something that is so horrible? I can't stop thinking about the anguish of those women: what happened to their dignity, what happened to their bodies, what happened, maybe, to their careers."[2]

The comedian Sarah Silverman spoke about *her* close friend and fellow comedian Louis C.K., accused by other female comedians of masturbating in front of them without their consent and then relying on a system of enablers to punish them professionally for telling the story. The process of exposing the culture of pervasive harassment, Silverman said, was like "cutting out tumors: it's messy and it's complicated and it is gonna hurt but it's necessary and we'll all be healthier for it." But, she went on, "It sucks. And some of our heroes will be taken down and we'll discover bad things about people we like. Or in some cases people we love." Describing her long friendship with C.K., she said, "I love Louis, but Louis did these things. Both of those statements are true. So, I just keep asking myself: can you love someone who did bad things? I hope it's okay if I am at once very angry for the women he wronged and the culture that enabled it, and also sad, because he's my friend."[3]

It was a dynamic that was not simply painful for female accusers and friends of the accused, but an obvious weak spot that those who were *not* supportive of the #metoo movement were eager to exploit, in an effort to defend against the female anger and put a stop to the campaign. "When we start conflating and putting all these things all in one bucket," warned the conservative Fox News personality Greg Gutfield of the breadth of complaints, "we're going to start hurting your fathers, your brothers, your sons, your grandfathers." The retired NBC anchor Tom Brokaw, defending himself against the claim of a former younger colleague that he had come to her hotel room and tried to forcibly kiss her in the 1990s, pounded out a middle-of-the-night, bathetic letter of self-defense in which he proclaimed, "I am proud of who I am as a husband, father, grandfather, journalist, and citizen."

In May Samantha Bee would joke darkly about the dynamic of emotional captivity to the men close to us, in both its personal and political forms, in a furious tirade against New York's freshly resigned attorney general Eric Schneiderman. Schneiderman had not only been a guest on Bee's show, but a prosecutor whom she'd previously hailed as a feminist super-hero, a man on whom feminist women were depending, and who had just been revealed as an allegedly violent abuser of his girlfriends.

"The good legal work that you did for women does not absolve you," she bellowed, during a nuclear-grade opening monologue. "It will not give me one second's pause about tearing you a new asshole on television. I give *zero fucks*. I would do an act entitled 'My Dad Is a Monster' if I had to. . . . Eric Schneiderman, you are trash and we do not *need* you."

Bee's rage resonated in 2018, in part because it reflected the liberating and livid surprise of having gotten to this point. It takes years, it takes emergency circumstances, it takes the electric shock of having so much injustice laid bare, to goad mass numbers of women into actually turning on the men in their lives — their elected officials or their dads or their partners or their bosses — and telling them what Bee told Eric Schneiderman over and over again in that seven-minute monologue: Fuck you, fuck you, fuck you.

It may have felt cathartic in its pop culture iteration, coming from a comedian in charge of her own show. But the catharsis stemmed in part from the fact that letting loose any comparable anger within workplaces or families might come at steep costs for women who did *not* have their own shows.

"I saw the people who spoke up evaporate," said public radio producer Kristen Meinzer, who publicly accused radio host John Hockenberry of sexual harassment, during a conversation with other #metoo storytellers. "I couldn't lose my job." She went on to note that "so much of how we're taught to live in this world as women is to keep the peace, to smile, to try and giggle it off, to say, 'Oh, that's fine' when it doesn't feel fine . . . How do you preserve your own job, how do you preserve your own space, and how do you preserve your physical safety as a woman? A lot of that is: we have

333

to be nice."[4]

NOT NICE LADIES

There is, of course, a long history of women who, in moments of political or personal crisis, make the revolutionary decision to *not* be nice, though the personal and political implications of this choice have rarely been obscure.

"Do not put such unlimited power into the hands of the husbands," Abigail Adams warned her own husband presciently in the spring of 1776. "Remember all men would be tyrants if they could. If particular care and attention is not paid to the ladies, we are determined to foment a rebellion."

Seventy-two years later, in 1848, two hundred women and forty-odd men convened in Seneca Falls, New York, to draft the Declaration of Sentiments, a document modeled on the colonists' Declaration of Independence, which Adams's husband John had signed. The Declaration of Sentiments was also a statement of independence — women's direct rebuke of male power and a seeming return on Abigail's promise of rebellion: "The history of mankind is a history of repeated injuries and usurpations on the part of man toward woman," the Declaration read in part, claiming that the

334

object of these injuries and usurpations had been "the establishment of an absolute tyranny over her."

And then they described that tyranny:

He has never permitted her to exercise her inalienable right to the elective franchise.

He has compelled her to submit to laws, in the formation of which she had no voice . . .

He has made her, if married, in the eye of the law, civilly dead.

He has taken from her all right in property, even to the wages she earns.

. . . In the covenant of marriage, she is compelled to promise obedience to her husband, he becoming, to all intents and purposes, her master — the law giving him power to deprive her of her liberty, and to administer chastisement . . .

He has so framed the laws of divorce . . . as to be wholly regardless of the happiness of women — the law, in all cases, going upon the false supposition of the supremacy of man, and giving all power into his hands.

He has monopolized nearly all the profitable employments, and from those she is permitted to follow, she receives but a scanty remuneration.

He closes against her all the avenues to wealth and distinction, which he considers most honorable to himself. As a teacher of theology, medicine, or law, she is not known.

He has denied her the facilities for obtaining a thorough education — all colleges being closed against her.

He allows her in Church as well as State, but a subordinate position . . .

He has endeavored, in every way that he could to destroy her confidence in her own powers, to lessen her self-respect, and to make her willing to lead a dependent and abject life.

It was a deeply subversive document. By making it a play on the Declaration of Independence, the suffragists were employing the language and logic of righteous rage that America revered — the rage of the founders, white men who were furious about limitations set on their liberty — and using that blueprint to express ire on behalf of a population on whose liberties those founders had, in their moment of righteousness, set about limiting.

It happens also, in its call for *in*dependence, to be an outline of the building

336

blocks of dependency, the very things that codified and enforced the imbalance of gendered power that got us straight to the present moment, one hundred and seventy years hence.

The women who wrote it knew that it wasn't going to be warmly received. "We anticipate no small amount of misconception, misrepresentation, and ridicule."

They anticipated correctly. As the historian Marjorie Spruill has noted, "Outraged newspaper editors denounced the convention as shocking, unwomanly, monstrous, and unnatural, or ridiculed them as Amazons or love-starved spinsters."[5] The *New York Herald* publisher James Gordon Bennett, Sr., a rabid opponent of both abolition and suffrage, called the activists a "motley gathering of fanatical mongrels, of old grannies, male and female, of fugitive slaves and fugitive lunatics." He predicted that "full consummation of their diabolical projects would reduce society to the most beastly and promiscuous confusion." More plaintively, one unsigned article in the *Daily Oneida Whig* of Utica, New York, wondered, "Was there ever such a dreadful revolt? This bolt is the most shocking and unnatural incident ever recorded in the history of womanity. If our ladies will insist on voting

337

and legislating, where, gentlemen, will be our dinners?"[6]

This same question would again reverberate in the wake of the uprising of feminists of the Second Wave, more than a century after Seneca Falls. That mass feminist movement, kicked off by Friedan's *The Feminine Mystique,* and then taken up by activists more radical and diverse in their priorities, coincided with the sexual revolution, and enacted material and legal changes in opportunities for women that would permit them to remap their lives in relation to men. Activists of the Second Wave demanded more educational and professional access for women, better legal protections against rape, harassment, and workplace discrimination. Feminists fought for the legalization of birth control and abortion and for laws that made it easier for them to leave bad marriages; they fought *about* pornography, and worked to acknowledge women's sexual appetites and establish their right to sexual autonomy and self-determination.

In many ways, the Second Wave was tackling the same laundry list of inequities laid out in the Declaration of Sentiments. In part this was because while the Declaration had been broad in its demands, and women of the late nineteenth and early twentieth centuries had succeeded in expanding educational and professional opportunities and altering some property laws, the major material win, more than seventy years after the Declaration's composition, had been the Nineteenth Amendment. So much was still left to be done.

Activists of the 1960s and 1970s, whose revolutionary movement lasted less than twenty years, made many changes in a short amount of time, challenging their own circumstances and assumptions so swiftly and dramatically that they altered the power dynamics within their own marriages and made their husbands uncomfortable and confused, suddenly rebuked for behaviors and attitudes which had never before been presented as problematic. Many men felt that they had entered marriages with a shared set of expectations but that the personal-is-political upheaval of the Second Wave had very suddenly rendered those expectations invalid. The men were not wrong: the rules had changed midgame; their dinners were no longer, necessarily, on the table.

Cecile Richards, the former president of Planned Parenthood, has written of how her progressive dad, a lawyer who'd fought on behalf of labor unions and for voting and civil rights, was undone by the subversions of the women's movement. Cecile's equally progressive mother, Ann, had experienced a change during the 1970s, campaigning on behalf of the Equal Rights Amendment. Her father, Richards wrote, was confused. "He had a wife who raised the kids, took care of every single dog and cat we brought home, threw dinner parties, and grew organic vegetables," wrote Richards. "Dad had grown up — and was living in a household where women threw themselves into volunteer work and didn't have careers. I realize now that for him (and so many other men of his generation) the prospect of total upheaval of the domestic scene must have seemed pretty frightening. Suddenly the tumult around women's roles and aspirations wasn't happening just on television; it was happening in our own home." The Richards' marriage, like so many of the era, ended in divorce.[7] And Ann went on to become governor of Texas.

It was surely not entirely fun to live through the era of quickly disintegrating marriages, though let's pause to acknowledge that it was *also* not fun to live through eras in which divorce was hard to obtain, and marriages, even abusive and unhappy ones, were not easy for women to extract themselves from. But the swiftness of the feminist rupture of early-married hetero expectation meant that the divorce wave was fast and big and produced many acrimonious splits; lots of kids suffered for it, lots of women and lots of men suffered through it. The chaos provoked by the divorce boom fueled an extremely potent antifeminist line: that feminists, in their political aims, were enemies of family, men, and marriage.

"If there's one thing feminists love, it's divorce," Phyllis Schlafly loved to croon, practically until her death.[8] What she did not acknowledge, of course, was that what feminists loved was equality of the sexes, and that the divorces that happened during the course of and in the wake of the Second Wave were often provoked by women's refusal to remain legally bound to men who did not want to have equal partnerships. Or by the realization that if they could attain economic security on their own, they did not *need* to stay in marriages that didn't make them happy, or in which they were treated badly.

As the historian Stephanie Coontz, who has written about the history of marriage, has pointed out, "Feminism didn't make good marriages go bad."[9] But it did challenge men to be better, and offered women

341

the opportunity to plan their lives around ambitions and desires not directly tied to husbands. These opportunities for escape and for alternate paths were, in fact, uncannily similar to what Elizabeth Cady Stanton had been clamoring for in the Declaration of Sentiments, what marriage reformers had been speaking about for more than a century.

Any time that men's power is questioned or tempered or rebuked or challenged, it seems, they are made to feel uncomfortable, and it often feels that any form of male discomfort is untenable.

The doctor Larry Nassar, accused of molestation by more than one hundred young gymnasts, complained about having to listen to multiple women's testimony against him, and about his fear that he might pass out on account of this ill-ease, during his 2018 trial; Senator Jeff Sessions squeaked about the way that Kamala Harris's intense questioning of him was making him "nervous" during a Senate hearing on Russian interference in the Trump campaign.[10] Recall that when Chuck Schumer was interviewed about his reaction to the Women's March by George Stephanopoulos, the host's question to the senator had been "Were you comfortable with everything you heard?" as if Schumer's sense of ease were the pressing concern.

More punishing is the increasingly common intimation that the discomfort women cause men by rejecting or challenging them is the thing that explains why some of those men enact violence against women. In the wake of the mass shooting at Marjory Stoneman Douglas High School by a former student, one survivor, Isabelle Robinson, wrote in the *New York Times* of the "disturbing number of comments I've read that go something like this: 'Maybe if [the shooter's] classmates and peers had been a little nicer to him, the shooting . . . would never have occurred.' "

Many powerful men, and the women who seek to retain warm association with them, strain to ease their discomfort. Part of that is understanding — seeing — whatever disruption has upset men as destructive, problematic, and unnatural, rather than as corrective or overdue.

"The public censure of women as if we are rabid because we speak without apology about the world in which we live is a strategy of threat that usually works," wrote Andrea Dworkin in the preface to *Intercourse,* her incendiary 1987 volume on the politics and power inequities of sex. "Men often react to women's words — speaking and writing — as if they were acts of violence; sometimes men react to women's words with violence. So we lower our voices. Women whisper. Women apologize. Women shut up. Women trivialize what we know. Women shrink. Women pull back."

Andrea Dworkin did not pull back, did not shrink herself or her words to be better in tune with male preference. She was a radical, lyrical, furious feminist writer whose thinking and prose were so provocative and so fiery that reading her work, even now, can burn.

Molested as a child, beaten by her first husband, Dworkin worked briefly as a prostitute in the Netherlands before coming to feminism after having been active in other social movements including the struggles against the Vietnam War and South African apartheid. As a feminist activist, she and the radical feminist lawyer Catharine MacKinnon — a kind of twentieth-century answer to Elizabeth Cady Stanton and Susan B. Anthony, with Dworkin as the scribe and MacKinnon as the action-oriented doer — stepped on a First Amendment third rail by proposing legislation to ban pornography.

Dworkin and MacKinnon were not alone in their fight against the pornography industry; Gloria Steinem, Audre Lorde, and others also argued for setting limits and exposing its misogynistic abuses. But Dworkin and MacKinnon went furthest, in 1983 writing a series of local ordinances, known as the antipornography civil rights ordinances, which sought to ban porn by treating it as a violation of women's civil rights. Their mission, which launched first in Minneapolis, and was later taken up, with varying degrees of success and failure, in Indianapolis, Cambridge, and Bellingham, Washington, set off an internal battle within feminism — again an echo of Stanton and Anthony — between self-described "prosex feminists" and the antiporn (though as they might clarify, not anti*sex*) work done by Dworkin and MacKinnon. The prosex feminists won, conclusively.

Perhaps most famously, Dworkin wrote, in *Intercourse,* that "violation is a synonym for intercourse," which was widely read and understood as an argument that *all sex is rape.* She would maintain staunchly for years after that this was a misreading of her sentiment, that what she believed was that "sex must not put women in a subordinate position. It must be reciprocal and not an act of aggression from a man looking only to satisfy himself." But the cruder reading

345

of her words was the one that stuck, largely because it did the job of discrediting her as a deranged fringe heretic, as somehow broken in her noncomportment with male-established aesthetic standards for femininity (Dworkin was obese throughout her life and often wore overalls). Her presumed dysfunction could be smeared into an understanding of her brazen anger at sexist power structures, and would thereby work to invalidate that anger.

"People didn't just disagree with Dworkin. They *hated* her," wrote one of her most elegiac later critics, the journalist Ariel Levy, a description that could be applied to lots of public, challenging women in America, including many who have shared almost none of Dworkin's radical politics, perhaps suggesting that it's not the specifics of the ideology but rather the threat to male comfort and supremacy that provokes the loathing. "To her detractors," Levy continued, "she was the horror of women's lib personified, the angriest woman in America."

The more pernicious and consequential threat of the censure Dworkin's ire provoked was the way that her unapologetic fury could be blamed for turning *other* women off and away from feminism. After her death in 2005, one writer for the *Guardian* suggested, horribly, that "Dworkin's true legacy has been that far too many young women today would rather be bitten by a rabid dog than be considered a feminist."[11] This was a terribly twisted knife: the suggestion that the legacy of willingness to express rage would be a generation of women less willing to voice their own fury, more willing to remain complacent.

Yet Dworkin's reputation was its own meta-testament to how right she was about so many things, even as she was wrong about other things, from pornography to sex work. Her medium was part of her message, and it explains why Gloria Steinem once called Dworkin feminism's "Old Testament prophet, raging in the hills, telling the truth."

She knew what she was doing; "I'm a radical feminist," she once said. "Not the fun kind." In a *New York Times* review of Dworkin's 1988 volume *Letters from a War Zone,* the reviewer, a woman named Lore Dickstein, wrote that "much of what Andrea Dworkin has to say is important . . . but how she says it tends to undermine her argument. . . . It rings in the ears, pummels the mind; one begs for release from this relentless harangue. But then, this is pre-

347

cisely Ms. Dworkin's point, her message as well as her method; to hound and harass, to respond to indifference or even civility with a shrill pitch of outrage."[12]

One of the hardest parts about writing this book, and about living through the #metoo movement, was realizing the sorrow I felt that Dworkin was not here to see what was happening. *Not* because I felt she would be wholly satisfied by #metoo; though I do hope she would be cheered that it was taking place. Far more than that, I was sad because during her career, as Levy has pointed out, Dworkin was unafraid to say that she longed to be read, to be *heard,* to be understood. And the tenor of the feminist conversation, as it bubbled over in the years after the 2016 election, was in moments so in the spirit of what she wrote that I have discovered, in returning to her work, sentiments that left her ostracized from popular political debate in her time, but which today — this week, this afternoon — might feel wholly appropriate in their tenor and pitch, even earn a bunch of fire emojis on Twitter.

"Feminism is dying here," wrote Andrea Dworkin, "because so many women who say they are feminists are collaborators or cowards." And "Men are shits and take pride in it." And, of the western canon of white male novelists and their sexism, "I love the literature these men created; but I will not live my life as if they are real and I am not," a sentiment I tweeted as I composed this chapter, and which quickly earned three hundred "likes."

The relentless, pounding march of #metoo — an angry surge that I expected to last only a few days or weeks but which stretched months, and then, even after briefly abating, came roaring back in the form of new relentlessly reported exposures of systemic power abuse, lawsuits, committees to push forward new legal protections for women who've been harassed — told me that contemporary women were in no mood to play nice, even when it would have been so much simpler, so much easier, to just let it stop, make all the risk and discomfort go away.

They reminded me of the bulldozing insistence of Dworkin, her determination not to give in to the easier path. Her work, she wrote, "does not say forgive me and love me. It does not say, I forgive you, I love you. . . . No. I say no."

349

CHAPTER TWO: TRUST NO ONE

During the three fall months at which #metoo was at its peak, I received somewhere between five and twenty emails every day from women wanting to tell me their experiences: of being groped or leered at or rubbed up against in their workplaces. They told me about all kinds of men — actors and midlevel managers; judges and philanthropists; store owners and social-justice advocates; my own colleagues, past and present — who'd hurt them or someone they knew. It had happened yesterday or two years ago or twenty.

"It's a 'seeing the matrix' moment," one woman told me in the midst of it all. "It's an absolutely bizarre thing to go through, and it's fucking exhausting and horrible, and I hate it. And I'm glad. I'm so glad we're doing it. And I'm in hell."

That period forced many of us to do that daily labor of sorting through our own anger

— at the men we liked, loved, worked with, and needed — examining the many angles from which our rage emanated, taking a hard look at how our lives and careers had been shaped by the systemic abuses of patriarchal power that any of us in the system had had to work around. And, at the same time, god damn it, managing the discomfort and injuries of the men who'd just recently been informed that women had reason to be angry at them.

I was challenged, in my exchanges with men — my own friends and colleagues, self-aware enough to be uneasy, to know they were probably on a list somewhere or imagine that they might be. They'd text and call, not quite saying why, but leaving no doubt: They had once cheated with a colleague; had once made a pass they suspected was wrong; they weren't sure if they got consent that one time. Were they condemned? What was the nature and severity of their crime? The anxiety of this — how to speak to guys seeking feminist absolution, the reassurance that I wasn't mad at them, but whom I suspected to be compromised — was real.

Some of my friends had no patience for men's sudden penchant for introspection, but I was always a sucker; I felt for them.

351

When they reached out, my animal impulse was usually to comfort, to forgive. Yet reason — and a Dworkinian determination not to placate, not now — drove me also to be direct, colder than usual: Yes, this is a problem. In fact, it's your problem. Seek to address it.

Then there were the men who were looking at the world with fresh eyes, wholly shocked by the unseemly parade of sexual molesters and manipulators. These men had begun to understand my journalistic beat for the first time: They hadn't known it was *this* bad. They hadn't seen how systemic, architectural, it was — how they were part of it, had benefitted from it, even if they hadn't pawed anyone, hadn't raped anyone. That faction included my husband, a criminal defense attorney who was certainly not ignorant of the pervasiveness of sexual assault, yet read the endless stream of reports with a furrowed brow. "Who does this?" he asked me. "Who *does* this?" Then one night, with genuine feeling: "How can you even want to have sex with me at this point?"

Months after I originally published this anecdote about my mate, Katie Roiphe would cite it, pairing it with anger I'd expressed elsewhere, to surmise that, given my fury and disgust, it was "not entirely surprising" that my husband would question my desire for him. It was a nonsensical elision — designed to cast me as castrating and my husband as a victim of wrathful feminist frigidity, rather than as my boon companion in fury and disgust.

In part Roiphe was simply reaching for the quickest, oldest, and most reliable weapon to turn on feminists: the aspersion that we don't want sex or men. But on some deeper level, she was flailing against a scarier possibility: that the exertions of #metoo were moving not only masses of women, but some men to empathize with women in very real ways, to consider the world through a female lens, destabilizing their own centrality and the argument that feminism is men's natural enemy — and in doing so, threatening generations of anti-feminists who'd made careers out of soothing the lacerations men had incurred under feminist siege.

As cheered as I was by the nervous self-reflection of some of my male compatriots, I was simultaneously frustrated by those who claimed they couldn't differentiate between harmless flirtation and harassment, because I believed that most women could. The rational part of me was glad that these guys were doing this accounting, examining the instances in which they wielded power. Maybe some simply hadn't understood the ways they were putting the objects of their attention at a disadvantage, but like Sarah Silverman and Gayle King and Judith Levine and Samantha Bee and every woman who has known and loved and relied on and trusted a man, I had to acknowledge that some of them, even my friends, surely had. One day, my friends and I learned that a man who'd been bemoaning the prevalence of harassment had also stuck his hand up a colleague's skirt when he was her boss. "It feels like Allison Williams with the keys in *Get Out,*" said my friend, the feminist journalist Irin Carmon, in reference to the recent horror movie about systemic racism. "Trust no one."

One of the revelations of #metoo — and the anger that it provoked in me, and in my friends — was the degree to which powerful men may have been behaving horribly for their entire careers, while it was women's reactions to that behavior that were regularly judged. Women were the cops, the ones held responsible for patrolling and controlling and adequately punishing and generously forgiving men's trespasses. And God help them if they chose wrong.

"Why do women think they have to support these guys?" Pat Schroeder wondered to me, recalling her fury at former Democratic presidential candidate Gary Hart, whose campaign she managed, until it was derailed when he was caught cheating on his wife and lying about it. "I couldn't have gotten out of the Hart campaign fast enough," she said, but Hart's wife stayed with him. And the worst part, she said, was that both Hart and his wife got angry at her for not sticking by him. "So I guess I was supposed to suck it up and come out and defend him," said Schroeder. "But I just can't believe that men are that weak. I'm really sorry, but if men are that weak and we have to defend them all the time, then why do *they* have all the power?"

Of course, the fact that they have all the power is precisely what permits them to turn every instance of their misbehavior into a referendum on whether the women around them are reacting appropriately. It's another way that women are asked to foot the bill for men's bad acts, another pattern that was being exposed and provoking a whole other level of anger in women who were seeing, some for the first time, what a crap position they'd been in, and how impossible it was to wiggle out — even now.

The degree to which the interest, after each revelation of male power abuse, turns to the women in his life — or even in his vague professional circle, past or present — could not have been made clearer than in electoral politics during the fall of 2017, when every time allegations were lobbed at a male politician, the headlines quickly turned to how his female colleagues were reacting.

After the much beloved liberal senator and former *Saturday Night Live* comedian Al Franken was accused by a woman of having kissed her against her will and groped her while she was sleeping on a USO tour, Franken apologized and asked for an ethics committee investigation into his behavior. His female peers in the Senate — especially those who had been openly supportive of the #metoo movement — were promptly asked what they thought and all agreed to wait for the ethics committee findings. But then more women began to come forward with stories about Franken: about ass-grabbing, boob-touching, and openmouthed kissing. These tales ate up daily headlines, particularly galling in the lead-up to a crucial senate election in Alabama, where Doug Jones, a Democrat, was looking to flip a seat by beating Roy Moore, a Repub-

356

lican who'd been accused by multiple women of having assaulted them when they were teenagers.

After his first statement, Franken did not respond at length to further allegations, but his female colleagues were regularly asked why — given their party's stated lack of tolerance for harassment and assault — they weren't calling on their own colleague to resign. The reluctance of the party to condemn Franken was giving cover to Republicans who wanted to go back to supporting the accused molester in Alabama. Franken's behavior, dubious and disappointing, but not violent, was redounding negatively to his party, eating up the time and energies of his colleagues, and in many ways echoing patterns of twenty years earlier, when then-president Bill Clinton had been revealed to have been having an affair with White House intern Monica Lewinsky. There had already been much talk in 2017 of the hypocrisy of the many feminists who had supported Clinton and not been kind to Lewinsky during the 1990s, including Gloria Steinem and Susan Faludi.

They had defended him in part because they had been forced to depend on him after twelve years of Reagan and Bush

357

administrations; he was the leader of the party that was invested in women's rights, the president who had appointed Ruth Bader Ginsburg to the Supreme Court, who had signed the Family and Medical Leave Act, who was married to a feminist many of them had then admired tremendously. But the choice not to condemn Clinton for his abuse of professional and sexual power had in fact worked to halt feminist momentum in the years after the Anita Hill accusations against Clarence Thomas had brought the term "sexual harassment" into the national lexicon.

This history meant that every contemporary feminist who wanted to make a point about #metoo — even those of us who had been in high school or college during the Clinton administration — had to answer for Clinton's behavior: Did we condemn it? Yes we did. But we were also called on to evaluate the feminists who had come before us and defended Clinton: Had this been a strategic and moral error? Yes it had been. Any of us who had supported Hillary Clinton in 2016 were additionally asked whether the feminist argument for her was compromised by her own complicity in defending her husband and denigrating Lewinsky to a friend in a conversation that would later be reported.

The answer to that last one — for me, anyway — was perhaps especially fraught, but at some point it was hard not to notice that there seemed to be an extremely wide circle of censure in which everyone — from old feminists to young feminists to Hillary Clinton to anyone who had ever said a good word about either Hillary Clinton or about feminism — was being asked to answer for Bill Clinton's shitty behavior . . . everyone that is, *except for Bill Clinton.*

Among those who had been caught up in this ricocheting trap of tenuous and retroactive culpability was New York Senator Kirsten Gillibrand, who had, as a legislator, concentrated on issues of sexual harassment and assault in the military and on college campuses, and was therefore asked regularly to answer for bad men, her associations with whom might prove her lack of actual commitment to the issues she advocated for.

During #metoo, Gillibrand was asked by the *New York Times* if she believed that Bill Clinton — whose wife Gillibrand had long cited as a mentor, and whose Senate seat she now held — should have resigned the presidency, and she said "Yes, I think that is the appropriate response." The fury she faced in response was intense. "Over 20 yrs

359

you took the Clintons' endorsements, money, and seat. Hypocrite," wrote the Clintons' longtime aide Philippe Reines on Twitter, while Democratic strategist Hank Sheinkopf called Gillibrand "traitorous" and a "disloyal" "political opportunist."

A week later, Democratic House minority leader Nancy Pelosi was being interviewed on *Meet the Press,* and spoke positively about #metoo as "transformative" and "wholesome." But when she was asked about allegations against one of her caucus members, longtime Michigan congressman John Conyers — that he had harassed former members of his staff and reached at least one cash-settlement with an accuser — Pelosi didn't condemn her colleague. Instead she praised him as an "icon." The resulting condemnation of Pelosi was harsh — and correct. Democratic strategist Lis Smith observed that, "we have no moral high ground against the likes of Roy Moore if we sit by in silence when Al Franken and John Conyers get to sit in their seats. . . . We can't be the party that says we stand up for women only when it's politically convenient. We have to apply the same standards to ourselves." And in its coverage of Pelosi's remarks, *NBC News* noted that they "raised questions about the credibility of the party's messaging and the degree to which its elected leaders are willing to put the protection of women ahead of political considerations."[13]

So one woman who had condemned a Democrat accused of harassment had been vilified as a traitor and another who'd defended one had been called a hypocrite. And each day brought Democrats closer to an election that might bring an accused assaulter of teenaged girls — not to mention another Republican — to the Senate.

On December 6, Al Franken's seventh accuser came forward. Hours before an eighth accuser would follow, Gillibrand released a statement saying that she believed that "while Senator Franken is entitled to have the Ethics Committee conclude its review, I believe it would be better for our country if he sent a clear message that any kind of mistreatment of women in our society isn't acceptable by stepping aside to let someone else serve." Within minutes, other women senators, including Washington's Patty Murray, California's Kamala Harris, Missouri's Claire McCaskill, and Hawaii's Mazie Hirono issued similar statements.

Some of the Senate's Democratic men would soon join the women, but it was unquestionably the women who had led the charge. One senate aide would eventually tell me that the Democratic women had been speaking angrily with one another — sometimes, truly, in the women's bathrooms in the Senate buildings — about their frustration at the situation, and the bad position it had put them in, for days.

Perhaps most difficult to absorb about the Franken decision was that it wasn't, in the end, about him. It was about the party, the caucus, the Alabama election, the women who'd come forward, the future of being able to advocate for harassment and assault protections. The maddening dynamic faced by Franken's colleagues, many of whom genuinely liked and respected him, was that they had a set of choices — to stand by and support him, or to ask for him to step aside — each of which left *them* imperiled. The women of the Senate chose to do what women had been unable to, or had chosen not to do, during the Clinton mess — they openly rebuked a powerful and widely beloved man, thus courting tremendous blowback.

But those senators surely understood that if they had *not* spoken out against Franken, they would have been tarred as self-interested hypocrites, only invested in zero-tolerance for sexual assault if allegations were made against someone in an opposing party. They would have hobbled the whole #metoo movement, since their failure to condemn one of their own would have given its critics fuel to say it was partisan-motivated, and not rooted in true objection to gendered power abuse. They certainly *also* understood that in speaking out against Franken, they would be viewed as self-interested executioners.

That they chose the latter path — that it was even an option, that they had the numbers, the strength, the confidence — spoke volumes about the unprecedented shifts in possibility this moment seemed to be heralding, and about the cumulative impact of increased women's participation in electoral politics: there were twenty-one women in the Senate, compared to the nine who'd been serving at the time of Bill Clinton's scandal.

Immediately after the call for Franken to resign, the *New York Times* Metro section's Twitter account asked of Gillibrand: "Is courage or opportunism at play?" A 2018 op-ed in the *Daily Beast* asked the same, wondering "whether she is too transparently opportunistic to be a viable presidential candidate." The charge that a woman who crosses a well-liked and powerful man is be-

363

ing opportunistic was illogical in part because there have rarely been plush opportunities on offer to women who transgress in this manner; a woman who *supports* a powerful man in the face of criticism is surely also being opportunistic, perhaps even more so.

But it also was kind of funny: opportunism is grabbing a woman's ass if she's near you at a party, or kissing her onstage because you have the *opportunity* to do so with impunity; it's taking advantage of a sleeping woman to make a funny joke about grabbing her tits because you're a comedian who came of professional age in the 80s when there was not only no price to be paid for objectifying women, but laughs and stature to be gained by it. Opportunism is converting a career as a comedian into a run for the Senate. But none of that is discernible as opportunistic because it is simply assumed that that's how white male power works, how it's *supposed* to work: it takes advantage of the opportunities at hand.

Most women I knew did not *want* the "opportunity" to patrol the borders of patriarchal overreach; we felt torn about both the vague prospect and the observed reality of these men losing their jobs. We thought of their feelings and their families, fretted that the disclosure of their misdeeds might cost them future employment, or even provoke them to harm themselves. But this was something else we were being compelled to notice: the ways in which we were still conditioned to worry for the men, but somehow not to afford the same compassion for women — their families, their feelings, their future prospects — even in a reckoning that was supposed to be about us, not them.

As the $n+1$ editor Dayna Tortorici wrote in 2017, "I imagine that some people feel good about bringing perpetrators to justice, such as it is under the system we have. But I imagine just as many do not want to be responsible for their offender's punishment. They might say: Please don't make it my decision whether you lose your job, are shunned by your peers, or get sent to prison. Prison, unemployment, and social exile are not what I want for men. I'm not here to be the police. I don't want to be responsible for you."[14]

And this was just some of what we were mad about.

CATEGORY ERROR

Women, of course, were doing our own accounting, attempting to classify moments

365

from our pasts to gauge how they fit into the larger picture. *Sure, he DM-ed me late at night asking me what my sexual fantasies were, but he didn't masturbate against my leg and then threaten to kill me; he didn't hire ex–Mossad agents to dig up dirt about my sex life; he didn't rape me.*

We *knew* there were differences. We were not dumb. We knew, when we looked at documents like the Shitty Media Men list and read social media accounts of everything from uncomfortable dates to physical assault, when we heard friends sift through their own churning memories, that there were legal distinctions between behaviors, as well as moral ones. There were the cheating dogs who propositioned us, the artless boy-men who made fumbling passes over work lunches, the bosses who touched us against our will, the men who retaliated professionally if we dared to reject them. These were different behaviors, with different costs, deserving of different reactions and repercussions.

Yet the rage that many of us were feeling didn't necessarily correspond with the severity of the trespass: Lots of us were, in those tumultuous months, as incensed about the guy who looked down our shirt at a company retreat as we were about Wein-

366

stein, even if we could acknowledge that there was something fundamentally nuts about that, a weird overreaction.

But even this feeling was rooted in the expectation, warped by generations of normalized patriarchal power, that we had nothing to be angry about to begin with. We had, all of us, spent decades being pressured to *under* react, our objections to the small stuff (and also to the big stuff) bantered away, ignored, or attributed to our own inability to cut it in the real world. Resentments had accreted, matured into rage.

"I stuffed all my harassment memories in an emotional trash compactor because there are just so many," said my friend, the writer and podcaster Aminatou Sow. "Now the trash compactor is broken, and everything is coming up." Sow said that among the things she'd recalled in the fall were an old boss "who definitely jerked off in the office and would make sure to let me see the porn on his computer. He has a bigger job now. And the man who pinned me to the wall in the copy room and told me I should be grateful he's paying attention to me because I'm a fat pig. I reported both those incidents, by the way, and nothing happened."

Part of it was that while there were infinite

gradations and varieties and severity of sexual and physical trespass, what they all had in common were their reflection of women's smaller share of professional, public worth.

Some, including the journalist Masha Gessen, writing for the *New Yorker,* worried that as we tried to parse how butt-groping and unsolicited kissing could exist on the same scale as violent rape, we risked transforming the moment of reckoning into a full-blown sex panic, and in doing so, reverting to ideas about women as inherently vulnerable, sexually infantilized. If all sexual contact, this fear went, was being categorized in this storm as dangerous for women, we were reverting back to Victorian ideas about women as victims, without sexual appetites and agency of their own.

But what Gessen saw as potential category collapse was in fact a crucial category *error.* Because the thing that united the varied revelations wasn't sexual harm, but *professional* harm and power abuse. Tarana Burke's original Me Too campaign had been about sexual assault and violence. But in the fall of 2018, the conversation being held under the umbrella of the hashtag #metoo was addressing a broader range of power abuses, chief among them, sexual harassment. Yes, sexual and professional damage were certainly related, and in some cases were combined. But the reason that they were sharing conversational and journalistic space during this reckoning was because sexual harassment is understood as a crime not because it is a sexual violation, but because it is a form of discrimination.

The term "sexual harassment" had been used for the first time in public in 1975 by feminist author Lin Farley, when she testified at a hearing on women in the workplace before the New York City Commission on Human Rights.

Farley, who was teaching a class on women and work at Cornell University, had helped to coin the term after hearing about Carmita Wood. Wood was an administrative assistant at the nuclear studies lab at Cornell University, the first woman to have held that job. After years of dealing with a boss who rubbed up against her, groped her, kissed her against her will, appeared to stimulate himself in front of her, and publicly put his hands under her shirt at a company Christmas party, and after having been denied transfer to another department by the university, Wood resigned her job. When she applied for unemployment benefits, the New York State Department of Labor rejected her claim; she appealed the decision, and presented testimony, which was corroborated by two of her former coworkers, but her claim was again rejected.[15]

Unsure of where else to turn, Wood had approached the office of the human affairs program at Cornell, where she encountered Farley and a group of other women. Compelled by her case, they held meetings to come up with a word that described the degrading, diminishing professional treatment Wood had endured, treatment that was all too common, yet so integrated into the life of women in the professional sphere that no descriptor had ever before been necessary. "It was something that we all talked about but because we didn't have a name," Farley has said, "we didn't know we were all talking about the same thing."[16] Farley and her colleagues searched for something all-encompassing, and eventually settled on "sexual harassment."[17]

In April of 1975, Wood published an op-ed in the *Ithaca Journal,* in which she wrote, "Women must be judged on their ability to perform their jobs — not on whether we maintain a sexual rapport with our bosses." Along with the women from Cornell's human affairs program, and the lawyer Eleanor Holmes Norton, then the chair on the New York City Commission on Human Rights, Wood formed a group called Working Women United, and they sent out a letter to hundreds of lawyers.[18] It crossed the desk of Catharine MacKinnon, who then began what would become a multiyear legal battle to assert that sexual harassment violates prohibitions against professional discrimination, which had been laid out in the Civil Rights Act with regard to race.

In 1977, an appeals court upheld decisions defining sexual harassment as sex discrimination, barred by Title VII of the Civil Rights Act. In 1979, as harassment cases worked their way up through the American legal system, MacKinnon argued that there was a link between sexual harassment and professional discrimination, citing among other things the siloing of women into lower-paying professions that demand their sexualization. "Sexual harassment perpetuates the interlocked structure by which women have been kept sexually in thrall to men and at the bottom of the labor market," MacKinnon wrote. "Two forces of American society converge: men's control over women's sexuality and capital's control over employees' work lives."

In 1986, the Supreme Court ruled in favor of Mechelle Vinson, an assistant bank manager who described being assaulted and raped by her boss in the bank's vaults and basements more than forty times. Justice William Rehnquist wrote in the unanimous decision, "Without question, when a supervisor sexually harasses a subordinate because of the subordinate's sex, the supervisor discriminates on the basis of sex." In other words, sexual harassment *might* entail behaviors that on their own would be criminal — assault or rape — but the legal definition of its harm is about the systemic disadvantaging of a gender in the public and professional sphere.

Those structural disadvantages did not begin or end with the actual physical incursions — the grabbing, kissing, or assault. In fact, the gender inequity that created the need for civil rights protections is what permitted so many of these trespasses to occur so frequently, and for so long. Gender inequity explained why women were *vulnerable* to harassment before they are even harassed — it left them with less stature, authority, and economic security, making it harder for them to resist or object to illtreatment. It explained why it was difficult for them to come forward with stories after they had been harassed, why they were often ignored or punished when they did. It clarified why so many women worked with or maintained relationships with harassers and why their reactions to those harassers became key to how they themselves would be treated, professionally — because when men, and specifically white men, have a disproportionate share of public, professional, and political power, women must act around and in reaction to them; they rely on men's approval for work, security, and any share of power they might aspire to. Gender inequity is cyclical, all-encompassing.

Many of the women who told their stories during #metoo explained that they did not do so before because they feared for their jobs. When women *had* complained, many had been told that putting up with these behaviors was just part of working for the powerful men in question. "That's just Charlie being Charlie" and "That's just Harvey being Harvey" were verbatim quotes cited in reported stories about the predatory behavior of Charlie Rose and Harvey Weinstein, offered as explanation for why those men had exposed themselves, attempted to coerce, berated, and pressed their penises onto younger female colleagues.[19] For years — forever — simply *being* the powerful man was plausible exculpation for monstrous behavior toward women.

Remaining in the good graces of these men — men who were just being themselves — because they were the bosses, the hosts, the rainmakers, the legislators, was the only way for those they'd aggressed against to preserve employment, and not just their own: Whole offices, often populated by female underlings, were dependent on the steady power of the male bosses. When a prominent alleged abuser lost his job, he wasn't the only one whose salary stopped; it often meant that his employees, many of them women, also lost their paychecks, which of course were smaller to begin with. When men held the most politically powerful posts, people who were less powerful depended on them for advocacy and representation. Complaints that imperiled these leaders immediately imperiled entire political parties, and ideological agendas on both the left and the right.

And that means that damage done by sexual and professional impropriety extended well beyond a harasser's colleagues, well beyond the actual object of harassment, sometimes to people the harasser didn't even know.

Consider the damage done to feminism,

to his wife, and by extension to the Democratic Party, by Bill Clinton's behavior. Consider the ways in which Franken's alleged groping imperiled his party's interests in Alabama, and was detrimental to his female colleagues' ability to do their work and not get labeled hypocrites, and how in calling him out, they lost stature with many of his loyal fans. Consider Ted Kennedy, the legendary liberal of the U.S. Senate. Kennedy sat on the all-male, all-white Senate Judiciary Committee that treated Anita Hill with such derision when she testified about the sexual harassment she'd experienced while working for Clarence Thomas. And Kennedy, on whom his party relied to do right, had to keep his mouth shut, both because of his own history of ill treatment of women — most notably the death of Mary Jo Kopechne, whom in 1969 he'd driven into a Martha's Vineyard pond and left to drown, after escaping himself — but also because at the same time that Anita Hill was testifying, Kennedy's nephew was about to be tried for rape in Florida. Kennedy's behavior — and his nephew's alleged behavior — had left him paralyzed, which in turn smoothed the confirmation of Clarence Thomas, a justice who would vote to dismantle injunctions against sexual harassment, as well as to make it easier to strip voting rights and make reproductive health care inaccessible.

But to get angry and challenge the authority of these men meant jeopardizing not just an individual job in an individual office; rather it risked far broader harm within whole professions where men hold sway. Lauren Greene, an ambitious congressional staffer who had accused her former boss, Republican congressman Blake Farenthold, of sexual harassment after he reportedly told another aide of his wet dreams about Greene and commented on her nipples, told reporters that her challenge to her boss had left her blackballed from politics, the profession she wanted to succeed in, and that in the fall of 2017, she was working part-time as an assistant to a home builder in North Carolina and babysitting on the side to make extra money.

These were the economics of sexual harassment, but also, simply, of sexism. The movement inspired by #metoo in 2017 and 2018 involved a recognition of and revolt against *sexism,* often in combination with white supremacy.

One of the reasons that a story about WNYC's radio host John Hockenberry had been particularly arresting was because it made clear that there was a web of ill treatment, a connection between his comparatively mild but still discomfiting come-ons to colleagues, and his ugly (but non-sexualized) treatment of his cohosts. To one of them, Farai Chideya, he reportedly said, "You shouldn't stay here just as a 'diversity hire.' " Another, Celeste Headlee, complained of how he'd interrupt and sabotage her on air. This man literally broadcast, on air, his disdain for the women — notably women of color — who were his professional peers. Headlee said she was told that her poor performance was to blame for Hockenberry's bullying behavior; she, like the two women who preceded her, eventually lost her post as cohost, while Hockenberry retained his position. All of that was public record. But none of it would have made it to print had there not *also* been an accusation of sexual impropriety.

How to make clear that the trauma of the smaller trespasses was not necessarily even *about* the sexualized act in question? It was also about the cruel reminder that these were still the terms on which we were valued, by our colleagues, our bosses, and sometimes our competitors. It's not that we were horrified — as some of the "sex panic" critics feared — like Victorian damsels; it's that we were horrified like women in 2017 who had briefly believed they were equal to their male peers but had just been reminded that they were not, like women who had suddenly had their comparative powerlessness, their essential inequality, revealed to them. "I was hunting for a job," said one of the women who accused Charlie Rose of assault. "And he was hunting for me."

A woman who was harassed, or who worked in a workplace where other women were, might feel vividly the full weight of the system that was not set up with her in mind, might see with clarity how much more difficult her professional path would be at every turn, how success might not be on her terms, but on terms set by powerful men. She might wonder if having laughed at her boss's degrading joke in a meeting had been the thing that earned her a reputation of willing to play along, had sped her success, or if *not* having laughed had earned her a reputation for humorlessness that had resulted in her not being invited to the next meeting, or on the next trip. After having accepted or rejected a boss's unwanted proposition, she might have felt shame, or embarrassment that wormed its way into her head, affected her confidence. She might have had her ambition sapped, might have removed herself from the profession in which she had hoped to succeed.

Heather McLaughlin, a sociology professor at Oklahoma State University, described in an interview with the radio show *Marketplace* her study showing that about half of women in their late twenties who've experienced harassment start looking for a new job within two years of the incident. For those who've endured more serious harassment, the figure is around 80 percent — and many opt to leave their chosen professions altogether: to start over, often in less male-dominated fields, which of course tend to be lower-paying. Ina Howard-Parker, a former book publicist who told me she was harassed at several progressive publishing houses, did just that. "I ended up deciding I'd rather work at Trader Joe's, where at least there's an HR department and rules of engagement at work." She now renovates houses in rural Pennsylvania.

Another reason that handsy colleagues existed on the same plane as violent predators was that the harm done to women simply didn't end with the original offense. It was also in how we were evaluated, punished, or promoted based on our reactions to it. Did we smile or remain stone-faced, reciprocate or retreat, ignore or complain? What became of us might hang on what we chose.

What became infuriatingly evident, through all of it, was how much time and energy women had been forced to spend maneuvering around the harasser, time and energy that might otherwise have been spent in service of their own ideas, work, advancement. This was a longtime cost for so many women who had dedicated percentages of their careers to fighting the many biases that kept their opportunities reduced and one of the true tolls of anger at injustice: the amount of time it takes away from the work we might otherwise be doing. "The very serious function of racism is distraction," Toni Morrison once said. "It keeps you from doing your work. It keeps you explaining, over and over again, your reason for being."[20]

Jennifer Scanlon, biographer of the civil rights organizer Anna Arnold Hedgeman, has written of how Hedgeman, a woman "raised to seek excellence and showcase her talents," had often wondered "what her life would have been like had she not felt the need to fight relentlessly for racial justice." Hedgeman herself recalled an exchange with a white woman, who'd been "taken aback when I told her that I had been forced to spend my whole life discussing the implications of color and that this was to me a waste of time and of whatever talent I had."

That sentiment was echoed in a story about one Harvard government professor's quest to hold the powerful head of her department accountable for the harassment and discrimination she experienced at his hands. According to the *Chronicle of Higher Education,* Terry Karl, who eventually left Harvard, despite the fact that her boss and alleged harasser, Jorge Domínguez, got to stay, "still resents the time she spent fighting this battle rather than focusing on her research and her students. She's still upset that it was her career that got derailed" and that "she had wasted precious time filing grievances rather than finishing her book."[21]

WEBS OF MALE POWER

Of course it's not a waste to fight for justice, to work to right wrongs; but it is an extra tax on those already working from power deficits. It's time and energy expended by people who could otherwise be advancing their own careers, doing their work, making their art, gaining economic security or perches in the public sphere — the very things that men seem to be able to do,

381

sometimes for decades, even if they themselves are the ones who have been alleged to have committed trespasses against these women.

Because networks — sometimes, literal television *networks* — of male power had worked to build, protect, and further reinforce male power. Fox News chief Roger Ailes had protected Bill O'Reilly, keeping him in a multimillion-dollar berth for years after public claims of harassment had surfaced; O'Reilly in turn had defended Ailes when Ailes was accused of serial harassment of the women at his network. And their network had defended Donald Trump, whose roles as birther and politician were built in part by the Fox News team — and he had defended both O'Reilly and Ailes — all against charges of sexual harassment of women.[22]

That both Ailes and O'Reilly had finally lost their jobs, and that Ailes himself was now dead, offered little relief from the compounding injustices. After all, the party and candidate Fox had labored to create and sell to America were now in power, installing judges and heads of agencies who would further reinforce the stultifying dominance of white men.

The female accusers of all these men had

received no such support, no such defense; instead they had been called liars from public, political, and media pulpits, had been chased out of the news business, hushed up with settlement money and nondisclosure agreements, insulted by the man who had become the president as being too ugly to grope. All while the men accused of harassing them had continued to draw paychecks and shape how our national narratives — including those about gender and power — were told.

Matt Lauer, accused of sexual misconduct by multiple subordinates at the *Today* show, had given Donald Trump an absolutely free pass at a 2016 presidential forum on foreign policy, failing to ask even a simple follow-up question about Trump's demonstrably false claim that he'd always opposed the 2003 invasion of Iraq. In the same forum, Lauer had grilled Hillary Clinton at length about her email server, interrupted her repeatedly, and then — after finally having asked her a question about policy — urged her to hurry up because her time was almost up.

In his years as cohost of the *Today* show, NBC's prize pig had amassed a long history of having been callous and dismissive to women on air, including his former cohost Ann Curry, whom he was rumored to have pushed from her perch. In 2014, Lauer had asked Mary Barra, the first female CEO of General Motors, whether she might have been hired for her job in part because the company was in trouble "and as a woman and a mom you could present a softer face and softer image for this company," and wondered, since she was a mother of two, "given the pressures of this job at General Motors, can you do both well?"

Lauer wasn't the only one whose alleged ill treatment of specific women seemed to correspond with public disregard for other women and their claims to equality. Amazon Studios president Roy Price, a man who had canceled the proto-feminist show *Good Girls Revolt* and passed on *The Handmaid's Tale* and *Big Little Lies,* resigned after being accused of making aggressively lewd comments toward a female producer. These kinds of decisions were certainly on a different scale than those that helped determine the outcome of a presidential election, but they nonetheless mattered: entertainment executives help to determine whose stories, what kinds of stories about women and power, audiences receive.

Leon Wieseltier, the former literary editor of the *New Republic,* had been a feared force within his highbrow institution, and he'd shaped the worldview of generations of journalists at what used to be called, only half-jokingly, the "in-flight magazine of Air Force One." Wieseltier also kissed women subordinates against their will and commented on the bodies and clothing of his young female colleagues, and spent portions of editorial meetings criticizing women — including Hillary Clinton and the writer Nora Ephron — whom he thought were stupid yet had somehow managed to get far in life. It seemed a rich irony, perhaps lost on Wieseltier, that the history of America had been one of wholly mediocre white men wielding unearned influence, often building their power by stoking resentments against nonwhite non-men via belittlement and vilification. Wieseltier's magazine had done just this on an editorial level, famously endorsing Bill Clinton's welfare reform, economic policy that had redounded terribly on America's least powerful populations, by deploying a cover image of a black mother smoking a cigarette.

In 2008, MSNBC anchor Chris Matthews said on television that Hillary Clinton had only become a senator and a candidate for the presidency "because her husband messed around . . . she didn't get there on her merits." In 2018, a tape turned up of

Matthews asking, on a hot microphone before interviewing Clinton during the 2016 campaign, for a glass of water and then joking, "Where's that Bill Cosby pill I brought with me?" in reference to the prescription medication Cosby is alleged to have administered to dozens of women before raping them. In 2017, it was also revealed that Matthews had been accused in 1999 of sexual harassment by a former assistant producer on his show.

Joel Achenbach, the *Washington Post* reporter who in 2008 had suggested that Clinton needed a bark collar, was temporarily suspended by the *Post* in 2018 for what was described as "inappropriate workplace conduct." Mark Halperin, an NBC commentator and author of the soapy political bestseller *Game Change,* had presented a view of Hillary Clinton as a grasping and scandal-plagued candidate, while his coverage of Trump in 2016 — an *actual* scandal-plagued candidate — had, by contrast, been notably soft, even admiring: Halperin once argued that the sexual harassment claims leveled at Trump would only help burnish the candidate's brutish brand.[23] In 2017, Halperin was accused by multiple women of having hit on them against their will when they worked for him, or as junior to him, at ABC News. One woman described how he had pressed his penis into her shoulder while she sat in a chair at the office.

The same power that had afforded Halperin the ability to press himself into younger colleagues — colleagues who had shared stories with one another but had never felt they had enough power to file a formal complaint at ABC, where he had held so much sway — also meant that he'd gotten to shape the nation's view of Hillary Clinton, whose political story had *already* been shaped by other men who had abused their power, including her husband and her 2016 opponent Donald Trump, not to mention Anthony Weiner, former New York legislator and husband of her colleague Huma Abedin, who in 2017 pled guilty after having exchanged sexts with a minor.

In hearing these tales of sexual harassment, we were getting a view of the architecture of sexism that had been holding everything up. We could see that the men who had had the power to abuse women's bodies and psyches throughout their careers were in many cases also the ones in charge of our political and cultural stories. And perhaps most chillingly, that part of the reason they had gotten so far was not simply that they

387

had cleared the field of competition by harassing or demeaning women around them, but because they had capitalized on a broad cultural desire to see women belittled, humiliated, diminished.

The reality was that in many, many instances, men had not succeeded in *spite* of their noxious behavior or disregard for women; they have often succeeded *because* of it. They'd been patted on the back and winked along — their retro-machismo hailed as funny or edgy — at the same places that were now dramatically jettisoning them.

"The incredible hypocrisy of the boards, employers, institutions, publicists, brothers, friends who have been protecting powerful men/harassers/rapists for years and are now suddenly dropping them," said one of my colleagues at *New York* magazine, at once both livid and depressed. "What changed? Certainly not their beliefs about the behavior, right? Only their self-interest. On the one hand, I'm so happy they're finally being called out and facing consequences, but there's something so craven and superficially moralizing about the piling on by the same people who were the snickerers and protectors."

Because while it surely felt cathartic to see

it all laid bare, even briefly, the view did not undo the damage. We could not go back in time and have the story of Hillary Clinton be written by people who had not also pressed their erections into the shoulders of young women who'd worked for them. We could not retroactively resituate the women who'd left jobs and whole careers because the navigation of the risks, of the daily abuses, drove them out. We would not see the movies or the art that those women would have made, could not live by the laws that they might have enacted, could not read the news as they might have reported it, had they ever truly had a fair shake at getting to tell it their way. The tsunami of #metoo stories hadn't just revealed the way that men had grabbed and rubbed and punished and shamed women; it had also shown us that they had done it all while building the very world in which we still were forced to live.

Chapter Three:
Collateral Damage

When I thought about my own history of having been harassed, I first recalled the restaurant manager who instructed me to keep my blouse unbuttoned as I served pizzas with fried eggs on top in high school, about the manager at Bruegger's Bagels who'd rub his dick against my ass as he passed me setting out the cream cheeses in the morning. I've never had a job in which there wasn't a resident harasser, but in my postcollege life, I believed I'd stayed out of his crosshairs.

Perhaps, in the story I'd told myself, it was because I was never wowed by powerful men, sensing on some visceral level that they were mostly full of shit. I had gravitated toward female mentors instead. But even given my wariness of Important Men, as a young woman I had had trouble *truly* believing that members of the opposite sex could be as cartoonishly grotesque as they some-

390

times were, even as I aged and acquired evidence.

I once heard that a choking person reflexively leaves the room, embarrassed for others to see her gasping for breath. I have no idea if that's true, but it's how I've dealt with harassment by men outside the workplace. Once on the subway, the man next to me wound his hand under my thigh and between my legs, and I sat there debating whether or not to stand up or scream because *I didn't want to embarrass him on a full train.* That's why, when an important writer took me to coffee, offering to help me find a new job, and asked if I'd ever fantasized about fucking a married man, I simply laughed maniacally, as if he'd just made a *joke* about a sixty-five-year-old man who suggests to a twenty-five-year-old woman that she fuck him during a coffee that was supposed to be about professional mentorship.

Once, when I was running down a sidewalk to hail a taxi in the pouring rain, an older, expensively dressed white guy had cut me off and jumped in; as he'd closed the door and just before it drove off, he looked at me through the window of the cab, put two fingers to his mouth and waggled his tongue, the gesture meant to

391

suggest cunnilingus, grinning meanly at me as he sped off. I'd just stood there, and then spent the next ten minutes — or maybe it was ten years — imagining all the better ways I could have responded, wishing that I'd given him the finger, or better yet, laughed at him. I thought of that anonymous man frequently during the fall of 2017. Bizarrely, the most gleefully punitive thoughts I entertained were toward him; I actively imagined him having been professionally humiliated and disgraced.

I thought about him again at a party at which a former colleague, *Slate*'s book critic Laura Miller, speaking of #metoo, recalled to me how badly men had reacted to the 1991 film *Thelma & Louise,* a gorgeous, flawed paean to women's fury. She remembered them being particularly upset by the scene in which the two heroines-turned-renegades blow up the oil tanker of a truck driver who'd waggled his tongue at them just as my dapper nemesis had at me. The scene was a perfect illustration of the fluid combustibility of women's rage, in the context of the film and the #metoo moment: about how women's fury at having experienced violent rape became murderous but also capacious, spilling over to crap husbands, lecherous truck drivers, all the men who'd ever treated them as objects. I'd been a teenager when I'd seen the film in theaters, but Laura had been an adult, and she recalled to me the scene of their blowing up the truck as one of the most exhilarating and cathartic moments she'd experienced in a movie theater, and how utterly terrified the men she'd known had been by it.

"But my feeling," she told me, smiling and shrugging, "was just, 'hey, don't go like this' " — and here she imitated the tongue-waggling — "to women, and you won't have to worry about us blowing up your oil tanker. It's really simple!"

At one of my early and formative workplaces, there had been a textbook harasser: a high-on-the-food-chain, late-night direct-messager who propositioned and sometimes slept with female subordinates, who could be vindictive if turned down, and who'd undertake elaborate, misogynistic pranks, including sending provocative emails under another staffer's name. One of the preyed-upon women was older than I: talented, glamorous, and definitely not game. She recalled to me in 2017 how she had initially believed that she could ride it out, but instead had been undone by her bewilderment and humiliation at having being played for a fool, for a *girl*. She'd quit after about a year at the company.

I remembered having watched her treatment, appalled, almost disbelieving that something this outrageous could happen. Yet I also remembered not wanting to get too close to her, as if her status as quarry might be catching. I remembered hearing company honchos say that they were well aware that they had a "walking lawsuit" in our midst. Even then, it struck me that the concern was for the potential tarring of the institution, not for the women who were suffering within it.

That harasser didn't sexually pursue me, but he did endeavor to undermine me. When I began dating a slightly older colleague, my direct supervisor (a married man on whom I had a fierce and never-requited crush, in part because it was safe; he had been a model mentor) pulled me aside to let me know that other people at the office — i.e., the Harasser — had been spreading rumors about how my work ideas were being fed to me by my boyfriend, trying to intimate that I was attempting to sleep my way to the top.

Just a few years ago, I was at another job. A new boss had been installed and wanted to hire the Harasser from my old workplace;

I told him I would not work in the same office as that man. I was on maternity leave; he promised that the hire was only temporary, that the Harasser would be gone by the time I returned. And he was. But soon after I got back, the office's youngest women began recounting to me that in the few months the Harasser had been in place, he'd creeped them out and sent them off-color, middle-of-the-night DMs. I had made a stand on my own behalf — I would not work with that man! — and yet had failed to consider or protect my less powerful associates.

So, no, I had never been serially sexually harassed. But the stink got on me anyway. I was implicated. We all are, our professional contributions weighed on scales of fuckability and willingness to go along, to be good sports, to not be humorless scolds or office gorgons; our achievements chalked up to male affiliation — the boyfriend who supposedly supplies you with ideas or the manager who was presumed to have taken you under his wing because he wanted to get inside your pants. We can rebuff the harasser; we can elect not to fuck the boss; we can be lucky enough to escape being targeted or directly punished. But in a world where men hold inordinate power, we were still in bed with the guy.

When I wrote about my own experiences, I struggled internally about whether to name the Harasser at my former job. I decided not to, largely because I understood something about how things had turned out. In a rare outcome, I — along with some of the women he pestered — had, in that moment, more power than he did. As Caitlin Flanagan would put it, in a piece that expressed anxiety about the perceived excesses and risks of #metoo, the women who were naming names were "temporarily powerful." She was right, we were. He was, as far as I knew, not in charge of any young women. And so I decided, in consultation with former colleagues, not to identify him.

But here was a crucial reason that he'd behaved so brazenly and badly for so long: He did not consider that the women he had tortured, much less the young woman who'd been mutely and nervously watching his performance and trying to steer clear of him, might one day have greater power than he did, however temporary it might be. He hadn't considered this because in a basic way, he had not thought of us as his equals.

That made me angry too.

My own reckoning got me close to one of the most complicated mind-fucks of them all: the recognition of how women, all of us, really, had participated in, were ourselves implicated in, this system.

After Leon Wieseltier lost his post at a new magazine after the exposure of his decades as a harasser, I heard from many friends and former colleagues who were pained about the situation. "He was, really, my champion," one woman told me. "All these things about him are true, but it is simultaneously true that if you were on his good side, you felt special — protected, cared for, like he believed in you and wanted you to succeed." In a profession where far too few women find that kind of support from powerful men, Wieseltier's mentorship had felt like a prize.

But many of even his most conflicted former admirers admitted that the stories about him — reportedly thanking women for wearing short skirts, kissing colleagues against their will, threatening to tell the rest of the company he was fucking a subordinate if she displeased him — had convinced them that sacking Wieseltier was the correct choice. They were sad for him, for his family, but acknowledged to me that he should not be in charge of women. It had left some of them reexamining how they had excused his conduct, worked around it. "I got so much from him intellectually and emotionally, but I wonder if part of it was because I was game," said one woman, "and what's the cost of that?"

Not all women who had played along with their bosses expressed shame or guilt; some spoke of it with pride. "Men have their fraternities and golf games to get ahead. Why shouldn't I have used the advantage of my sexuality to my benefit? God, what else was I supposed to do?" said one woman in her early fifties.

And then there were the many women who said nothing at all, or if they did speak, spoke up on behalf of the men who were being called out, criticized, or accused. In the *New York Times,* the writer Daphne Merkin described how her "feminist friends" of all ages had been whispering about women angry at harassment, "Grow up, this is real life" and "What ever happened to flirting?" Merkin argued that "stripping sex of eros isn't the solution" — again, mistaking the moment as being about objecting to erotic fun, not inequality.

Several of these women seemed to view their critiques of the #metoo movement as transgressive and dangerous; in her dissenting piece, Katie Roiphe claimed to be channeling the terrified whispers of friends afraid that they'd be the victims of violent feminist retribution should they dare to bring nuance to the conversation. Merkin framed the #metoo movement as reliant on a kind of "political correctness" that stifled dissent.

In Merkin's and Roiphe's view, they were the brave outsiders, heretics storming the feminist battlements. They were wrong on a couple of levels, including in their claim the #metoo conversation had been one-dimensional and unnuanced: all of it, including pieces by the most radical feminist critics of harassment, including Shitty Media Men list creator Moira Donegan, had been full of contradiction, self-doubt, ambivalence, anxiety, and worry. #metoo had produced some of the richest and most complex feminist writing I'd ever read. It was also simply a lie that the voices of dissent had been muffled: these women, along with plenty of other #metoo critics (some of whom were *also* #metoo proponents! Because the conversation was varied and self-interrogating!), had been published in major magazines and newspapers, given the same real estate the #metoo reporters and opinion writers had been given.

But more crucially, the ideas that Roiphe and Merkin were presenting as transgressive and edgy objection were anything but. What they were serving up, in the guise of concerned feminist critique, was in fact a giant helping of white patriarchal justification. They were simply giving voice to the same arguments and defenses that had quelled broad objection to a culture of harassment and denigration up until that moment. And in doing so, as women, they were performing a valuable service on behalf of the system in which they had risen, and specifically on behalf of the powerful men whose power they were protecting.

These women could say things that would, and did, sound defensive coming from men: that the anger of the #metoo-ers was hysterical and vicious, that men's incursions on women's bodies were natural and normal; they could be the women who assured men that they *liked* being treated as men wanted to treat them. They did men's work of confusing groping for eros, and workplace coercion for flirtation.

Women who are willing to defend white patriarchy and its abuses — usually women with proximity to powerful men and the chance to gain from it, and who are therefore themselves often white — have historically found reward from those powerful men, in the form of sexual or romantic attention, marital alliances, as well as jobs and stature, in exchange for their defense of the very power structure from which they benefit.

Part of the defense they've offered has long been the reassurance that whatever *other* women are angry at the powerful men about isn't quite real, or justified, or rational. Part of it is modeling cheerful and affectionate allegiance to those men, appreciation for their behaviors as natural and even exciting in their unreconstructed adherence to old masculine norms.

Perhaps the most popular iteration of the woman who makes herself more valuable to patriarchy by adhering to its every expectation for femininity, and distancing herself from other kinds of women who challenge it, is the figure of the "cool girl." The Cool Girl is a type of woman, imagined nearly uniformly as young and white, who raises no querulous objection to — and indeed embraces — masculine norms, conforming to a kind of ideal femininity imagined by men to best suit and support male dominance. The best-known literary description of the Cool Girl is from *Gone Girl,* Gillian

Flynn's novel about women's rage turned psychopathic. In it, Flynn's narrator describes how being called a Cool Girl is "the defining compliment" from men, and entails being a "hot, brilliant, funny woman who adores football, poker, dirty jokes, and burping." Crucially, she continues, "Cool Girls never get angry . . . and let their men do whatever they want. Go ahead, shit on me, I don't mind, I'm the Cool Girl."

But where the Cool Girl has been presumed to be in it for personal — often sexual or romantic — affirmation from men, there was another version of this figure who emerged during #metoo: the women, many of them older and professionally powerful themselves, who spoke out in defense of the men who were being accused of assault. In France, a group of women, including the actress Catherine Deneuve, wrote a petition defending men's "right to bother" from the incursions of #metoo and its French sister, #balancetonporc (expose your pig). Deneuve's petition explicitly distanced herself from the kind of woman who would object to sexual harassment: "As women we do not recognize ourselves in this feminism, which beyond denouncing the abuse of power, takes on a hatred of men and sexuality."

Less aggressively antifeminist, but still

troubling, was the public performance of support for retired NBC anchor Tom Brokaw after a former NBC reporter, Linda Vester, told reporters that Brokaw had come to her hotel room and tried to kiss her against her will in the 1990s. Vester had corroborated her tale with contemporaneous diary accounts and the word of a friend who said she'd spoken to her on the night of the alleged encounter. Her story was in fact just a small part of a far larger *Washington Post* piece about a male-dominated culture at the news network that had been home to Matt Lauer and Mark Halperin; yet no one was calling for Brokaw to be fired. But the day after the story broke, a letter circulated, signed by sixty-four women, many of them prominent NBC figures including Andrea Mitchell, Mika Brzezinski, and Rachel Maddow, assuring the world that "Tom has treated each of us with fairness and respect. He has given each of us opportunities for advancement and championed our successes throughout our careers."

The letter was mysterious in a couple of ways: the spate of #metoo stories should have put to rest the idea that man's good treatment of some women assures that he has treated all women well. Many of the same men who'd been great mentors to women had also harassed or assaulted women. And while their letter didn't directly defend Brokaw against Vester's claim, it certainly acted as a suppressant to any *more* women who might want to come forward with her own story about Brokaw to corroborate Vester's: Why risk crossing a man that these powerful, admirable women — *Rachel Maddow?!?* — had taken such pains to stand alongside in solidarity?

But the letter was clarifying in certain ways. It made explicit what had been implicit in much of the internal feminist criticism of #metoo: that some of the accused men's staunchest female defenders were defending in part their own ascension within the system that had permitted the men to be abusive. The appreciation of the man in question hinged on women's experiences of having been personally offered opportunities for advancement by him; they owed him. Never mind that this same power — the chance that he might champion her, and that his ability to offer women at the network opportunities for advancement — was exactly what Vester understood, what she said kept her from barring him from her hotel room, or crossing him earlier in her career by telling people what had happened there or filing a complaint.

My friends and I, including Irin Carmon, who had made the "trust no one" reference to *Get Out,* began to describe female defenders of powerful men as Women of the Sunken Place, a reference via that same film to their inability to resist the powerful pull of white patriarchy. It was just a dumb joke, memed in other contexts on social media, but I thought about it a lot. Lots of people talked about Weinstein and some of the other guys as monsters, but the real horror-movie terror wasn't about individual Freddies or Jasons. It was the revelation of systemic menace: that everyone around you was in on the threat.

Plenty of people, including me, initially understood the divides between some feminists on the usefulness and righteousness of #metoo as breaking along generational lines — between the angry young women and a more sanguine older generation. On one side of this divide, I thought for a while, were women who had come of age before Anita Hill's testimony against Clarence Thomas, who had perhaps been raised to assume they'd encounter harassment and had resolved to tough it out, whose own desires and turn-ons had been shaped by assumptions about power and sex, masculinity and femininity, and were very different from what younger women wanted and assumed them to be. To this contingent, younger women's complaints could sound hand-wringingly excessive: What did those girls expect? Wasn't part of the *thrill* of a heterosexual encounter tied to domination and power differentials?

But here was a sharp irony: as a feminist journalist, I'd for years been interrogated by older women about what was wrong with young women: *Why weren't they angry?* Why didn't they identify with feminism? Why were they complacent? Why didn't they want to go further toward changing the world?

Well, now those young women had gotten angry. And some older women were rearing back in horror at the force of their rage, and at the fact that a lot of that rage involved interrogating the whole system within which their feminist elders had risen. This moment was asking not just men but the pioneering women who'd succeeded alongside them to reckon with what had *not* been changed by feminism, how much gendered inequity older feminists had decided to live with, to participate in.

In other words, what the feminists who'd long yearned for a wave of youthful fury had not expected was that some of that fury

406

might be directed toward them, or at least toward the men who had become their friends, lovers, husbands, and colleagues; that a fresh generation of enraged activists would be looking straight at them, their feminist foremothers — the generation from which younger women had run for decades, imagining them to have been wicked old man-hating hysterics — and pretty much accusing them of not having been angry *enough.*

But the generational explanation for division over harassment wasn't quite right: for one thing, there were plenty of older women cheering the movement on with joy and satisfaction, and plenty of young women who were wary and put off by its intensity. Polling would confirm that there w*asn't* much of a difference of opinion on #metoo dependent on age.

What was true was that the skeptical intrafeminist voices that had been in a position to get blared by cable TV networks and in newspapers and magazines, the women who were prominent enough to serve as useful critics of the movement, were women who had achieved a certain notoriety, accrued a degree of power themselves, had benefitted from the system they were now prepared to defend against #metoo's wrathful censure. That system had been run by the men whose honor they were now upholding; their defenses were inherently defenses of the institutions in which they themselves had flourished. And some number of those women were older, simply because by definition the most successful had been at it longer.

And to be fair, for many of those women, women who'd spent years breaking ground in their industry, there'd been plenty of evidence that there were certain behaviors, certain realities of male-dominated culture and institutions, about which they simply had not ever been *allowed* to be angry.

I'd felt that, as a young woman, wide-eyed at the realization that this kind of thing — coercion, harassment, assault — happened to lots of people, regularly, and that no one else around me in the adult world seemed to treat it like it was worth objecting to, making a big deal about. In the *New York Times,* film critic Manohla Dargis had written about how, since reading about the women who claimed that Harvey Weinstein had raped them, she'd been thinking about her own experiences, including a time that a film director had lurched at her during an interview and she'd simply kept talking, calmly. "In the moment . . . he was just another man trying to wield power over a woman. It wasn't traumatic — it was *ordinary.*" Dargis continued, observing that it is "the perverse, insistent, matter-of-factness of male sexual predation and assault — of men's power over women" and "this banality of abuse" that she understood, now "haunts the movie industry," the revelation of which had given way to her realization that now was the "time for rage."[24]

Irin Carmon, who reported two *Washington Post* pieces about Charlie Rose's harassment of more than thirty young female employees, said that she had been thinking a lot about how when she'd arrived at Harvard as a young feminist undergraduate, she had been aghast at the elite all-male final clubs there. She had refused to attend events at the clubs for her first two years of college. But with time, after years of watching those around her behave as though the existence and exclusions of the clubs were normal, *ordinary,* just part of college life, she had surmised that she was the crazy one and acquiesced to their presence, eventually giving in and going to parties there.

When, in the years after her graduation, students began protesting the clubs in earnest, leading Harvard's then president, Drew Faust, to announce a plan to impose penalties on those who joined them in 2017, Irin's reaction had been to think, "Wow, I didn't know I'd been allowed to be angry about that."

Irin's perplexity, as a teenager, about why more women weren't angry about things that it seemed they had every right and reason to be angry about, is discernible in a question she asked as a freshman journalist at the *Harvard Crimson,* while interviewing visiting speaker Andrea Dworkin three years before Dworkin's death.

"How do you save people who don't think very much is wrong?" Irin had inquired of Dworkin.

Dworkin's response had been prophetic. "That's where first-person testimony of women has been so important," she'd said. "Because the mainstream will say 'Oh, that doesn't happen,' and then a group of women will say, 'Well, it happened to me.' "[25]

Yeah. Me too.

That is what the movement had done. It had offered women the chance to hear from others that it had happened to them too, and that they too were angry, and that they too could say it aloud.

Kristen Meinzer, the radio producer who'd leveled allegations at WNYC's John Hockenberry, said in a conversation conducted by the *Cut,* that she felt "fortunate" for the women who'd first broken their silence on Weinstein, who'd helped create a world "where we're allowed to be angry finally." She went on, "I feel that for the longest time, we weren't allowed to be furious. And my god, shouldn't we *all* be enraged? And I don't just mean the women in this room. But shouldn't everybody be?"

Yes, everyone should be. But it wasn't that simple. It had mattered that the women whose experiences had finally stirred a nation to feminist fury, the women who had given other women — white women — *permission* to finally recognize and express their anger had themselves been wealthy, white, famous, beautiful actresses who'd first gone on the record against Weinstein. It mattered, structurally, that they had had the social, professional, and economic ability to risk crossing their powerful tormentor; that they had had access to the media and platforms and that their power — derived from a combination of their beauty, fame, and in most cases, whiteness — ensured that they had a hold on public sympathy.

The fact that *they* of all people had figured out that they were allowed to be angry and had voiced that anger had been

411

critical in helping other women recognize their own fury. For years, women — and again, especially white women, *especially* economically privileged white women — had been assured that there was no reason for them to be legitimately furious about anything having to do with gender inequity: not about social clubs, not about sexual harassment, not about lack of representation in politics.

But as with Hillary Clinton's defeat at the hands of Donald Trump, there was something about the recognition that even these powerful women — women who had "won" at white patriarchy — still sustained harm, that laid bare the truth of it. If *they* had been discriminated against, had been assaulted, had lost jobs because of the bad behavior of men more powerful than they, if *they* had something to be pissed about, then perhaps other women — toiling in cubicles and restaurants and on factory floors, working multiple jobs without equal pay or a humane minimum wage or paid leave or affordable health care — weren't in fact delusional in their suspicions that they had something to be mad about too.

These sleek, beautiful movie stars and the powerful establishment presidential candidate had given ordinary women the permis-

412

sion to explode with the rage they'd been pressured to keep inside for so long. From some angles, the original Harvey accusers were benevolent emissaries, sent to set loose the rage of the masses.

Except, of course, the fact that it took these privileged white women's stories to get anyone to take sexual power abuse seriously also made them emblematic of the stark, maddening inequalities in place when it came to which kinds of women's stories were of interest, and which kinds of women were readily believed.

"You're a farmworker? A lady who cleans offices? You're a prostitute or an immigrant? You're not going to tell your story," said one Democratic lawmaker to me in exasperation in the fall of 2017. Lin Farley, the woman who'd coined the term "sexual harassment" to begin with, had agreed. "If it's Angelina Jolie, it makes headlines," she told the *Washington Post.* "If it's a woman on the assembly line at Grayson Heat Control, she doesn't make headlines and it goes unnoticed and unseen."[26]

These omissions were particularly galling given that it had been black women's willingness to get mad and press for change that had created sexual harassment law to begin with, starting with the cases brought by

413

Carmita Wood and Mechelle Vinson and Paulette Barnes and Diane Williams. These women had been first to engage a legal fight in part because they had applied the logic of race-based discrimination law to sex discrimination. "Racism may well provide the clarity to see that sexual harassment is neither a flattering gesture nor a misguided social overture but an act of intentional discrimination that is insulting, threatening, and debilitating," Kimberlé Crenshaw has written."[27]

It had been Anita Hill who had made the term sexual harassment a familiar one, and other black women — Angela Wright, Rose Jourdain, Sukari Hardnett — who had been willing to corroborate her story, not that the Senate Judiciary Committee ever asked. It had been Tarana Burke, a lifelong advocate for the rights and health of women of color, who had first coined the term "me too" *precisely because* she wanted to let women, "particularly young women of color, know that they are not alone."[28]

And yet, the earliest iterations of the contemporary #metoo wave were about exposing abusers of predominantly white women, men in white-dominated industries — movies, television, art, restaurants, politics — while too little attention was paid

414

to factory workers, tipped employees, women in the service industries, and low-wage employees, among the most economically precarious, therefore the most vulnerable to harassment, and also far more likely to be nonwhite.

CHAPTER FOUR:
SYMPATHY FOR THE DEVILS

It was Woody Allen who first called it "a witch hunt," publicly at least, in a particularly ill-thought-out interview given ten days after the Weinstein allegations came to light. Professing his sadness for the women who'd accused Weinstein, the producer of several of his films, Allen had warned, "You also don't want it to lead to a witch-hunt atmosphere, a Salem atmosphere, where every guy in an office who winks at a woman is suddenly having to call a lawyer to defend himself."

The analogy was inane for several reasons, primarily that the atmosphere in Salem, Massachusetts, between 1692 and 1693, during which twenty people, fourteen of them women, were executed and four others died in prison after having been accused of witchcraft, was probably not at all like the atmosphere in the office where the guy winked at a girl that one time and then had to call his lawyer.

But even putting aside these niggling details, the many, many critics who would follow Allen's lead by describing the #metoo movement as a "witch hunt" — and this august group included the actor Liam Neeson, the Austrian film director Michael Haneke, one of Bill Cosby's defense attorneys in his trial for raping women, and Missouri Governor Eric Greitens, himself under investigation for allegedly having tied up, assaulted, and then threatened to blackmail a woman in his basement, which led to his resignation in 2018 — failed to grok some of the key differences between witch trials and stories of sexual assault.[29]

Witch hunts entailed agents of the state prosecuting and trying civilian women and some men for — and this part is important — *a crime that was not real.* Those same powerful agents of the state, magistrates and governors, would then sentence those civilians, often to long-term imprisonment or death, based on fantasized evidence of meetings with the devil in the dark woods.

The movement spurred by #metoo, by contrast, involved civilian women, and some men, telling reporters the stories of how men more powerful than they had discrimi-

417

nated against them, assaulted them, coerced them, touched them, and damaged their careers. In the cases in which those accused faced repercussion, the sentence — often a firing or a forced resignation — was decided not by the state, or by the accusers themselves, but by individual employers and institutions, many looking to cover their own asses and obscure their own complicity. As of this writing, none of the men accused, even of violent rape, had yet been summarily executed or imprisoned; only Weinstein had been indicted, though it remained unclear whether he would ever go to jail. None had ever been asked to return the hefty salaries or advances they'd earned while they'd been allegedly groping their colleagues; some were still being paid out the terms of their thick contracts, and others had already returned to work.

It was not a witch hunt.

But it was an instance in which some men had lost their jobs or sustained reputational damage, and apparently that felt to many men as if they were being massacred. Their hyperbolic language offered a hint of how instinctively men *understood* the potentially revolutionary power of women's anger, and provided clues about what had prompted them to work to suppress it via so many strategies for so many years. Because apparently, when women raised their voices with rage — or even critique — of these men's behavior, these men got *terrified.*

"I was ambushed and then perp walked," Tom Brokaw had written in his letter to colleagues after Linda Vester had told a story about him trying to kiss her against her will, "taken to the guillotine and stripped of any honor and achievement I had earned in more than a half century of journalism and citizenship." (There had been no guillotine or perp walk or stripping of honor, at least not until this stupid letter.)

MSNBC commentator Mike Barnicle had mourned publicly for the injury done to his friend and former colleague Mark Halperin: "He deserves to have what he did deplored," Barnicle declared on television. "But does he deserve to die? How many times can you kill a guy?" (Halperin was not dead.)

When people were mean to Matt Damon on the internet for being patronizing and reductive about what he perceived as #metoo's shortcomings, the British director Terry Gilliam described the actor as having been "beaten to death" (he was fine) in the same interview in which Gilliam shrugged off the experiences of the women who'd been raped by Weinstein by suggest-

419

ing that they'd known what they were getting into.

The view of a man's lost job as a death had become so much a part of our mindset, that while reading an ordinary news report the day after the resignation of Eric Schneiderman from the post of New York attorney general after accusations that he'd beaten and demeaned multiple girlfriends, I noticed that the *New York Times* casually referred to his "abrupt demise."[30] (He was still alive.)

Of Charlie Rose, a wholly mediocre journalist who'd been elevated in part by an industry built on the sidelining of women, the business magnate Barry Diller told Maureen Dowd, "You get accused, you're obliterated. Charlie Rose ceases to exist." Rose had certainly not ceased to exist. In fact, just days before Dowd's interview with Diller had run, Rose had butt-tweeted the letter "H" and received a torrent of supportive replies from men and women, asking how he was holding up, telling him that they missed him, that they wanted him back, that they were worried for him. Rose would soon be profiled by the *Hollywood Reporter,* the headline describing him as "brilliant," "broken," and "lonely."[31]

The fact that lots of people could extend

such sympathy for Rose, a man who'd been reported to have trapped young assistants at his fancy waterside mansion and forced himself on them, to have exposed himself to multiple female employees, to have called subordinates in the middle of the night to tell them his fantasies about them — yet extend none of the same sympathy toward the women he'd chased out of his business — affirmed a bunch of things. First, that the world is stacked in favor of men, yes, in a way that is so widely understood as to be boring, invisible, just life.

But more deeply, it was a reminder of how easily we can see in men — even in the bad ones — talent. Brilliance. Complexity. Humanity. We manage to look past their flaws and sexual violations to what value they bring to the world. It is the direct opposite, in many ways, of how we view women, whose successes can still be blithely attributed to the fact that the boss wanted to fuck them.

During the spring of 2018, there was a spate of stories about disgraced men who were working to stage comebacks: a rumor floated that Rose would host a show on which he interviewed other accused men. There were tentative "comeback" feelers put out by *Today* host Matt Lauer, and chef

Mario Batali. One of Batali's accusers described reading a piece on what the chef would do next. " 'He gets to choose: Will he go back into business? Will he go to Rwanda? Or does he just want to retire in Italy? Those are his choices,' " she said through gritted teeth. Another woman, a Weinstein accuser, added, "Most of us never got a first chance to have the careers we dreamed of."[32]

And still more: when white men have had such a disproportionate share of public, political, and social power, when they have been allowed and encouraged to be the leaders, the celebrities, the bosses, the voices that explain the news to us and make our movies and tell our stories, they have a disproportionate grip on our sympathies, imagination, and affection. Other kinds of people, people we don't hear and see as often, who are not sent to us to comfort and explain and reassure and lead, people with less access to the kind of fame that breeds familiarity and a sense of humanity, are simply not valued, or even acknowledged, in the same way.

We just don't consider, don't even see, the loss of all the women who — driven out, banished, self-exiled, or marginalized — might have been *more* talented or brilliant or comforting to us, on our airwaves or in our governing bodies, but whom we have never even gotten the chance to know.

The writer Rebecca Solnit has noted that this dynamic was also in play when the *New York Times* called Robert Lewis Dear, who shot and killed three people in a Colorado Springs Planned Parenthood facility in 2015, "a gentle loner," what led the Associated Press to describe a 2018 Maryland school shooter as a "lovesick teen," and the *New York Times* Twitter account to describe an Austin, Texas, mail bomber who'd set out to kill and terrorize black people a "quiet, 'nerdy' young man who came from 'a tight-knit, godly family.' " It's what led police to buy a hamburger for Dylann Roof — who'd just killed nine people in their church — because he felt hungry.

It's not that the compassion for these criminals is wrong; it is morally correct. But it is not applied to those who are not white men, who are routinely and easily described in the press as "terrorists" if they are Muslims, and who, if they are black, are lucky to be arrested alive.

It's a disproportionate dynamic that the philosophy professor Kate Manne has written about extensively, calling it "himpathy," connecting this impulse to the way in which

423

we've been directed to feel for the white working-class male voters so fetishized by a political media since 2016. "We need to look . . . not just at the domineering 'successful' misogynists," Manne said in an interview at *Slate,* "but [at] this disappointed, aggrieved, down-on-his-luck, ripe-for-empathy kind of proverbial working-class white guy . . . who gets a heck of a free pass for all sorts of terrible behavior because he's disappointed and feels in various ways like he's been shortchanged."[33]

In other words, the dynamics of understanding white male aggrievement as paramount to our national interests, and as a justification for racism and misogyny — via, say, the election of a man who promises to ban Muslims, deport Mexicans, and who brags of grabbing women against their will — are related to the dynamics that lead us to reflexively worry about the men who drove women out of careers by waving their penises at them till they fled, and by our comparative inability to imagine, let alone prioritize, the humanity of Muslims, Mexicans, or women.

The ability to narratively flip the dynamics of aggression and abuse — to view the less powerful as a menace to the aggressors — has been key to how white patriarchal structures have persisted. It's how police can systematically kill black people, but when black people protest those killings with Black Lives Matter marches, those protesters can be called "terrorists" on the news, or a "hate group," by the Republican pundit Meghan McCain. It's why, when Baltimore resident Freddie Gray was hauled into a van by police in Baltimore in 2015 and taken on a rough ride that resulted in his death, multiple news reports asserted that the "violence started" when protesters threw rocks in protest of his killing, and not when he was murdered.

The violence done by the more powerful entity — the police and the state — to the less powerful entity is often so normalized, so banal, so expected as to not even be discernible, not even visible. But angry resistance to that violence, coming from the less powerful and directed at the more powerful, is automatically understood as disruptive, dangerous, electric. The upset of power dynamics creates chaos.

Women's anger, publicly and loudly expressed, is all of that: unnatural, chaotic, upsetting to how power is supposed to work. Women's determination to voice that fury toward men in 2017 and 2018 had led those men to feel some fraction of the anxiety that nonwhite non-men feel daily.

That these men experience any anxiety or discomfort is intolerable enough that in 2018, a Canadian clinical psychologist named Jordan Peterson became a mega-bestselling author of a kind of men's manifesto, called *12 Rules for Life: An Antidote to Chaos.* "Order is where the people around you act according to well-understood social norms. . . . Chaos, by contrast, is where — or when — something unexpected happens." And just in case it wasn't clear, Peterson sexes both sides of the paradigm; according to Taoist symbolism, he claims, "Order is the white, masculine serpent; Chaos, its black, feminine counterpart." Chaos is the thing that Peterson and his devout readers were searching for an antidote to in their struggle to reimpose . . . order.

These structural assumptions are why calls for civility almost always redound positively to the oppressors, because incivility against the oppressed is not only so normalized, it is also so comforting that it can barely be detected as oppression; while even the most trivial challenge from the less powerful sets off alarms. Donald Trump can call women pigs and cows and dogs and call Mexicans rapists and promise to build walls and encourage racist violence and still be elected president. But a female comedian makes a joke about the dissembling of a White House press secretary and gets instantly reprimanded for having "grossly insulted" her by Andrea Mitchell, who also signed the NBC letter in support of Tom Brokaw.

During the period in which newspapers were initially reporting on how asylum-seeking immigrants were having their young children ripped from them, presidential daughter and advisor Ivanka Trump tweeted a photograph of herself beatifically embracing her small son. When Samantha Bee performed a fierce excoriation of Trump's incivility in both supporting her father's administration, and posting such a cruel celebration of her own intact family, she called her a "feckless cunt." It was this epithet, one that Donald Trump had himself used as an insult against women on multiple past occasions, that sent the media into a spiral of shocked alarm and prompted Trump himself to recommend, via Twitter, that Bee's network, TBS, fire her. But neither Trump's past use of the word to demean women, nor his possible violation of the First Amendment, provoked as much horror as the feminist comedian's deploy-

427

ment of a slur that she had used before on her show often in reference to herself.

Typically only the incivility of the less powerful toward the more powerful can be widely understood as such, and thus be subject to such intense censure. Which is what made #metoo so fraught and revolutionary. It was a period during which some of the most powerful faced repercussion.

The experience of having patriarchal control compromised felt, perhaps ironically, like a violation, a diminishment, a threat to professional standing — all the things that sexual harassment feels like to those who've experienced it.

Frequently, in those months, I was asked about how to address men's confusion and again, their discomfort: How were they supposed to flirt? What if their respectful and professional gestures of affiliation had been misunderstood? Mothers told me of sons worried about being misinterpreted, that expression of their affections might be heard as coercion, their words or intentions read incorrectly, that they would face unjust consequences that would damage their prospects.

The amazing thing was the lack of acknowledgment that these anxieties are the normal state for just about everyone who is not a white man: that black mothers reasonably worry every day that a toy or a phone or a pack of Skittles might be seen as a gun, that their children's very presence — sleeping in a dorm room, sitting at a Starbucks, barbecuing by a river, selling lemonade on the street — might be understood as a threat, and that the repercussions might extend far beyond a dismissal from a high-paying job or expulsion from a high-profile university, and instead might result in arrest, imprisonment, or execution at the hands of police or a concerned neighbor. Women enter young adulthood constantly aware that their inebriation might be taken for consent, or their consent for sluttiness, or that an understanding of them as having been either drunk or slutty might one day undercut any claim they might make about having been violently aggressed upon. Women enter the workforce understanding from the start the need to work around and accommodate the leering advances and bad jokes of their colleagues, aware that the wrong response might change the course of their professional lives.

We had been told that our failures to extend sympathy to the white working class — their well-being diminished by unemployment and drug addictions — had cost

429

us an election; now we were being told that a failure to feel for the men whose lives were being ruined by harassment charges would provoke an angry antifeminist backlash. But with these calls came no acknowledgment of sympathies that we have *never* before been asked to extend: to black men who have *always* lived with higher rates of unemployment and who have faced systemically higher prison sentences and social disapprobation for their drug use; to the women whose careers and lives had been ruined by ubiquitous and often violent harassment. Now the call was to consider the underlying pain of those facing repercussions.

Rose McGowan, one of Weinstein's earliest and most vociferous accusers, recalled being asked "in a soft NPR voice, 'What if what you're saying makes men uncomfortable?' Good. I've been uncomfortable my whole life. Welcome to our world of discomfort."[34]

Suddenly, men were living with the fear of consequences, and it turned out that it was not fun. And they very badly wanted it to stop. One of the lessons many men would take from #metoo was not about the threat they had posed to women, but about the threat that women pose to them.

BACKLASH

Everyone, including me, was waiting for the backlash from practically the first moment that #metoo kicked off. And then, with every dissenting piece, came the tremor of a question: Was this it? The backlash?

Enough of us knew enough about our history to know that it was on its way. Any minute, coming to swallow us up and feed us to Phyllis Schlafly's ghost for dinner before we knew what hit us. And there *was* plenty of backlash. Lots of it contained in predictions about the instability of the moment, the self-inflicting dangers of mass fury and chaotic social upheaval. "This kind of mania will always at some point exhaust itself," wrote the conservative columnist Andrew Sullivan calmly, even as he himself was being driven to irritated paroxysm by the #metoo crusade.

"You may . . . have noticed that we're starting to lose the crowd," wrote Caitlin Flanagan, simultaneously a #metoo supporter and one of its sharper critics. "This gets called 'backlash,' which makes it seem [to be] a product of sexism, but to a significant extent it's also a product of the rage itself, and the irrational, score-settling things it can make people do." Flanagan was very worried about the intensity of women's

431

rage. "How many women have alienated the very people they need to make this movement successful because they are so blinded by rage that they can only speak in radical and alienating terms?"[35]

Laurie Penny wrote, "This was always how the counternarrative was going to unfold: It was always going to become a meltdown about castrating feminist hellcats whipping up their followers into a Cybelian frenzy . . . We know what happens when women get out of control, don't we?"[36]

Yes. That's when we change the world.

It seemed that a good deal of the pushback to the frenzy of #metoo was either blind to — or perhaps all too aware of — the fact that the destabilizing disorder of the period was a sign that it was at least potentially a *part* of an actual revolution.

Chaos was what former senator Barbara Mikulski had remembered in 1991 when the women of the House had banged on the door and insisted that Senate leader George Mitchell talk to them about letting Anita Hill testify against Clarence Thomas. "There was a sense that the whole process, if not spinning out of control, was getting very chaotic," Mikulski remembered of that day,[37] in an oral history in which Hill recalled that Senator Mitchell's approach had been " 'Let's keep things under control, under his control.' " The women's insistence they get to talk, that they got to insist that Hill get to tell her story, was the moment that George Mitchell lost control.

Yes, things were out of control. That was the point. Because *control* was when no one was able to report the story of Harvey Weinstein raping women; *control* was Donald Trump getting elected president, thanks to voter suppression and the electoral college systems designed to suppress, and thus better control, nonwhite populations. *Control* was the unchallenged reigns of Bill O'Reilly and Roger Ailes and Bill Cosby. *Control* was women being too terrified to defy Eric Schneiderman by telling of how he hit them; *control* was ensuring that no one cared about the abuses sustained by Ford factory employees or flight attendants; *control* was all male presidents and vice presidents; *control* was only two black women senators and no black women governors in the history of the country; *control* was marital rape being legal to the seventies; *control* was slavery and locking women in unsafe shirtwaist factories. *Control* was Jordan Peterson's Taoist white serpent, thrust at us against our will.

And women, ordinary women, understood

433

this. The pollster Tresa Undem, carefully tracking Americans' attitudes about gender, told me in 2017 that her polling had shown a huge majority of voters — 86 percent — who connected the notions of harassment and assault to a "desire for power and control over women." Undem told me that she'd also seen a very sudden and striking shift after years of polling on reproductive rights: for the first time, she had begun to hear voters use the words "control" and "controlling women" when discussing efforts to restrict women's access to abortion and to contraception.

To some extent, women who wanted liberty and equality knew they had to create some chaos. And yes, it was moving with such velocity and intensity that it was terrifying in its unpredictability. But it had to be radical and wrathful and energetic to get people to pay attention and to actually alter the power dynamics. Rules had to be changed, as they had been in the Second Wave, when marriages entered into on unequal terms were no longer acceptable and the fact that some of them ended was a sudden shock to the system and some men felt they had been unfairly victimized by swiftly changing expectations. Now butt-groping and salacious come-ons and harassment were no longer going to be acceptable and some men were going to lose their jobs and some of them would no doubt feel that they had been unfairly victimized.

But this was what it meant to say that we wanted the world to be different: not in some hazy future after all the old not-different men had retired from their perches and died peacefully in their sleep. We wanted it to be different now, and that meant dethroning some of them early. Things had to get out of control.

"The law cannot do it for us," Shirley Chisholm had said. "We must do it for ourselves. Women in this country must become revolutionaries."

Women knew they'd be punished. In every conversation was the threat: men won't mentor you anymore; they won't have lunches with you; they won't hire you. But these threats — while surely correct — didn't seem to stop the steady march of #metoo.

In part that was because many of us understood that part of the problem here was that the men who weren't going to invite women to lunches anymore were the same men who would have harassed us over them anyway. The idea that we could have protected ourselves from these men's subju-

435

gation of women by being nice to them was *also* part of the control they tried to exert over us.

We also understood that the backlash to female empowerment wasn't on its way; it was already here. It was Donald Trump. "The backlash is here," said Tarana Burke at a conference in 2018. "We have millions of women pouring their hearts out, and you think it's about taking down individual powerful men? This is about the system that held them up."[38]

That system was working away, even as men were balking at being taken to the guillotine, to further disempower women, socially, professionally, politically, and economically. As Susan Faludi observed in the *New York Times,* Trump had "signed into law a tax bill that throws a bomb at women . . . [it] systematically guts benefits that support women who need support the most: It means an end to personal and dependent exemptions (a disaster for minimum-wage workers, nearly two-thirds of whom are women). An expiration date for childcare tax credits and a denial of such credits for immigrant children without Social Security cards. An end to the Affordable Care Act's individual mandate. And, barely avoided, thanks to Democrats' objec-

436

tions: an enshrinement of 'fetal personhood' in the form of college savings accounts for unborn children, a sly grenade lobbed at legal abortion."[39]

The agencies that were supposed to protect women from harassment and discrimination were being headed by people who didn't believe harassment and discrimination existed. The administration had asked to stop getting reports on pay inequality, and had rolled back protections that prevented car dealerships from discriminating against minority buyers; a domestic gag rule had been proposed, withholding federal funds from Title X health clinics that provided pregnant patients referrals to abortion providers; Donald Trump was separating immigrant children from their families and housing them in warehouses; and Jeff Sessions was declaring that domestic abuse no longer qualified women for asylum in the United States. Trump was promising to fill the retiring justice Anthony Kennedy's Supreme Court seat with a judge likely to overturn Roe vs. Wade. The highest court in the land, shaped by Donald Trump, was likely to outlaw abortion, curtail contraceptive access, roll back affirmative action, further erode voting and collective bargaining rights, and strengthen anti-immigration policy.

Being scared of the coming backlash was nothing compared to the one we were in the midst of, which was itself the reaction to the disorder represented by a black president and a would-be female president, to the increased educational and professional and entertainment space taken up by women and people of color. This was the backlash to *Ghostbusters* and *Mad Max* and lady Jedis and Beyoncé. Backlash was Elliot Rodger, who had killed six people in 2014 because women had refused to have sex with him, and become a patron saint to other so-called incels (involuntarily celibate men), including Alek Minassian, who in 2018 drove a car onto a Toronto sidewalk and killed ten people.

So it wasn't as if threats that our bosses were going to stop having lunch with us were quite enough, at this juncture, to slow down the anger of women. Many of them were less anxious about going too far than about not going far enough.

"What bothers me is that this moment, as good as it is, prompts the question: What are women getting out of it?" Kristen Gwynne, a woman who had worked for multiple harassers, told me. "I lost time. It affected my self-esteem and my ability to produce work. So even if the people who did target me were punished, I still feel like I deserve some sort of compensation. I don't want them to release a public apology — I want them to send me a check. I wish we could storm the offices of these men, kick them out, and change the locks. We should demand something different of men that's not just them going to rehab. Put women in power."

That was what many women wanted: a remaking of the structure, of the systems and the institutions. And given what was happening on election nights in 2017 and 2018, it wasn't such an outlandish request. Because all around us, in special elections and in primaries, women were running for office. And winning. Perhaps #metoo wasn't going to be about retribution, rather it might be about *replacement.*

On election night in the fall of 2017, Virginia seated a record number of women in its general assembly, including its first Asian-American woman, its first two Latina women, and its first transgender woman, Danica Roem, who had run against the Virginia delegate who had written the state's transphobic bathroom bill. In New Jersey, Ashley Bennett had run against a Republican city county freeholder because he'd openly mocked women who'd attended the women's march — via a meme asking whether the protest would end in time for them to cook him dinner — and beaten him.

Watching the returns, I got a text from an old friend, a woman who'd worked on the Clinton campaign and who'd been there next to me, shell-shocked, on that night that Clinton had lost. She told me she'd been crying while watching the Virginia results come in.

"Maybe *we're* the backlash," she wrote.

■ ■ ■ ■

PART IV
THE FURIES

■ ■ ■ ■

After the election, first I felt totally numb, just deflated. But soon I felt angry. And I was out on the street in New York when the election happened and I went to meet a friend for lunch, and I was walking down the street and there were just all these big white guys in suits in New York City and I was just mad at every single one of them. I have no idea what their political affiliations were, who they voted for, but I just felt betrayed by every single one of those people. And I remember thinking, *I'm in New York City, I'm in this place that is supposed to be so liberal and I know that some of you voted for this guy* and that made me so, so mad. Anyway, I walked down the street stiff-shouldered and I didn't move out of the way for any of those people, and that meant that I got knocked in the shoulder a bunch of times because usually you're playing that kind of dodging game down the street and I was just like, *No, today I am not moving for you because I am pissed and I own this street as much as you do, so I'm gonna walk down it with even more of a straight back and a straight line than I have before.* I've sort of kept that up, I have to say. Because it feels pretty good when you realize how much you dodge out of other people's way when you walk down the street and it's a little victory to get someone else to move for you.

— Cortney Tunis

CHAPTER ONE:
THE EXHILARATION
OF ACTIVISM

I'm turning my anger into action.
I'm trying to convert my anger into
    inspiration.
I've taken my anger and channeled it into
    activism.
My anger has hardened into determination.

Throughout conversations about this book, with women candidates and activists and feminists and #metoo accusers and friends and colleagues and strangers, this was something I heard again and again: the desire to take anger and transform it into something else, something that was *not* anger.

"There's something about feeling sadness, and nurturing sadness, that makes you want to be alone in a quiet room," said Cortney Tunis, one of the administrators for Pantsuit Nation, the formerly private Facebook group of Hillary Clinton supporters that had mushroomed in the days before the election, and later became the springboard for some women to engage in postelection organizing. Tunis was mulling the differences between the anger and the grief that so many of the women in Pantsuit Nation felt after the election. "But there's something about anger that makes people want to — metaphorically — break a window. Really what that means is they are showing up at a town hall and telling their story about how the immigration ban is bullshit."

In other words, anger should not *need* to be transformed in order to count as worthy; anger on its own can have progressive value. As Amanda Litman, a young Clinton campaign staffer who after the election launched an organization called Run for Something, which recruits and supports millennials running for office, has written, "Instead of resisting [anger] or avoiding it, let your fury push you to action. Embrace your anger and put it to work."[1]

I often found that by the time women were talking, or acting, out of political or feminist rage, the anger itself had already been a productive or catalytic force. Their fury was already a tool they used in speaking to me and to one another. It had offered them a lens through which to see and understand the world and its inequities anew; its expression had already been a mode of introduction and connection to other angry women; it had already spurred the making of art or telling of a story or the filing of a lawsuit or an HR complaint; it had already prompted a vote or volunteering for a campaign or attendance at a protest or a run for office or a desire to become civically engaged and educated.

It's the choices to work together, to talk about shared dissatisfactions and frustrations, to begin to organize or strategize or learn more about the forces that have provoked our rage and how to dismantle them, that are the stuff of rebellion. They're the makings of insurgency, of the kinds of political upheavals that can change, and have in the past changed, the nation and its power structures.

The ability to feel the anger and convey it to others is itself the transformative experience for many women. Women's anger spurs creativity and drives innovation in politics and social change, and it always has.

In the nineteenth century, women who previously had been kept largely isolated in their domestic spheres, bound by the gendered responsibilities of wifeliness and motherhood in the agrarian economy of the

447

early Republic, began to come together thanks both to the religious revivals of the time and the industrialization that brought many of them into factories as workers and into schools as students and teachers. Once they gained access to one another, the ability to communicate their anger — over the enslavement of African Americans, over their lack of a franchise, over the dangerous working conditions many of them faced, over the drunken domestic abuse many women suffered at home — quickly produced agitation that would become the abolition, suffrage, labor, and temperance movements.

Sometimes the mere public expression of women's anger was its own innovation. Female suffragists of the nineteenth century, including Maria Stewart and the Grimké sisters, were among the first women to lecture in public spaces to audiences of mixed genders and races. Their speeches themselves provided a radical new model for women's participation in civic and political life. Suffragists' open-air rallies and parades in support of the vote upended expectations for female behavior and decorum.

In the early twentieth century, young suffragist reformers Alice Paul and Lucy Burns studied new modes of resistance abroad with militant British feminists, and returned to the United States prepared with new strategies, including hunger striking, chaining themselves to the White House fence, and burning President Woodrow Wilson's speeches. Suffragist Carrie Chapman Catt took another tactic: supporting Woodrow Wilson's entrance into World War I, enraging her pacifist sisters, but perhaps greasing the wheels for Wilson's signing off on the Nineteenth Amendment in 1920.

Suffragists made pragmatic inroads in other ways as well. The Polish-born Jewish suffragist and abolitionist Ernestine Rose, angry that her inheritance had been forfeited when she refused to marry the man her father had betrothed her to against her will, dedicated herself in part to a legal campaign to reform women's property laws in the United States. She lobbied through the 1850s alongside Stanton and Anthony for a set of reforms called married women's property acts, which would eventually pass in New York and be adopted by other states, and permit wives to retain more rights to inheritances and property than ever before.

The politicized female educators of the late nineteenth and early twentieth centuries, frustrated by the reduced educational

449

opportunities for women and African Americans, would open, run, and teach at many of the land-grant, women's, and historically black colleges that would educate future generations; they pioneered new fields — such as teaching and nursing — and later unionized and strategized alongside male-dominated unions to become politically powerful. The civic education schools started by Septima Clark in the Jim Crow South would become a training ground for many civil rights activists.

Female activists of the civil rights movement not only organized marches and sit-ins, they pamphleted and mimeographed and strategized; their thinking was fundamental to the legal strategies that enshrined racial and gender equality. The civil rights lawyer Pauli Murray's writing on race, gender, and discrimination was so original and crucial that it would be cited both by Supreme Court Justice Thurgood Marshall as the "bible for civil rights lawyers" and by Ruth Bader Ginsburg, who credited Murray as one of the "brave women" whose intellectual efforts had been the basis for the sex discrimination protections Ginsburg was fighting for as a lawyer arguing in front of the Supreme Court.

Anger has driven women to develop a million approaches to changing the world.

It's prompted some to put the sources of their pain and suffering on display: from Mamie Till's determination to show the world her son's battered dead body to the editors of *Ms.* magazine, who in 1973 published a photo of Geraldine Santoro, a Connecticut woman who'd bled to death after an illegal abortion, to Diamond Reynolds, who in 2016 live-streamed the murder of her boyfriend, Philando Castile, by policemen, as her four-year-old daughter watched in terror from the back seat.

Anger has prompted women to make radical art — from novels of sexual liberation, like Erica Jong's *Fear of Flying,* to poetic theater, like Ntozake Shange's *For Colored Girls Who Have Considered Suicide/When the Rainbow Is Enuf* — and to create better medical and sexual education materials, like *Our Bodies, Ourselves,* which taught generations of women around the world about their anatomy, about sexual pleasure, and about their reproductive options. Anger has led academics to recover and reclaim women's share of the academy, creating new fields of women's and gender studies and remaking university curricula.

Women's anger has led to entirely new forms of civil disobedience: In 1965, a

University of Chicago student named Heather Booth helped a friend's sister get an illegal abortion. When other women began to call for help, she and a cohort of young feminists began to develop an elaborate system of phone numbers, code words, and houses that would be known as the Jane Collective; they would assist more than eleven thousand women in getting safe abortions between 1969 and 1973.

The 2016 presidential victory of an unqualified and monstrously abusive white patriarch over a qualified female competitor provoked rage in direct response to that loss, rage that quickly prompted political reaction and certain kinds of creative new activism.

Everywhere you turned in 2017 and 2018, new ideas arose, fueled by women's fury, including the TIME'S UP movement and its Legal Defense Fund, established by the women of Hollywood as an attempt to redistribute economic resources to afford women in other industries more stability to come forward with harassment claims.

The media's slow but steady acknowledgment of the role of black women's catalytic, foundational, leading roles in progressive and feminist politics has spurred boosts in attention to organizations like Higher

Heights and Jessica Byrd's Three Point Strategies, which aim to center issues of racial justice and transform them into electoral victories for black women running for mayor, for House seats, for the Senate and governors' mansions.

Newly minted activists created new kinds of organizations: Kat Calvin quit her job in Los Angeles and founded Spread the Vote, in which volunteers do the arduous work of helping prospective voters get the materials they need to obtain IDs in states with restrictive voter ID laws; Rita Bosworth, Gabrielle Goldstein, Lala Wu, Candis Mitchell, and Lyzz Schwegler came up with the Sister District Project, which matches energetic volunteers in deep blue America with "sister" races in red districts that need more fund-raising and volunteer help.

In special elections and primary campaigns, newly angry women brought skills they'd learned in the PTA to canvassing and organizing. After an early primary in Georgia, a pharmaceutical research employee and mother of three young children named Jessica Zeigler, frustrated by low turnout of millennial voters, began implementing a plan to reach older high school students and recent graduates who were eligible to vote in the district, but who might live with conservative parents unfriendly to Democratic door-knockers, by setting up a text-banking system via seniors and recent graduates of all the local high schools. By the time the post-primary run-offs happened, 1,800 additional voters between the ages of eighteen and twenty-three had been registered in her district.

A Missouri copywriter and former lawyer named Michele Hornish, furious and wanting to do something, began a website called Small Deeds Done, which offers weekly small tasks that other angry women can undertake, from writing postcards and calling representatives, to learning about the history of civil rights, labor, and feminist activism. With a partner, Hornish also developed a new fund-raising structure via a website called It Starts Today, through which people can make monthly small donations that get evenly distributed between the whole slate of Missouri's Democratic candidates, circumventing the larger party establishment that tends to divert funds only to districts it deems "winnable."

And in 2018, Liuba Grechen Shirley, who entered politics after the 2016 election to challenge her local Long Island congressman Pete King, furious after he supported Trump's Muslim ban, successfully petitioned the Federal Election Commission to be able to use campaign funds to pay for childcare, a potentially game-changing structural shift for women candidates who happen to be mothers. "I was enraged," she said of her entrance into politics, and her realization, as she was mounting a campaign while trying to juggle and pay for care of two young children, about "why there are so many millionaires in office."

Around the world, women have come up with innovative forms of protest and expression, from the black actresses who protested "Noire n'est pas mon metier" on the red carpet at the 2018 Cannes Film Festival to Frances McDormand, who used her 2018 Oscar acceptance speech to introduce the world to the term "inclusion rider," a clause by which those with power in Hollywood — the actors and directors — might leverage their heft to guarantee racial and gender diversity by demanding it in their contracts. At the spring March for Our Lives, the young, furious activist Emma González dared to make everyone terribly uncomfortable by holding them in silence, without explanation or apology, until the six and a half minutes it had taken for a student to kill seventeen of his former classmates had ticked out.

Hashtag campaigns, die-ins, senators demanding reform to Congress's *own* rules about sexual harassment; these are all strategies and ideas being pushed by women who are upset, who are mad, who are angry about the conditions as they have been.

Meanwhile, angry art of the new era — from Naomi Alderman's bestselling novel *The Power;* to *Dietland,* a television show about a women's magazine . . . and a feminist terrorist group that throws men out of planes; to Hannah Gadsby's cult stage show *Nanette* and the exhibition of Adrian Piper's art at MoMA and the feminist street art of Tatyana Fazlalizadeh — captures the furious female energy of contemporary America.

Some of the ideas are very old, some are brand-new; some will transform the world, others will fail. But the anger is moving women and their thinking on inequality forward, in ways that are both legal and tangible, and also imaginative and ideological. And sometimes the anger is working its magic simply by existing, persisting, unrelenting and unapologetic.

As Catharine MacKinnon herself declared in 2018 about the innovations of the #metoo movement, it "is accomplishing what sexual harassment law to date has not . . . This mass mobilization against sexual abuse . . . is eroding the two biggest barriers to ending sexual harassment in law and in life: the disbelief and trivializing dehumanization of its victims."

In MacKinnon's view, it was the surging movement itself, and the emotions — the rejection, the unwillingness to look away any longer; in short, the anger it had drawn forth — that was shifting what the law had not been able to: the culture, our shared assumptions. "Revulsion against harassing behavior . . . could change workplaces and schools. It could restrain repeat predators as well as the occasional and casual exploiters that the law so far has not . . . this uprising of the formerly disregarded . . . has made untenable the assumption that the one who reports sexual abuse is a lying slut, and that is changing everything already."[2]

LET'S GET ELECTED

And then there have been the women pushing for more power in electoral politics, traveling a path long forged by furious women.

Shirley Chisholm didn't win the Democratic nomination in 1972, but she knew that she was creating a precedent that might bear fruit deep into the future. Writing in

457

1973, Chisholm averred, "What I hope most is that now there will be others who will feel themselves as capable of running for high political office as any wealthy, good-looking white male."

Chisholm had been the first black woman elected to the House of Representatives. Twenty years after her presidential bid, Carol Moseley Braun would become the first to be elected to the Senate. "I was absolutely offended," Moseley Braun recalled to me in 2017, of how she had felt, in 1991, when Clarence Thomas was nominated to the Supreme Court. "No, that's too light a word. I was appalled. I was apoplectic about it." Moseley Braun, who'd served in the Illinois state legislature and in the U.S. Attorney's office, decided to run for the Senate in 1992.

"It was such a complete repudiation of Thurgood Marshall's legacy," she said. "Marshall had been so important to the liberation of black people, and this was turning the table over on everything the Warren court did. I had had a lifetime of possibilities because of the Warren Court; my husband was not black, and our marriage would have been illegal but for the Warren Court; I had marched with Dr. King. The Clarence Thomas nomination was a repudiation of everything I had fought for or worked for and it would not stand was my attitude."

Moseley Braun was especially livid at the Illinois senator, Democrat Alan Dixon, who was planning to vote to confirm Thomas. She went to meet with him about it. "He was so obtuse about the whole thing, that the conversation lit a fire in my belly. Then came the Hill hearings and then women said, 'Okay. Enough of this.' " The hearings, and the view of the "tired, old white men on this committee," she said, "became the wind under the wings of my candidacy."

Moseley Braun challenged Dixon in a primary and beat him, becoming the first candidate to successfully topple a sitting senator in a primary in more than a decade.[3] One of her campaign slogans was the unapologetically frank, "We don't need another arrogant rich guy in the Senate."[4] It worked. When she won her seat, she not only became the first black woman ever elected to the United States Senate, but only the second African-American senator elected since Reconstruction. In the Senate, Moseley Braun became the first woman to ever sit on the Finance Committee, and she and Dianne Feinstein became the second and third women in history to ever join the Judiciary

459

Committee, that group whose pale homogeneity had prompted their attack on Washington. "There was great anger," Moseley Braun said of the time. "There were people really, really mad and rightly so."

Between 1931, when Hattie Wyatt Caraway of Arkansas had been appointed to fill her husband's seat as senator, and 1992, only six women had ever served in the United States Senate for more than about a year. In 1992, four women were elected to the Senate, tripling the number of women in that chamber; since then, thirty women have been sent to Washington as senators, including six by appointment. Of the roughly 290 women who have ever held a seat in the U.S. House of Representatives, nearly 60 percent of them have been elected since 1992, when twenty-four won seats at the same time; this was the same number of congresswomen as had been elected in the entire previous decade.

In 2018, all previous records were being broken. By the spring, 309 women had announced that they were running for seats in the House of Representatives, a number higher than any other time in American history and nearly twice the number that had run just two years before. More broadly, according to the Black Women in Politics database, forty-seven black women were running for federal seats in total, at least twenty-four of them nonincumbent black women running for the House of Representatives, then home to only twenty black women.

Kelly Dittmar at Rutgers University Center for American Women and Politics has cautioned that that historic number still only represented 22 percent of the total number of House candidates, and that many of the women running will be up against incumbents in general elections. More women running does not always translate to more women winning. Everything is still changing. There is no predicting.

And yet.

The rise felt meaningful, and 2018 saw wave after wave of long-shot primary wins by underestimated women, many of them nonwhite, sometimes against entire fields of men.

"Women have been the leaders of the Resistance," Lauren Underwood, a young black candidate who beat six white male opponents in the Illinois House race, said the week before her primary, in a podcast interview in which she expressed what she understood to be so many of her fellow female candidates' frustration with the fact that current members of Congress, so many without the life experience of women, would not even convene to vote on policy issues like paid leave or equal pay. "Part of the reason that we're seeing women running is we know that our voices are needed to see the change we're looking for," she said, "because we can't count on someone else to be the advocate."[5]

Everywhere you turned, there were women running for office for the first time: military wife Tatiana Matta beat out other Democrats to challenge House Republican Majority Leader Kevin McCarthy in California; Nebraska's Kara Eastman, a president of a nonprofit organization, staged a surprise win in a Democratic House primary over former congressman Brad Ashford.

The challenge wasn't just crossing partisan lines, either. Angry liberal women were challenging the men, and some of the other women, in their own parties. The actress Cynthia Nixon mounted a primary campaign against New York governor Andrew Cuomo, while Alexandria Ocasio-Cortez, a twenty-eight-year-old former organizer for Bernie Sanders running on a Democratic Socialist platform, staged a shocking upset of ten-term incumbent New York City congressman Joe Crowley.

While the vision of women storming the ramparts of government was radical from one vantage point, it was as American as the idea of representative democracy laid out by our forefathers. "Representative citizens coming from all parts of the nation, cobblers and farmers — that was what was intended by the founders," said Marie Newman, a former small-business owner and antibullying advocate who challenged longtime antichoice Illinois incumbent Democrat and machine politician Dan Lipinski in a 2018 primary and came within three percentage points and less than three thousand votes of beating him. "You come to the House for a while and bring your ideas and then you probably go back to your life."

What Newman and her fellow female candidates were challenging were often the structural realities of patriarchal power in its purest form: her opponent had been in office himself for thirteen years, and his father had held the same seat for twenty years before that. "It's a family that has reigned supreme, like a monarchy, for over thirty years," she said during her race, her frustration with the bonkers unfairness of it unhidden. "He's an old white man who doesn't understand what his district wants, and it doesn't matter what party you're in. We are more than half the population, but only twenty percent of Congress."

And while Marie Newman may not have won her primary, the closeness of the race, against such an entrenched example of inherited white male power, offered some hope that it could be done.

In the wake of Trump's defeat of Clinton, a gang of women were eyeing the aging cast of men who'd been hogging America's political power . . . forever, and imagining that they might replace them. Replacement. It was a particularly charged concept, exactly the threat that seemed to have been motivating so many Trump Republicans and the voters who supported them. "You will not replace us" had been the chant of white supremacists marching in Charlottesville in the summer of 2017, and the fear that white male power might be redistributed had been the symbolic motivator behind the rhetoric of so much of the Trump campaign, as well as the Republican Party's efforts to disenfranchise precisely the voters — nonwhite voters, nonwealthy voters — most likely to vote them out.

CHAPTER TWO:
RESTORATIVE JUSTICE

The fantasy of restorative justice was particularly resonant in the midst of the cascade of #metoo revelations of sexual abuses by those who've had too much power, in too many industries, for too long. "Let's make a full-blown trend out of replacing predatory men with women who were long overdue to hold their jobs in the first place," one writer had crowed in *Vogue.* "It's really the least the patriarchy can do."

The idea of replacing the bad men, the ones who'd been removed from power by #metoo, with women — many of them nonwhite women — was not just imaginatively attractive; it was happening, at least in some industries. Alex Wagner stepped in for Mark Halperin on *The Circus;* Hoda Kotb replaced Matt Lauer on *Today,* and Kitty Block took over the Humane Society of the United States after former head Wayne Pacelle stepped away after charges of sexual misconduct. One day in June 2018, I turned on the television and saw Christiane Amanpour, the woman hired to host Charlie Rose's PBS show, interviewing Barbara Underwood, the woman who replaced Eric Schneiderman as New York's attorney general, about the lawsuit she'd just filed against the Trump Foundation.

Of course, in most fields, altering power ratios is neither swift nor easy. Even when men are pushed from lofty perches, those waiting to take their places, the ones who've accrued seniority, expertise, and connections, still tend to be mostly men. Women who've been driven out or self-exiled from their chosen professions often cannot simply reenter them — not as partners or managers or even midlevel employees.

This is one of the relative virtues of politics: It can be swiftly responsive to change. You can, in theory, run for local or state or even federal office, even if you've never been so much as a student council secretary. If you're a preschool teacher or a law professor or a sanitation worker, there will be substantial obstacles — yes, weaker networks, fund-raising disadvantages, party machinery, institutional obstruction, and identity bias — to push past. Yes. But you can run. And if you win, whether the office is small or large, you might be able to shake things up. Ocasio-Cortez, brilliant and charging into Congress with a righteously leftist agenda, had until recently worked as a bartender.

The people who control state and local legislatures often determine who in their communities gets to vote easily, who has access to health care or to legal sanctuary; local governing bodies around the country have in recent years passed legislation for paid leave and paid sick days and higher minimum wages. No, not all women candidates want to determine those policies in ways that benefit nonwhite men, and numbers of Republican women running for office in 2018 were up too. But the vast majority of the female candidates storming the polls in 2018 were Democrats.

More broadly, the idea of replacing men with women would be a way to alter one of the most deeply entrenched structural realities of how the nation has been built, who makes its rules, and who enforces them. It would be a seismic shift toward representational democracy.

In the wake of #metoo, and the view it offered of the corroded and corrupted layer of male power, women had already stepped into political space left by men. Tina Smith took Al Franken's Senate seat; not only was Solicitor General Barbara Underwood named to fill Schneiderman's job, within a few weeks of his resignation, at least two other women had announced that they would run for his seat in the fall. In Pennsylvania, a woman named Mary Gay Scanlon won the primary to fill the seat of Patrick Meehan, who resigned after harassment allegations,[6] and two women ran for the seat vacated by John Conyers in Detroit. Debbie Lesko, a Republican woman, defeated Hiral Tipirneni, the Democratic woman who ran against her, for the seat left open by Trent Franks, a congressman who repeatedly asked a female staffer to be a surrogate mother for his child.

In May 2018, Rachel Crooks, one of the women who'd accused Donald Trump of sexual misconduct before the election, claiming that when she'd been a twenty-two-year-old receptionist at Trump Tower, he'd kissed her against her will, won a Democratic House primary. When Trump had denied her claim on Twitter, Crooks had shot back, daring him to find security footage of the day and stating that "It's liars like you in politics that have prompted me to run for office myself."[7]

It felt like an avenue toward something

like the unimaginable: reparations for all the power that had been denied to women for so many centuries. "What if women hadn't been taken out of the pool like this?" asked Erin Vilardi, the head of VoteRun-Lead, which trains and supports women running for state and local office. "Imagine having had our first woman president run and win in the 1980s! We're still not allowed to be mad about this. These guys need to *resign.* They *all* need to resign. If you are not willing to work *for* gender equality, you must step aside. We need all those open seats because research shows that women are more likely to win open seats. If you've groped or harassed, step aside right now. Pick a young woman as your successor."

The video game developer Brianna Wu, who'd been a target of the coordinated misogynistic mass attack called "Gamergate" in 2014, told me in 2018 of her "unmitigated anger at the way that women had been treated" in her field, from groping to not being taken seriously by the men who dominated gaming. After becoming a target of harassment and threats during Gamergate, Wu wrote to male peers asking them for help; she said she received none; the FBI closed its investigation into the dozens of threats she had received, provoking in her

469

an "unbelievable fury" that she said was the catalyst for her to run for Congress, challenging a moderate congressman in Massachusetts in the state's primary.

"It turns out those were angry tears everybody cried on November 8, and nobody knew they were angry tears until later," said Vilardi, who also noted that until recently, women have had no road map for what to do with their resentments and furies. "Women are not allowed to scream from podiums, not allowed to slam doors in workplaces," she said, acknowledging that this expressive limit is part of what's earned women the reputation as more benevolent bosses. "But that's bullshit," she went on. "Because if you look at all those studies about how women are better bosses, they're better at everything *except* in areas of decisiveness, and that's because we don't get to *have* that split-second, I'm-the-goddamn-boss-that's-why gut reaction. We have zero role modeling in channeling our anger into decisiveness or 'That's just the way he is' stuff people said about Harvey Weinstein. We don't get *any* of those passes."

Brianna Wu told me that her battle, as a candidate, was also in learning to communicate her anger, which she longs to simply lay out for audiences, point by point,

470

but which she refrains from doing. "If you say things like that to men, they shut down; they think you're being a bitch. Anger terrifies men." Wu said that she has one particularly visceral memory from her campaign, at a town hall at which an elderly woman asked her about women's health-care access "because she was angry about it." As soon as Wu began to answer her question, "the three men sitting beside that woman, the instant I started talking, pulled out their phones on cue and started surfing." Wu said she recalled standing in the midst of the town hall, "this fury boiling up in me. But because I was in front of a whole crowd, it was so hard to stay professional."

Despite the efforts to suppress or disguise anger, Amanda Litman, the cofounder of Run for Something, said that she believed that angry candidates make the *best* candidates, because their passion propels them out the door every day to do the work of knocking on doors and making calls, producing the most crucial result: getting out the vote.

Litman's theory was that the anger of the women in the Virginia elections had had a reverse coattails effect: the first-time women candidates had done such a stellar, driven job of canvassing and pavement-pounding that they had produced a higher turnout and helped Democrat Ralph Northam defeat Republican Ed Gillespie for governor. "Getting those candidates out there knocking [on] doors, speaking from a place of fury and commitment to change, gets more voters up, drives up turnout," said Litman.

"When we started," said Patricia Russo, the head of the Women's Campaign School at Yale, which had begun training women candidates in 1994, in the wake of the Year of the Woman, "the median age for women attending our school was midforties. Now the median age is around thirty." That shift reflected new attitudes about when women were "allowed" to enter politics. They didn't have to wait until their kids were grown anymore, and there was a better chance that they'll be taken seriously in their thirties or even twenties — being young and single was no longer a deal-killer, nor was being the mother of little children. Also different now, Russo said, is that the majority of those who enroll in the school are women of color.

Other groups had also gotten into the candidate-training-and-support business over the past two decades, and registered exponential growth in the wake of 2016. For Higher Heights — founded in 2011 to harness the power of black women as voters, organizers, and candidates — a slow rise in engagement in the months after Trump's win became an enormous spike with the fall 2017 elections in Virginia, New Jersey, and Alabama, when the role of black women *voters* as responsible for Democratic wins had been heralded by the political media. "Black women were really acknowledged as political drivers of change, as first-time candidates and as the voters who made the difference," said cofounder Kimberly Peeler-Allen. Peeler-Allen recalled attending a candidate training in Minneapolis in the fall of 2017, at which she'd been told to expect forty or fifty black women. When she walked in she'd been greeted by seventy. "Nearly sixty percent of the women who were there were women of color," she recalled. "It was mind-blowing!"

VoteRunLead's Erin Vilardi said that in a typical year, two-thirds of the organization's resources were devoted to persuading women to run, with a goal of tapping two thousand nationwide. In 2017, 3,200 women were trained by VoteRunLead and over ten thousand had contacted the group completely unsolicited. EMILY's List, meanwhile, had nearly tripled the size of its state and local team and doubled its digital staff to handle the forty thousand inquiries they'd received about jumping into the electoral fray post-Trump.

"I think there's a disgust," Vilardi said, "when women find themselves running against a guy who hasn't changed the photo on his website since the 1990s — these men have been in office for so long." Then there was another kind of disgust, increasingly articulated by at least some of the rookie politicians she'd met: "There's disgust very much about the abuse that men in power have systematically been engaging in unchecked, and disgust with the people who continue to keep those men in power."

The anger that was bubbling to the surface over so many injustices — incursions on reproductive autonomy, the shootings of African Americans by police officers, the stranglehold of the NRA over American politics and thus the inability to enact gun control legislation, the gerrymandering and voter suppression efforts that left nonwhite voters with so much less electoral power, the pervasiveness of sexual harassment and assault, the paucity of women and nonwhite officials in representative government — was propelling women to run. The idea that the election of more women, especially more nonwhite women, was structurally, architecturally corrective, was clear.

But persuading the kinds of organizations and institutions that had long held up the party system in the United States that this was an opportunity for a major overhaul was difficult. Marie Newman, the challenger to antichoice, anti-immigration incumbent Dan Lipinski, had a hard time getting party machinery to support her, even against a politician who often voted against his party. While she garnered early support from Senator Kirsten Gillibrand, the National Abortion Rights Action League (NARAL), and Gloria Steinem, it took Planned Parenthood and EMILY's List a long time to start diverting money toward her. Newman's eventual primary loss to Lipinski was so close that it seemed possible that an earlier willingness to take a chance on her candidacy could have meant a different result.

"This is a moment to take significant risks, and we're hedging our bets," Vilardi said to me at one point, in reference to the foot-dragging in Newman's race, and also to the Democratic Congressional Campaign Committee and state parties, all cogs in a political machine that tended to be slow about directing money toward new kinds of candidates in crowded primaries. "Not throwing every dollar behind the exciting new women candidates, especially women

475

of color," Vilardi says, "is missing the political moment if I ever did see it."

The throng of disgusted women, most of them brand-new to politics, did require the investment of time and resources. And many of the mechanisms in place to train women candidates were quickly at capacity, thanks to the rush of women who knew mostly that they were furious, but did not know much beyond that.

Across the nation, on practically every weekend in late 2017 and early 2018, women who hoped to one day lead their communities and perhaps their country were getting crash courses in civic participation. On a Saturday in late October 2017, as EMILY's List's president Stephanie Schriock was addressing potential candidates at the Detroit Women's Convention, the group's executive director, Emily Cain, was doing the same for a hundred women in Manhattan. "If you wake up in the morning caring about something," Cain told the potential future leaders of America crowding the wood-paneled room, notepads out, "you are qualified to run for office." The message echoed one delivered by Higher Heights cofounder Peeler-Allen to the black women she advises, many of whom lack confidence: "Each one of you is beyond prepared to run for public office. You need to channel your inner mediocre white boy and use that to run."

If that seemed a depressingly low bar for entry, consider that one of the grim gifts of the Trump administration was the recognition of how low the bar could go for political plausibility. As Jennifer Carroll Foy, a public defender who won a Virginia House seat while pregnant with twins, replacing a Republican white man, said in a short documentary about her candidacy, "If *he* can do it, I know that I can do it."[8]

The whole training curriculum of VoteRunLead was overhauled in 2017 and could now be summed up with its call to action: "Run As You Are." Vilardi mentioned Eve Hurwitz, a Navy reservist and small-business owner running for state senator in Maryland. She'd long colored her hair a vivid shade of purple, but, said Vilardi, "Everybody told her that you can't run with purple hair, so she lost it, but other people said, 'How are you not going to run with purple hair? That's who you are!' So she dyed it back." Similarly, Peeler-Allen recalled reassuring a recent candidate who was fretting about whether she had to code-switch — alter her speaking style and mannerisms — to speak before different audi-

477

ences. "Be genuine in what you're saying," Peeler-Allen said she advised. "As long as people feel you have their best interests at heart, it won't matter whether you twang or drawl or drop a consonant here or there."

Which is not to say that the political waters would suddenly part, allowing women to walk serenely into office. "You can know you're the best person for the job, and come out of a tearjerker of a training session, having just been inspired by the first Somali refugee to gain elected office," Vilardi said. "But the world is still gonna come at you and tell you that Jim Smith, Jr. has been waiting for ten years and is next in line for that seat you want to run for."

For all the obstacles first-time female candidates face, Vilardi noticed a refreshingly new mind-set post 2016. "The 'Am I qualified?' stuff we used to hear, when women would talk themselves out of running for office — what is the time management going to be, wondering how they'll talk to their husband or partner or boss about this, worrying that they can't make this work with their job, or that legislatures pay crap — now all of that is being negotiated in a positive way." Instead of talking themselves out of it, they're talking themselves into it. "It's like lightbulbs are going

478

off everywhere," Vilardi said. "Prior to the 2016 election, two-thirds of VoteRunLead women would tell us they wanted a five-year plan. Now sixty percent want to run by 2020."

Part of it was a feeling of urgency in response to what had recently been exposed, after years of the myth that it was in abeyance: sexism. When Tresa Undem conducted a poll in December 2016 asking if the Trump campaign and election had made voters "think more about sexism in our society," 40 percent of respondents said yes. In November 2017, when she asked whether the news about sexual harassment and assault made people think more about societal sexism, 73 percent said that it did. In December 2016, 52 percent of those surveyed by Undem said that the country would be better off with more women in office; in November 2017, 69 percent gave that answer. And in 2016, 65 percent of people Undem had polled had felt that men held more positions of power in society than women; in 2017, that number had risen to 87 percent.[9] "As pollsters, we don't see shifts in attitudes this big," Undem said, also noting that women were using the word "misogyny," a word she'd rarely, if ever, heard in previous years.

479

The sight of so many women rushing to occupy elected office is almost sure to draw out antagonists. All reassurances to the contrary, this is a zero-sum game: If women gain greater political power, white men lose some of theirs. After a 2018 Indiana primary propelled multiple women to wins, a law professor named Kenneth Dau-Schmidt wrote to his local paper, describing how "disturbed" he was by the results. "The fact that all women candidates won, even against accomplished male incumbents," he wrote, "was troubling." It was clear to Dau-Schmidt that "hundreds of Democratic women are voting just for female candidates based on their gender." It had apparently never occurred to him that the history of electoral politics in America was one of voters pulling levers for candidates based on their gender, but he was certainly not alone in his irritation, and his response felt particularly resonant as we lived through the potent and damaging backlash to the election of Barack Obama and the symbolic threat of Hillary Clinton, the real and presumptive victories that had landed us with the Tea Party and eventually the Trump presidency.

Andrea Steele of Emerge America, which trains Democratic women candidates in twenty-four states, worked on Carol Moseley Braun's campaign in 1992 and remembered the drop-off in women candidates that happened *after* 1992. "We thought everything was going to change," she said, recalling the deep disappointment when it didn't. "The difference between then and now is we have infrastructure. EMILY's List is stronger, Emerge is growing its support structure, there are state organizations helping to fund candidates. And a big part of what we've seen over the years is that when women get into politics, they start bringing other women in."

CHAPTER THREE:
MY SISTERS ARE HERE

Of course, change, even political change, won't come simply from the women who are running for office; it will also come from the women who are engaging in their campaigns, volunteering, paying attention, educating themselves, becoming activists for the first time in their lives. And in the years since Donald Trump became president, those women are legion. A 2017 Pew survey found that nearly six in ten women said they were paying increased attention to politics since the 2016 election, a greater share than men.

The self-styled "Resistance" that grew up in response to the Donald Trump administration was made of, built on, the efforts of women. Women were running the local chapters of Indivisible, one of the biggest organizations to rise in opposition to Trump and Republicans, at a rate of two to one, according to one of Indivisible's founders;

more than three quarters of Indivisible's email subscribers were women.[10] Journalist Charlotte Alter reported that Planned Parenthood said its volunteers, the majority of them women, had made more than 200,000 phone calls to members of Congress and organized more than 2,200 events across the country opposing the repeal of the Affordable Care Act, as well as having delivered more than a million petitions to members of Congress, asking them not to defund women's reproductive health care. One 2017 survey found that 86 percent of the people using an anti-Trump text-messaging service were women. In a survey of twenty-eight thousand people who'd contacted Congress in 2017 to protest the administration, Democratic pollster Celinda Lake found the same percentage were women.

Yes, progressive politics had long relied on the labor of women, many of them women of color, the hard-working base of state and local political organizing. But what happened after Clinton's loss, and grew through the #metoo movement, and the fury over mass shootings, was the activation of another population, long dormant: suburban white women.

I'd met and spoken to some of them,

traveling to Georgia in June of 2017, in the lead-up to the special election campaign of Jon Ossoff, and landing among them was like walking onto the set of *Thelma & Louise,* encountering women who had just been rousted from political somnambulence and were certain that they would never be the same. "Something's crossed over in me," says one of the heroines in that old cinematic testament to the alchemical changes brought on by wrath, "I can't go back." And then, in another scene, "I feel *awake.* I don't remember feeling this awake. Everything looks different."

"If I'm not knocking on doors, I'm making calls; if I'm not making calls, I'm writing postcards; if I'm not writing postcards, I'm replacing my lawn sign," I heard one woman saying at a suburban restaurant outside Atlanta. She and her peers were using a language of awakening and liberation that was redolent of past insurgencies.

"I am no longer in the closet," Ann White, a sixty-four-year-old former speech pathologist told me. "I am out, I am out blue. Everybody knows now that I'm a Democrat, that I'm liberal. And they're kind of tired of it, but that's okay. I'm not done. I'm just getting started." White, like so many previously complacent white women, had simply believed that Hillary Clinton would beat Donald Trump. When she hadn't, White said, she had felt herself transforming. "The profanity filter on my mouth totally went away," she said, recalling cursing like a sailor on the phone with a friend, shocking her teenaged children, who'd "never heard me say the F-word before." She attended the Women's March in Atlanta in January, and said that "it was the very first time since the election that I felt empowered." She'd also realized, for the first time, that "there's a whole lot of people like me who are not going to take this lying down!"

White joined a group called Liberal Moms of Roswell and Cobb Counties. "My favorite slogan," she told me, trying not to cry, "is 'You Are Not Alone.' I found my people."

This is one of anger's most important roles: it is a mode of connection, a way for women to find each other and realize that their struggles and their frustrations are shared, that they are not alone, not crazy. If they are quiet, they will remain isolated. But if they howl in rage, someone else who shares their fury might hear them, might start howling along. This is, of course, partly why those who oppress women work to stifle their anger.

Woman after woman spoke to me of how

the loud eruption of their rage had brought them into a community they'd never known existed. "I never even put a sign in my yard because I wasn't sure how it would be received if it wasn't a Republican sign," said Cherish Burnham, forty-four, of her life as a Democrat growing up in a red suburb. On the morning of November 9, consumed by hopelessness, she'd gone to volunteer at her sons' elementary school science class and seen two other mothers who also looked stricken. After tentative inquiries, the trio realized they were all upset about the same thing; they stood outside the school in conversation for an hour.

Them too.

The expression of primal, agonizing anger that followed Trump's election meant that for the first time, some women — even those who'd been living in proximity to one another for years — could hear one another for the first time.

"Every time I see an Ossoff sign I feel like I have an ally," said Tamara Brooking, a fifty-one-year-old research assistant to a novelist. A lifelong Democrat who voted for Bernie Sanders before she voted for Clinton, Brooking said that after the election, "I was fucking furious. I was insanely mad." Now that she's become active in Democratic organizing, she said, "I'm feeling like I'm working toward something. After the anger and depression faded, the motivation kicked in."

Many women had put magnets with the logo of their activist group on their cars; if they spotted a magnet on the parked car, they turned it 180 degrees as a kind of greeting and signal of communion. "It's to let each other know, 'my sisters are here,' " said Jennifer Mosbacher, forty-four, reaching for the language of sisterhood evocative of the 1970s, or more activist spheres. "It's this feeling of camaraderie in an area where you have often felt very isolated and disenfranchised. But now you can go to your neighborhood grocery store and get flipped, and you're like, *'Cool, someone else is here.'* "

Women spoke with the youthful fervor of having found new friends and new love — of politics and one another. Several described how they'd not been sleeping, staying up all night scrolling through Facebook and message boards, reading political posts and messaging one another.

Their ardor echoed the recollections of the feminist writer Vivian Gornick in a 1990 essay, in which she recalled the period of second-wave feminism in which "Every

487

week, there was a gathering of some sort at which the talk was an exhilaration. There wasn't a woman in the room whose conversation did not engage. . . . We saw our inner lives being permanently marked by the words we spoke. We were changing before each other's eyes, taking our own ideas seriously, becoming other than we had been."[11]

The language I heard in Georgia was audible in interviews with women all over the country. The *Washington Post* reported on Kim Drew Wright, a forty-six-year-old writer and mother of three who, the week after the 2016 election, had invited local members of Pantsuit Nation to join her for a drink at a local bar; ninety people had come. She'd become a leader of liberal women in her conservative suburb, and helped to drive Democrats to victory in the fall 2017 elections in Virginia. "I wouldn't have done this every day for the past year if I hadn't gotten so angry about Trump," Wright told the *Post*. "Once you wake up and see how important local elections are, it's hard to go back to the shadows and stick your head in the sand."[12] To another outlet, Wright explained, "On election night, a switch got flipped in me. I'm starting to call it my 'I'll be damned' switch. I'll be damned if I'm going to be quiet anymore."

488

The sheer amount of time these women were devoting to political organizing was staggering, especially given that most of them worked full-time and had children. "My business [and] my family have suffered from the work we're doing," Mosbacher told me. "Our fridge is barren; my daughter is like 'Are we going out *again*?' "

"I tell people that I am fresh out of fucks," Tamara Brooking told me. "I'm done. I'm done pretending that your hateful rhetoric is okay. I'm done pretending that people like us must be quiet to make you feel comfortable."

There's that willingness to discomfit again; it turns everything upside down, disturbs the equilibrium of households and partnerships that had been built around earlier states of complacency and quiet. And in this too, there were other kinds of reminders of the Second Wave, the kinds of intimate upheavals it had provoked.

The writer and professor Amy Butcher would describe the tolls of some of this in her essay "MIA: The Liberal Men We Love," which she published in the weeks after the second Women's March. "*I'm frustrated and embarrassed,* my boyfriend of three years said to me, *with how worked up you are.* He didn't find palatable my rage, the anger I felt for Trump, for the men and women who voted for him, was . . . embarrassed that I led ninety students from my small Ohio university through the streets of Washington with half a million Americans . . . when I returned, delirious for sleep but feeling righted, in some small way satiated, he stood there in the hall and told me he was overwhelmed. *All of you women with your labia hats,* he said. *All of you with your clitoris signs.*"[13] Butcher and her boyfriend broke up.

And still she wrote, she wished that the men who were put off by this surging fury could know what it was like to feel communion with the other women, the angry women on the road back with her from the Washington march. "I woke that night to a thousand taillights — many cars but far more buses, thousands of stories packed onto wheels — as we traced the edges of America, making our way home . . . as we climbed the smudged dusk of West Virginia — the heart of America, indeed, the heart of Trump Country — it seemed, if only for that evening, as if the porch lights had been left on for us . . . and how amazing it was, truly, to watch our steady stream of red lights blink and brake as we led one another home."

The connection women were feeling in shared fury was its own home, its own reward, its own community, and for some the pushback to their activism, the losses it incurred — money, domestic comforts, relationships built in other circumstances, based on earlier expectations for comportment — were not worth retreating for.

"I know five people who are getting divorced over it," Dawn Penich-Thacker told me in the spring of 2018. "Because it has fundamentally changed how they see themselves as women." Penich-Thacker was a thirty-eight-year-old college professor and former Army public affairs officer in Tempe, Arizona. She became energized in the wake of the Trump election to become more civically involved, led a petition to reverse a universal voucher program in Arizona, and assisted in the teachers' strike there in 2018.

She had been a Democratic voter, but not much of an activist, and had joined Pantsuit Nation in the run-up to the election. After Clinton's defeat, local members of Pantsuit Nation discussed taking the group offline and turning it into a live and in-person activist organization; they formed Stronger Together Arizona. In December of 2016, "we called a statewide meeting and eight hundred people showed up, mostly women,"

Penich-Thacker recalled. "It was a surprise to the organizers; the museum we'd booked couldn't even accommodate that many people." During the meeting, attendees divided up according to policy interests and Penich-Thacker headed over to a group discussing education. She began making trips to the capitol to protest planned changes in state funding for schools. When the state legislature passed a bill to privatize education, a mission to expand vouchers spearheaded by Trump's Education Secretary Betsy DeVos, Penich-Thacker and five other women, all mothers of varying ages, who had seen one another over and over again, gathered together and asked what they could do next. They realized the state permitted a right to referendum; if they collected enough signatures they could block a law.

"We had the blessing of ignorance," said Penich-Thacker, noting that they had no idea how unlikely it would be that they could collect more than seventy-five thousand signatures in ninety days. "We literally did not have a penny, and we were six people. But we knew all these other pissed off people, the lion's share of them women, ninety percent through Stronger Together, Facebook, and Indivisible." They collected more than one hundred ten thousand signatures and successfully blocked the law. Sued by organizations with ties to DeVos and the Koch brothers, the group soldiered on, winning their court cases. "We kept education in the headlines and our network kept growing and growing," she said. "We have about five thousand volunteers now." When teachers went on strike in West Virginia and Oklahoma, the grassroots group that moved to strike there had been involved with Penich-Thacker's volunteers, circulating the original petitions. In May, Arizona teachers won a 19 percent pay raise.

"I would be lying if I said I see an end to this," Penich-Thacker told me she had said to her husband the night before our conversation. "It's not going to be over in November. It's not going to be over next year, because you don't change things overnight." When she and her five original coconspirators started working together, she said, she believed that it was just to fight and roll back the one bad law. "But it's now clear to all of us for various reasons that there's way more work to do than stopping one law." She paused. "But also, I think that in many ways, we actually love this. It has consumed our lives."

The marital, romantic, domestic tolls were

real, she said. But her relationships with her fellow activists, she said, "are the deepest friendships I've ever had. These women in this movement are my battle buddies. I can't imagine leaving this behind, even if it ravaged my life." Penich-Thacker said that part of the intensity of the bond is living through the aftershocks of such personal transformation. "There is the bond over the shared political vision, the bond over doing *work* together: we set out to do something, we accomplished it, we feel good. But also the spiritual and emotional bond of saying 'My partner is basically done,' or 'I'm struggling at work.' We have each other to talk through that."

"That is a moment of joy," Gornick wrote in 1990, looking back at the 1970s, "when a sufficiently large number of people are galvanized by a social explanation of how their lives have taken shape, and are gathered together in the same place at the same time, speaking the same language, making the same analysis, meeting again and again in restaurants, lecture halls and apartments. . . . It is the joy of revolutionary politics, and it was ours. To be a feminist in New York City in the early 70s — bliss was it in that dawn to be alive. Not an I-love-you in the world could touch it. There was no other place to be, except with each other. We lived then, all of us, inside the loose embrace of feminism. It was as though we'd been released from a collective lifetime of silence."[14]

When women awaken in their thirties, Penich-Thacker told me, "I think some men are like, 'This isn't who you were when I met you.' Well, it's who I am now and for any future I can foresee."

"I believe this is the beginning of a new wave of feminism," Mosbacher told me. "And I hope by the time my nine-year-old daughter is in college, she'll be reading books about this movement and how it changed the tide in this country."

So many of the newly hatched activists, describing their previous ennui and isolation, and their subsequent rebirth in sisterhood, could indeed sound like the quivering start of a women's movement, and bring to mind the first paragraph of Betty Friedan's *The Feminine Mystique,* about the "strange stirring," and "sense of dissatisfaction [and] yearning" that "each suburban wife struggled with . . . alone."

Stacey Abrams, then Georgia's House Minority Leader, who in 2018 would win a primary to become the nation's first black female gubernatorial nominee, told me that women "understand that this has to be the beginning of something. . . . Because they've seen, for the first time, the real consequences of inaction. So you have women who are waking up and seeing that they don't have the luxury of going back to sleep."

She acknowledged that "among African-American women there's been a long consistency of action, which has moved our communities closer and closer to political power over time. What you're seeing in the suburbs now is a version of that."

For some, these repetitions of history were intolerable.

Aditi Juneja said that she had been working with newly active white women throughout the summer of 2017, and "so many of them don't realize they're not the first people to be activists and organizers." When she speaks to them, she said, "I try to make an effort to say, 'Well, Black Lives Matter dealt with this; Dreamers dealt with this.' I try to reference these other people-of-color-led organizations, to let them know that they are not the first women to do this."

Juneja had noticed that the white activists were very focused on rules. "They ask questions I've not ever heard from women-of-color organizations, like 'Do we need permits to canvas?' They are very hierarchy-oriented, very rules-oriented in a way I have not seen when organizing with people of color." She suggested that one of the reasons the town-hall format had caught on in 2017 was that "white people, even white women, have faith that if they voice their opinions to their representatives, that they will be heard, that they will have influence, that they have a political voice to which officials will be responsive." Black and brown people, Juneja said, know that they have representatives, and know how government works. "But there is no faith that politicians will see that there is any cost to disappointing black and brown people. But these women believe that you work through making calls and going to town halls because you assume that they will *care* what you have to say."

There were other forms of structural bias underpinning some of the activism, including the fact that the vast majority of women giving up their lives to work for campaigns and around policy issues — often offering some of the most innovative ideas and fresh thinking about how to reach members of their own communities, all while balancing kids and full-time jobs — were doing so on a volunteer basis, while so many of the highly paid party consultants were men.

Jessica Morales noticed that the resistance groups that sprang up at the end of 2016 and throughout 2017, many of them led or organized by women, were operating at strategic odds with the better-remunerated "thought-leaders," who, she said, "somehow kept coming back to: You know what we should do? Focus on white men." To those activists who pushed back at this, Morales said, the message was clear: " 'You don't understand the math; you're not being technical; you're so emotional about this election.' " To that, Morales herself said, "Literally go fuck yourselves."

Morales believed that political professionals were dismissing the impact of resistance groups in part because they're so often led by and comprised of women. "They're just not seeing, not understanding, the impact of these organizations," she said. "But there simply have not been organizations before this that could drive millions of calls in one day, just like that. And that's what's been happening."

But the repetition of unequal history, hierarchical patterns, and internal marginalization cannot be the end of the story if angry women are to move forward. And so, the task for activists and candidates and participants in the political struggles of the

Trump era is to find the places where there can be long-awaited growth.

"The question we have now in this resistance movement," said Juneja, "is: Are white women going to use their power to defend their own interests or are they going to use it to transform systems so that we all have more power? If this movement is going to be sustainable, once you stand shoulder-to-shoulder with someone who's not quite like you, can you see how connected your fights are? Do you realize: I have to show up for them? Because our liberation is intertwined. And that's not a meme that I retweeted. That's actually really a thing."

That struggles were connected was not a new idea: it's how the suffrage and abolition movements kicked off together; how suffrage bled into labor and settlement house movements, how civil rights and the New Left informed — in part through their sexist shortcomings and in part through their approach to structural inequality and liberation — the women who would drive the Second Wave.

The idea that anger at injustice is contagious, transferable to other contexts, has long been a principle of progress. As the education reporter Dana Goldstein wrote in the *New York Times,* in reference to the

2018 wave of teachers' strikes, "the politics of teacher strikes shift over time, but in every generation, their leaders have forged ties to broader social movements." Nineteenth-century Chicago Teachers Federation leader Margaret Haley, Goldstein noted, had been "inspired by Susan B. Anthony and other suffragists," while "many of the union leaders who led the nation's most famous . . . teacher strike, in New York City in 1968, were first active in the civil rights movement." The seven-day Chicago teachers' strike, Goldstein wrote, had come in the wake of Occupy Wall Street. And in 2018, West Virginia teachers had told her that they'd "come to activism through the 2017 Women's March, the #metoo movement or Black Lives Matter," a sentiment echoed by one West Virginia striker who told *Times* journalist Michelle Goldberg that the Women's March, "as well as the explosion of local political organizing that followed it" had been a "catalyst" for her and other strikers.

Jessica Morales hoped that connections can be forged by those who've never made them before. She told a story of a woman who contacted her by direct message on Twitter, as she was trying to organize protesters on social media to stand against

Trump's travel ban. "She was this nice teacher in St. Louis who wrote me and said 'I've never started a protest but I am willing to go to the airport and I can leave right now. I really want to do this; I feel passionate about this, but I don't know how to protest.'"

Morales sent her a list of things to do: "get in your car; get friends, fit as many as you can; if you can, make signs; when you get there sing some songs and do some chants, here are examples; don't leave; they are going to tell you that you have to leave, but don't; make a Facebook event and I'll promote it and that's a protest." The woman made the Facebook event. And hundreds of people went to the airport in St. Louis, as they did to airports all around the country, by the tens or perhaps hundreds of thousands.

"I don't think that woman probably knew a lot of immigrants," said Morales, months later. "But it goes to show what we are learning, which is that morally, she knew that this was the wrong thing. And that is really good. We can move forward with that."

By 2018, the rising generation of activists seemed to be absorbing these messages faster than their foremothers and forefathers

501

ever had.

The March for Our Lives, held in March 2018 and organized by the high school students of Parkland, Florida, in the wake of the mass shooting at their school, was a model of interconnected anger. Officially a protest against gun violence and the NRA's grip on American politics, its speakers seemed to see it as all part of one piece: "We need to arm our teachers with . . . the money they need to support their families and to support themselves,' " said one speaker, while eleven-year-old Naomi Wadler named the too-often forgotten names of African-American girls, "whose stories don't make the front page of every newspaper."

The protest felt effortlessly integrated in its concerns. Signs about gun violence acknowledged how deeply white patriarchy was embedded in the crisis of mass shootings, and read things like "White Men Are Terrifying (Statistically)" and "Your Guns Have More Rights Than My Vagina" and "We Live in a Country Where Guns Matter More Than Black Women's Lives." Common rapped, "I stand for peace, love, and women's rights." One young woman, nervous about speaking in front of millions, simply leaned over in the middle of her speech and vomited, while speakers wept, and their noses ran; it was astounding, moving to see the viscera of women's passions on display, without apology or shame — its own testament to urgency and fury and the will to change.

That march recalled the explosive drive behind a 1917 statement written by Lavinia Dock, a suffragist, called "The Young Are At the Gates," a phrase that would become the National Women's Party banner in the suffrage fight.

"What is the potent spirit of youth?" Dock asked. "Is it not the spirit of revolt, of rebellion against senseless and useless and deadening things? Most of all, against injustice, which is of all stupid things the stupidest? Such thoughts come to one in looking over the field of the Suffrage campaign and watching the pickets at the White House and at the Capitol, where sit the men who complacently enjoy the rights they deny to the women at their gates . . . A fatal error — a losing fight. The old stiff minds must give way. The old selfish minds must go. Obstructive reactionaries must move on. The young are at the gates!"

In 2018, it was both the literally and the more metaphorically young — those whose willingness to give voice to rage was nascent

503

— who were at the gates, challenging the men who complacently enjoy the rights they deny others.

As Ann White, the suburban Georgia sixty-four-year-old woman who'd been newly woken from her carapace of political apathy, told me, she was feeling the responsibility of taking a stand, not on her own behalf, but "for people of color, for those who cannot afford health insurance, who are lesbian, gay, and transgender, for immigrants. I'm a white older woman. There's a lot of old white people that are on [the Republican] side right now. Well I'm an old white person and I can be vocal too."

On the day of Trump's first State of the Union address, Jessica Morales wrote to me, excited about a response event being put on by the National Domestic Workers Alliance, at which leaders including head of the Domestic Workers Alliance Ai-Jen Poo, Black Lives Matter's Alicia Garza, Planned Parenthood's Cecile Richards, Congresswomen Barbara Lee and Pramila Jayapal, Tarana Burke, and Mónica Ramirez of the National Farmworker Women's Alliance, who'd stood in solidarity with the #metoo actresses, were coming together to respond to the president's speech.

"It's so powerful and kind of reminds me

504

that the other side of the anger is the hope," Morales wrote to me. "We wouldn't be angry if we didn't still believe that it could be better."

And if it gets better in part because of women's ability and willingness and need to feel their anger and to let it out into the world, then what we would be living through right now would not be a trend or a fad or a witch hunt, but an insurrection — a righteous revolution, led by angry women.

CONCLUSION

Men literally have no idea how to even legitimately recognize or name our anger — largely because we don't either. This is new territory for everybody. Women's rage has been so sublimated for so long that there's simply no frame for what happens when it finally comes to the surface.

— Sara Robinson

I first met the activist Amanda Litman, fifteen years my junior, when she was an undergraduate, studying with a beloved college professor of mine, writing a thesis on women in politics and looking to me, who had written a book on the 2008 presidential election, for guidance. It was with tremendous pleasure, in the months before I began this book, that I found myself reading her words — printed in *Women's Health* magazine — and realized that she was offering guidance to me.

In an essay about how devastated she had been by the 2016 election, as a dedicated member of Hillary Clinton's campaign staff, she described how she had moved forward, founding Run for Something, one of the most successful new political organizations in the country.

"My anger is my cup of coffee in the morning," she wrote. "It gets me out of bed and keeps me focused. . . . Simply doing the damn thing has soothed me and brought me back to myself. Every memo I write, every donor I meet with, every reporter I speak to, each conversation I have, is guided by strategy but fueled by the fury I feel at my country, at dangerous men, at my party, and at the very system of democracy I love that painfully let me down."

When I first read these words, I was already thinking about this book, which I had decided to write in the months after the election, but had intended to report slowly, imagining that it would chronicle the steady evolution of women's rage in the age of Trump. But by the fall of 2017, as the wildfire of female fury was spreading, it had become clear that I needed to work swiftly, to capture this rebellion before its sharp, spiky contours got retroactively smoothed and flattened by time. And so I wrote these pages over the course of four months.

I mention this because as I was finishing them, I realized that those four months — while enormously stressful, professionally — had comprised one of the physically healthiest periods of my adulthood. Yes, I was sickened and terrified by the world around me, the ravages of the Trump administration, the dangers to the democracy and the harm being done to the people in it. Yes. Of course I was.

But while I was pouring some of that fear — and all of my anger — into this project, I realized that I had begun to sleep well and deeply at night; I had wanted to exercise more than I ever had before. My appetite was healthy; I was communicating well with the people I loved; I was having great sex. It certainly wasn't about the good effects of book-writing; I had, after all, done this twice before, under far less punishing deadlines, and had not found either process salutary — quite the opposite. But as Litman had described of her own experience, there had been something about spending my days and nights immersed in anger — mine and the anger of others — that had been undeniably good for me.

It seemed to fly in the face of everything I had ever been taught about fury's ill-effects on the human body, things I had believed to be true on some level even as I had begun this book's introduction, four months earlier. Yes, I wanted to reclaim and excavate the value in women's anger, I had written in an early February draft, but I also understood the emotion to have other, damaging dimensions, the ones that had been affirmed to me so often by culture, by my sources, that I had absorbed as truth. What I wrote when I started this book was that while anger might be politically useful, catalytic, thrilling, and communicatively indispensable, I knew that too much of it was *also* bad for you . . . poisonous, internally corrosive.

By June, I no longer believed that it was deleterious. In fact, I returned again and again to a proclamation made by Elizabeth Cady Stanton, nearly two centuries earlier, that "if women would indulge more freely in vituperation, they would enjoy ten times the health they do. It seems to me they are suffering from repression."

My fitness had not been buoyed simply by my ability to loose my ire; it had also been the chance to take seriously *other* women's rage, the fact that I'd been forced — encouraged — to really examine those emotions that we spend so much of our lives being told to avoid or look away from or laugh at. Writing this book had permitted me to stare straight at them, to think hard about them and consider the credit they deserve for shaping the nation.

I confess that I am now suspicious of nearly every attempt to code anger as unhealthy, no matter how well meaning or persuasive the source. I believe that Stanton was correct: what is bad for women, when it comes to anger, are the messages that cause us to bottle it up, let it fester, keep it silent, feel shame and isolation for ever having felt it or rechannel it in inappropriate directions. What is good for us is opening our mouths and letting it out, permitting ourselves to feel it and say it and think it and act on it and integrate it into our lives, just as we integrate joy and sadness and worry and optimism.

I had been given a gift: the opportunity — the incentive — to explore the dimensions and be curious about and respectful of my own anger, as well as the rage of other women. It felt *great. I* felt great. In getting to voice and appreciate fury, I had found relief, release, inspiration, and exhilaration.

But I was also aware that my experience was unusual, that it could not be converted into advice that might apply to others. So while sure, I urge those who can comfortably do so to scream, yell, curse, write it out, phone a friend, and not keep themselves from *feeling* their own anger, you will find here no exhortation to lean into your own rage as I have into mine.

I was not paying any price for expressing my ire, in fact I was *being paid* for it; it was my work, my job to take women's anger seriously. My editors, bosses, friends were taking this project, and therefore the fury it was unpacking, seriously. It was glorious. But it was not replicable.

To suggest to other women that they should simply let it out, channel their fury and scream it to the world, would be to repeat a long history of well-intentioned, idealistic, but ultimately impractical approaches to feminist strategy: the urging of individual women to work around or within the systems that have not been built to accommodate or even acknowledge them. I can't tell women to express their anger as I have and not acknowledge that in the real world, this rage might get them fired, denied raises and promotions, incur punishments and violence. We live in a world in which a black woman, angry at being pulled over for no reason, risks arrest, and a woman angry at being unjustly arrested risks death; in which young women are shot, or run down by cars, because they — or because another woman — have rejected the advances of a man.

Having had the rare and privileged experience of having had my anger taken seriously, valued on its merits, I no longer believe that it is *anger* that is hurting us, but rather the system that penalizes us for expressing it, that doesn't respect or hear it, that isn't curious about it, that mocks or ignores it. *That's* what's making us sick; *that's* what's making us feel crazy, alone; *that's* why we're grinding our teeth at night.

And so it is not women (or not *only* women) who must change our behaviors; it's the system built to suppress our ire, and thus our power, by design. We can change it by protesting and marching and calling and sending postcards; by donating money and knocking on doors for candidates and running for office, and making demands of our government and in our workplaces, on behalf of ourselves and, crucially, alongside and on behalf of those with more reason to be furious and less ability to leverage that fury than we have.

But more immediately, we can change it by doing what the world does *not* do: by acknowledging, paying attention to, respecting, and not shying away from *other* women's anger. Seek it out, notice it, ask women what makes them angry and then listen to them when they tell you. If part of what they're angry at is you, take it in, acknowledge how their frustrations might mirror your own, even if they are refracted at you.

Consider that the white men in the Rust Belt are rarely told that *their* anger is bad for them. Rather, and correctly, we understand that what's bad for them are the conditions that have provoked their frustration: the loss of jobs and stature, the shortage of affordable health care, day-care, the scourge of drugs. We understand their anger to be politically instructive, to point us toward problems that must be addressed. What we all — in the media, and in politics, and in our personal lives — can endeavor to do is to treat the anger of women as we treat the anger of white men. That also means considering its potential: understanding that the fury of contemporary women at inequity, at sexism and racism and lack of representation, is made of the very same stuff that Thomas Paine's anger was, and that the demands it prompts might be just as transformative. Rage birthed this nation — along with its attendant, baked-in inequities, the very strictures against which members of its majority population are now furiously straining.

Consider what Catharine MacKinnon wrote in February of 2018, arguing that #metoo has made a kind of progress that decades of legal reforms had not: "It is . . . this uprising of the formerly disregarded . . . that is changing everything already . . . [T]oday's movement that is shifting gender

518

hierarchy's tectonic plates."

Of course we must not underestimate the pushback to any shift that can be reasonably described as tectonic. The desire to push disruptive social fury back down underground is strong. The rage must be stronger still, to resist the pull of apathy, the censure of the powerful.

Martin Luther King, Jr. understood that as well as anyone, and it's what made him insist, in his most famous speech, that "this sweltering summer of the Negro's legitimate discontent will not pass until there is an invigorating autumn of freedom and equality. Nineteen-sixty-three is not an end, but a beginning. And those who hope that the Negro needed to blow off steam and will now be content will have a rude awakening if the nation returns to business as usual. . . . The whirlwinds of revolt will continue to shake the foundations of our nation until the bright day of justice emerges."

What King commanded we too must command: that this not get written off as a summer storm, an aberration or fad or period of hysteria until our demands have been met. We must insist on our discontent, not permit it to be muffled or put behind us swiftly. We must emerge on its other side with substantive victories: changes in law,

519

policy, representation, power, a remaking not only of rules to better support equality — via criminal justice and environmental reform, the expansion of reproductive justice, of workers' rights and strengthening of a social safety net — but a reformation of the very attitudes that have permitted inequality to be codified again and again.

Repeatedly, during 2017 and 2018, I was asked — of the Women's March, of #metoo, of women's drive toward elected office: "Is this a moment or a movement?" In part, the questioners craved reassurance that this hard work, these difficult feelings, this fear and pain and risk, was in service of something big, long-term, and important.

But the question, and the binary on which it relies, doesn't track. Because movements are made up of moments, strung out over months, years, decades. They become discernible as movements — are made to look smooth, contiguous, coherent — only after they have made a substantive difference. It was nine years between Emmett Till's murder and the passing of the Civil Rights Act. It was more than eighty years between the first 1830s meeting of abolitionists and suffragists and the passage of the Nineteenth Amendment, more than 130 years before the passage of the Voting Rights Act. That law was recently gutted by the Supreme Court, a body that in 2018 also defended states' rights to purge voter rolls, disproportionately targeting minority voters. Which means that the movement for full democratic enfranchisement in the United States is ongoing, two centuries hence. It's easy to feel defeated by this, but more worthwhile to instead feel inspired: to know that in resisting and dissenting today, we are playing our parts in a story with long, righteous, proud roots.

No deus ex machina is going to appear to announce to those agitating for revolutionary change in the United States and around the world that the project we have embarked upon is a movement; no one can promise that our work now will remap our landscape and remake our future. That burden is on those of us who want desperately for it to do so. *We* determine whether or not we change the world.

The task — *especially* for the newly awakened, the newly angry, *especially* for the white women, for whom incentives to renounce their rage will be highest in coming years — is to keep going, to not turn back, to not give in to the easier path, the one where we weren't angry all the time, where we accepted the comforts of racial

521

and economic advantage that will always be on offer to those who don't challenge power. Our job is to stay angry . . . perhaps for a very long time.

"It is probably going to be years," Emma González told reporters in 2018 about her battle against the gun lobby. "And at this point, I don't know that I mind. Nothing that's worth it is easy . . . We could very well die trying to do this. But we could very well die *not* trying to do this too. So why not die for something rather than nothing?"

González seems to know in youth what it took some activists ages to figure out: what's ahead of her. Vivian Gornick has written of her initial delight, as a woman in the 1970s, discovering the writing of the first wave feminists who had preceded her by a century: "We were . . . reincarnating as the feminists of previous generations," she wrote. "I remember reading Elizabeth Cady Stanton and feeling amazed that a hundred years ago she had said exactly what I was now saying. Amazed, and gratified. Not sobered. That would come later."

What should have been sobering, of course — what was sobering to me, in the summer of 2018, reading Andrea Dworkin and Flo Kennedy and Audre Lorde and Gornick herself — is that if women have been here before, yet we had to get here again, the process of change was going to be slow, hard, and often circular.

As Gornick recalls of how she thought in the 1970s, "Any minute now the whole country would be converted to the rightness of our cause. After all, it wasn't as if it hadn't all been said before. Now, surely, it was being said fully, freely, and for the last time. Women and men alike would set quickly about correcting the painful imbalance and then, existentially speaking, let the chips fall where they may." But as the years wore on, she began to hear in the glibness of her own assured analysis — of "how frightened we all are to look clearly at the meaning of sexism, how difficult it is to reverse the emotional habits of centuries, what anxieties the effort induces" — a stark and defining truth. She had been correct in her assessment of the challenges. "I began to see it was going to take longer than any of us had expected. Much longer."

That it will take a long time shouldn't scare us. It should fortify us. It *must* fortify us, as it seems to fortify Emma González. And we should remember that with each imperfect, and eventually stalled, stage of major social change has come some real progress: expanded enfranchisement, in-

523

creases in liberty for more kinds of people, greater bodily autonomy. And yes, after each step has come the siren song of not-anger — of complicity and satisfaction and fealty to the traditional structures that soothed the burns left by the revolt. But it's nowhere near time for that yet.

We need to work to ensure that this moment will have spurred real change, to know that the changes we make will reverberate far into the future. Consider Shirley Chisholm, who cried when she was mad, and who didn't win. She lost. And yet. She pulled Barbara Lee into politics. Barbara Lee, who was the only person in Congress to vote against the AUMF, which she has been trying to repeal ever since; a fight she has also lost. Barbara Lee, who pioneered a bill in 2015 that would overturn the Hyde Amendment — a major step forward for poor women on an issue that no one had dared to touch since the 1970s. Lee's bill went nowhere. But enthusiasm for her efforts would help opposition to Hyde to find its way into the presidential agenda of Hillary Clinton. Who lost. And whose loss helped spur the entry of perhaps tens of thousands of women into electoral politics and provoked this country to take women's experiences of sexual harassment seriously for the first time. Some of those women will lose, too. But that will not be the end of the story either.

At all the marches, all the rallies, you'll see one sign over and over again. It is a Mexican proverb, apparently taken from the Greek: "They thought they could bury us; they didn't know we were seeds." Women's anger has been buried, over and over again. But it has seeded the ground; we are the green shoots of furies covered up long ago.

If you happen to be reading this in the future, having stumbled across it in an attempt to find out if you're allowed to be angry about whatever you're angry about, let me say: yes. Yes you are allowed. You are in fact compelled.

And if you're reading this now, in its moment, with me; if you've gotten to this page because you've been feeling rage at the unfairness and injustice and at the flaws of this country and because your anger is making you want to change your life in order to change the world, then I have something incredibly important to say: Don't forget how this feels.

Tell a friend, write it down, explain it to your children now, so they will remember. And don't let anyone persuade you it wasn't right, or it was weird, or it was some quirky

525

stage in your life when you went all political — *remember that, honey, that year you went crazy?* No. No. Don't let it ever become that. Because people will try.

The future will come, we hope. If we survive this, if we make it better — even just a little bit better, but I hope a lot better — the urgency will fade, perhaps the ire will subside, the relief will take you, briefly. And that's good, that's okay.

But then the world will come and tell you that you shouldn't get mad again, because you were kind of nuts and you never cooked dinner and you yelled at the TV and weren't so pretty and life will be easier when you get fun again. And it will be awfully tempting to put away the pictures of yourself in your pussy hat, to stuff your protest signs in the attic, and to slink back, away from the raw bite of fury, to ease back into whatever new reality is made after whatever advances we achieve now.

But I say to all the women reading this now, and to my future self: What you're angry about now — injustice — will still exist, even if you yourself are not experiencing it, or are tempted to stop thinking about *how* you experience it, and how you contribute to it. Others are still experiencing it, still mad; some of them are mad at you. Don't forget them; don't write off their anger. Stay mad for them. Stay mad *with* them. They're right to be mad and you're right to be mad alongside them.

Being mad is correct; being mad is American; being mad can be joyful and productive and connective. Don't *ever* let them talk you out of being mad again.

ACKNOWLEDGMENTS

Many thanks to everyone at Simon & Schuster, especially to my exceptional editor, Marysue Rucci. She, along with Jonathan Karp, Carolyn Reidy, Zachary Knoll, Sarah Reidy, Christine Pride, and Cary Goldstein have given my work a supportive and enthusiastic home, for which I'm so grateful. My agent, Linda Loewenthal, has long guided me, and this time brought me to Jane Isay, whose sharp and joyous editorial eye I could not have done without. Further gratitude to Meredith Tax, Alice Walker, and to the Women's Film Archive for permissions and access.

My colleagues at *New York* magazine helped shape many of the ideas in this volume, especially Noreen Malone, Laurie Abraham, Stella Bugbee, Jared Hohlt, Adam Moss, Pam Wasserstein, and Lauren Kern; Ann Clarke's support and humor buoyed this project. I am grateful for the thorough, speedy fact-checking of my colleague Jordan Larson, and the research assistance of Aubri Juhasz. Thanks to Bonnie Siegler for the cover and to Amy Bass for checking my history (fast!). For sustaining insight throughout these terrible years, thanks to Brittney Cooper, Katha Pollitt, Michelle Goldberg, Liz Meriwether, Rebecca Solnit, Lisa Miller, Emily Nussbaum, Bene Cipolla, Edward McPherson, Tom McGeveran, Dahlia Lithwick, Lizzie Skurnick, Jen Deaderick, Amy Goldwasser, Melissa Harris-Perry, Greg Veis, Jamelle Bouie, Joan Walsh, Geraldine Sealey, Lori Leibovich, Zoe Heller, TaNehisi Coates, Chris Hayes, Jean Howard, Jim Baker, Pheroze Wadia, and Aaron and Karel Traister.

I thank especially Heather McPherson, Sara Culley, Kate Shaw, and Krista Williams, all of whom read portions of this book as it was being written. I'm beholden to the furious, hilarious women whose voices are in my head every single day: Irin Carmon, Anna Holmes, and Aminatou Sow; I'd be a different thinker without them. And I'd be no thinker at all without Marion Belle, whose humor, political enthusiasms, and hard work brighten my days and make my work possible. I am lucky, too, to have Zoe Reich and Paul Margarites, Peter

Koechly and Krista Williams, all of whom have offered friendship, ideas, and logistical help. It is inconceivable to me that this book was written and will be published in a world without my lifelong comrade, Michael Friedman, in it. The echo of his voice — and his prescience about this period — are contained in this volume.

My parents housed and fed and urged me to go outside while I wrote; my debt to them, like my love for them, is incalculable. To my daughters: I adore you, am proud of you, and am grateful for your patience and good humor, as well as for your impatience and ill humors. This book is dedicated to you in part because I want you to know that it is okay to be mad; it is *important* to be mad. My husband, Darius Wadia, is a finer partner, better friend, and kinder man than I ever expected to find in this world; he worked to make this book real every bit as hard as I did, all while doing his own difficult and important work, of which I am so proud. I am lucky to navigate this world alongside him.

NOTES

Introduction

1. See the National Women's Political Caucus website at: http://www.nwpc.org/about/nwpc-foundation/.
2. Nan Robertson, "Democrats Feel Impact of Women's New Power," *New York Times,* July 15, 1972, http://www.nytimes.com/1972/07/15/archives/democrats-feel-impact-of-womens-new-power-womens-power-has-an.html.
3. Douglas Rogers, "Lights, Camera, Sexism!," *Washington Post,* July 4, 2004, http://www.washingtonpost.com/wp-dyn/articles/A16333-2004Jun29.html.
4. John Stauffer and Benjamin Soskis, *The Battle Hymn of the Republic: A Biography of the Song That Marches On,* (New York: Oxford University Press, 2013), p. 22. The folk musician Len Chandler rewrote the lyrics to the "Battle Hymn of the Repub-

lic" as "Move on Over" in 1965, at a commemoration of the Harpers Ferry uprising; its chorus was adopted as a slogan by the Black Panther Party.

5. Leymah Gbowee, "Leymah Gbowee in Her Own Words," PBS.org, September 13, 2011, http://www.pbs.org/wnet/women-war-and-peace/features/the-president-will-see-you-now/.

6. Alice Kessler-Harris, *Out to Work: The History of Wage-Earning Women in the United States* (New York: Oxford University Press, 2003), p. 41.

7. "Rosa Parks Essay Reveals Rape Attempt," *Huffington Post,* July 29, 2011, https://www.huffingtonpost.com/2011/07/29/rosa-parks-essay-rape_n_912997.html.

8. Sarah Kaplan, "A Scientist Who Studies Protests Says 'The Resistance" Isn't Slowing Down," *Washington Post,* May 3, 2017, https://www.washingtonpost.com/news/speaking-of-science/wp/2017/05/03/a-scientist-who-studies-protest-says-the-resistance-isnt-slowing-down/?utm_term=.758284a8c17d. First brought to my attention in a tweet by Zeynep Tufekci, from a panel she was on with Dana Fisher at the 2017 American Sociological Association Annual Meeting.

9. Myisha Cherry, "Anger Is Not a Bad

Word," TEDxUofIChicago, June 2, 2015, http://www.myishacherry.org/2015/06/02/my-tedx-talk-anger-is-not-a-bad-word/.

10. Kathy Spillar, "Not Backing Down," *Ms. Magazine,* August 31, 2017, http://ms magazine.com/blog/2017/08/31/not-backing-down/.

Part I

1. Susan Sarandon with Elizabeth Day, "Susan Sarandon: Feminism Is a Bit of an Old-fashioned Word," *The Guardian,* June 29, 2013, https://www.the-guardian.com/theobserver/2013/jun/30/susan-sarandon-q-and-a.

2. For a good discussion of the impact of Waters's riot statements, listen to Janet Mock's podcast, https://janetmock.com/podcast/.

3. Evans Rowl and Robert Novak, "No Insurrection in Los Angeles," *Washington Post,* May 4, 1992, https://www.washing tonpost.com/archive/opinions/1992/05/04/no-insurrection-in-los-angeles/1ff2c017-9674-4bc8-8667-51e7325f43ce/?no redirect=on&utm_term=. 30f1bab1d799.

4. Taryn Finley, "Maxine Waters: '92 L.A. Rebellion Was a 'Defining Moment' for Black Resistance," *Huffington Post,* April

535

27, 2017, https://www.huffingtonpost.com/entry/maxine-waters-la-rebellion-was-a-defining-moment-for-black-resistance_us_58fe2861e4b00fa7de165e18.

5. Mychal Denzel Smith, "The Rebirth of Black Rage," *The Nation,* August 13, 2015, https://www.thenation.com/article/the-rebirth-of-black-rage/.

6. "Tea Act," History.com, https://www.history.com/topics/american-revolution/tea-act.

7. Kenneth P. Vogel, "Face of the Tea Party Is Female," *Politico,* March 26, 2010, https://www.politico.com/story/2010/03/face-of-the-tea-party-is-female-035094.

8. "New Demographic Profiles of Occupy Wall Street vs. Tea Party Movements," prri.com, December 1, 2011, https://www.prri.org/spotlight/new-demographic-profiles-of-occupy-wall-street-vs-tea-party-movements/.

9. Tina Dupuy, "The Occupy Movement's Woman Problem," *Atlantic,* November 21, 2011, https://www.theatlantic.com/politics/archive/2011/11/the-occupy-movements-woman-problem/248831/.

10. Quinn Norton, "A Eulogy for #Occupy," wired.com, December 12, 2012, https://www.wired.com/2012/12/a-eulogy-

for-occupy/.

11. Karen McVeigh, "Occupy Wall Street's Women Struggle to Make Their Voices Heard," *The Guardian,* November 30, 2011, https://www.theguardian.com/world/2011/nov/30/occupy-wall-street-women-voices.

12. Ren Jender, "When the Stupidity about Rape Wouldn't Stop, I Quit the Movement I Loved," xojane.com, January 14, 2013.

13. Patrisse Khan-Cullors, "We Didn't Start a Movement. We started a Network," Medium.com, February 22, 2016, https://medium.com/@patrissemariecullorsbrignac/we-didn-t-start-a-movement-we-started-a-network-90f9b5717668.

14. Cavan Sieczkowski, "Feminist Activist Says Beyoncé is Partly 'Anti-Feminist' and 'Terrorist,' *Huffington Post,* May 9, 2014, https://www.huffingtonpost.com/2014/05/09/beyonce-anti-feminist_n_5295891.html.

15. Barbara Marcolini, "Trump Voters, One Year Later," *New York Times,* video, n.d., https://www.nytimes.com/video/us/politics/100000005538314/trump-voters-one-year-later.html.

16. Laura Barrón-López, "Donald Trump Adviser Says Hillary Clinton Should Be Shot by Firing Squad," *Huffington Post,*

July 20, 2016, https://www.huffington post.com/entry/al-baldasaro-donald-trump-hillary-clinton_us_578fa150e4b07 c722ebd2fd1.

17. Daniel Denvir, "The Betrayal That Should Haunt Hillary Clinton: How She Sold Out Working Women and Then Never Apologized," *Salon,* https://www.salon .com/2015/11/02/the_betrayal_that_ should_haunt_hillary_clinton_how_she_ sold_out_working_women_then_never_ apologized/.

18. Rebecca Traister, "The Left Is Borrowing Hillary Clinton Hate from the Republican National Convention — with Dangerous Consequences," *New York Times,* July 25, 2016, http://nymag.com/daily/ intelligencer/2016/07/left-is-borrowing-hillary-hate-from-the-rnc.html.

19. Michelle Goldberg, "Men Explain Hillary to Me," *Slate,* November 6, 2015, http://www.slate.com/articles/double_x/ doublex/2015/11/hillary_clinton_bernie_ sanders_sexist_coverage_some_men_want _to_mansplain.html.

20. Alexis Okeowo, "The Writing Life of Warsan Shire, a Young, Prolific Poet," *New Yorker,* October 21, 2015, https://www .newyorker.com/culture/cultural-com ment/the-writing-life-of-a-young-prolific-

poet-warsan-shire. For the complete poem, "For Women Who Are 'Difficult' to Love," see https://genius.com/Warsan-shire-for-women-who-are-difficult-to-love-annotated.

21. Thomas E. Patterson, "News Coverage of the 2016 General Election: How the Press Failed the Voters," Shorenstein Center, December 7, 2016, https://shoren steincenter.org/news-coverage-2016-general-election/?platform=hootsuite.

22. Jonathan Mahler, "For Many Women, Trump's 'Locker Room Talk' Brings Memories of Abuse," *New York Times,* October 10, 2016, https://www.nytimes .com/2016/10/11/us/politics/sexual-assault-survivor-reaction.html?action= click&contentCollection=Politics&module =RelatedCoverage&region=Marginalia& pgtype=article.

23. Natasha Stoynoff, "Physically Attacked by Donald Trump — a *People* Writer's Own Harrowing Story," *People,* October 12, 2016, http://people.com/politics/don ald-trump-attacked-people-writer/.

24. Megan Twohey and Michael Barbaro, "Two Women Say Donald Trump Touched Them Inappropriately," *New York Times,* October 12, 2016, https://www.ny times.com/2016/10/13/us/politics/donald-

trump-women.html.

25. Ibid.

26. NTK Staff, "Claire McCaskill Lacks Specifics on Goals of the Women's March," *NTK Network,* January 23, 2017: https://ntknetwork.com/claire-mccaskill-lacks-specifics-on-goals-of-the-womens-march/.

27. Margaret Hartmann, "What Happened to the 19 Women Who Accused Trump of Sexual Misconduct," *New York* magazine, December 12, 2017, http://nymag.com/daily/intelligencer/2017/12/what-happened-to-trumps-16-sexual-misconduct-accusers.html.

28. Mark Lilla, "The End of Identity Liberalism," *New York Times,* November 18, 2016, https://www.nytimes.com/2016/11/20/opinion/sunday/the-end-of-identity-liberalism.html.

29. Eliza Newlin Carney, "Who's Behind the Women's March," *American Prospect,* January 19, 2017, http://prospect.org/article/who%E2%80%99s-behind-women%E2%80%99s-march. See also: Nina Agrawal, "How the Women's March Came into Being," *Los Angeles Times,* January 21, 2017, http://www.latimes.com/nation/la-na-pol-womens-march-live-how-the-women-s-march-came-into-1484865755-

htmlstory.html.

30. Annelise Orleck, *Rethinking American Women's Activism* (New York: Routledge, 2015), pp. 112–13.

31. Lawrence O'Donnell, "Something Is Happening: Women's March Makes History," MSNBC.com, "The Last Word," video, January 23, 2017, https://www.msnbc.com/the-last-word/watch/-something-is-happening-women-s-march-makes-history-861237315678.

32. Annelise Orleck, *Rethinking American Women's Activism* (New York: Routledge, 2015), pp. 112–13.

33. ABC News, "Kellyanne Conway Interview: 'Didn't See the Point' to Women's March on Washington," YouTube Video, 17:15, January 22, 2017, https://www.youtube.com/watch?v=H8tErpLLFbE.

34. ABC News, "Chuck Schumer on Women's Marching 'Part of the Grand American Tradition,' " YouTube Video, 7:33, January 22, 2017, https://www.youtube.com/watch?v=tTLcREwdNp0.

35. Micah White, "Without a Path from Protest to Power, the Women's March Will End Up Like Occupy," *The Guardian,* January 19, 2017, https://www.theguardian.com/world/2017/jan/19/womens-march-washington-occupy-protest.

36. "Don't Just March, Run!" EMILY's List, https://emilyslist.org/pages/entry/getting-ready-to-run.
37. Edward-Isaac Dovere and Elana Schor, "Will the Women's March Be Another Occupy, or a Democratic Tea Party?" *Politico,* January 21, 2017, https://www.politico.com/story/2017/01/womens-march-organizing-strategy-233973.
38. Ibid.
39. "McCaskill on Women's March: I Hope Trump Pays Attention," *Morning Joe,* January 23, 2017, https://www.msnbc.com/morning-joe/watch/mccaskill-on-women-s-march-i-hope-trump-pays-attention-860604483733.
40. Matt Ford (@fordm), "Leaving Dulles now to file from home. Gender disparity was striking: Probably 70 percent of lawyers volunteering there are young women," Twitter, January 29 2017, 6:53 pm, https://twitter.com/fordm/status/825899790785454083.
41. Patty Murray, Kamala D. Harris, et al., "Letter to President Donald J. Trump," United States Senate, January 30, 2017, https://www.harris.senate.gov/imo/media/doc/013017%20Harris-Murray%20Letter.pdf.

42. Nora Mcinerny Purmort, "How I Accidentally Convinced 100 Strangers to Get Matching Tattoos," *Cosmopolitan,* March 1, 2017, http://www.cosmopolitan.com/politics/a9078317/how-i-convinced-100-women-to-get-matching-tattoos/.

43. Megan Garber, " 'Nevertheless, She Persisted' and the Age of the Weaponized Meme," *Atlantic,* February 8, 2017, https://www.theatlantic.com/entertainment/archive/2017/02/nevertheless-she-persisted-and-the-age-of-the-weaponized-meme/516012/.

44. Sady Doyle, "New Survey Says Women Are Leading the Resistance, Because of Course They Are," Talk Poverty, April 11, 2017, https://talkpoverty.org/2017/04/11/new-survey-says-women-leading-resistance-course/.

45. Catherine Pearson, "Women Wore 'Handmaid's Tale' Robes to the Texas Senate," *Huffington Post,* March 20, 2017, https://www.huffingtonpost.com/entry/women-wore-handmaids-tale-robes-to-texas-senate_us_58d034bee4b0ec9d29de74f5.

46. Ruptly, "Torched Confederate Flag & Witch Costumes: Activists Protest Against 'Free Speech' Rally in Boston, YouTube

Video, 2:10, August 19, 2017, https://www.youtube.com/watch?v=gg5Mkiv_djA.

47. Timothy Bella, "Patrisse Khan-Cullors on 5 Years of Black Lives Matter," *New York* magazine, January 18, 2018, http://nymag.com/daily/intelligencer/2018/01/patrisse-khan-cullors-on-5-years-of-black-lives-matter.html.

48. Kirsten Gillibrand (@SenGillibrand), "It is an honor to announce that Mayor@ Carmen YulinCruz of San Juan, Puerto Rico will join me at the #SOTU. Throughout the crisis in Puerto Rico, Mayor Cruz has shown extraordinary leadership and fearless advocacy for her city," Twitter, January 29, 2018, 6:21 am, https://twitter.com/SenGillibrand/status/957982123377545216.

49. Samhita Mukhopadhyay, "2017: The Year Women's Anger Was Unleashed," Mic, December 22, 2017, https://mic.com/articles/187016/2017-the-year-womens-anger-was-unleashed#.XymO8o0op.

50. Laurie Penny (@PennyRed), "Most of the interesting women you know are far, far angrier than you'd imagine," Twitter, July 18, 2017, 2:27 am, https://twitter.com/pennyred/status/887423515892342786?lang=en.

51. Manohla Dargis, "Harvey Weinstein Is Gone. But Hollywood Still Has a Problem," *New York Times,* October 11, 2017, https://mobile.nytimes.com/2017/10/11/movies/ harvey-weinstein-hollywood .html?hp&action=click&pgtype=Home page&clickSource=story-heading&module=first-column-region&region=top-news&WT.nav=top-news&_r=0&referer =https://t.co/Jl3eXTRHqT?amp=1.

52. Oluo Ijeoma, "Does This Year Make Me Look Angry?" *Elle,* January 11, 2018, https://www.elle.com/culture/career-politics/a15063942/ijeoma-oluo-women-and-rage-2018/.

53. Melissa Harris-Perry, "Women Are Angrier Than Ever Before — and They're Doing Something About It," *Elle,* March 9, 2018, https://www.elle.com/culture/career-politics/a19297903/elle-survey-womens-anger-melissa-harris-perry/.

54. Amanda Arnold, "Steve Bannon Is Really Worried About the 'Anti-Patriarchy' Movement," *The Cut,* February 10, 2018, https://www.thecut.com/2018/02/steve-bannon-is-worried-about-the-anti-patriarchy-movement.html.

55. Caitlin Flanagan, "The Conversation #MeToo Needs to Have," *Atlantic,* Janu-

ary 29, 2018, https://www.theatlantic.com/ politics/archive/2018/01/the-right-conversation-for-metoo/551732/.

56. Michelle Goldberg, "The Teachers Revolt in West Virginia," *New York Times,* March 5, 2018, https://www.nytimes.com/ 2018/03/05/opinion/west-virginia-teachers-strike.html?action=click& contentCollection=opinion%C2%A Eion=rank&module=package&version= highlights&contentPlacement=3&pgtype =sectionfront.

57. "Florida Student Emma González to Lawmakers and Gun Advocates: 'We Call BS,'" CNN.com, February 17, 2018, https://www.cnn.com/2018/02/17/us/ florida-student-emma-gonzalez-speech/ index.html.

58. Leon Stein, ed., *Out of the Sweatshop: The Struggle for Industrial Democracy* (New York: Quadrangle/New York Times Book Company, 1977), pp. 196–97.

Part II

1. John Nichols, "16 Years Ago, Barbara Lee's Warning Against the AUMF Was Ignored. Nevertheless, She Persisted," *The Nation,* June 30, 2017, https://www.the nation.com/article/16-years-ago-barbara-

lees-warning-against-the-aumf-was-ignored-nevertheless-she-persisted/.

2. Austin Wright, "How Barbara Lee Became an Army of One," *Politico,* July 30, 2017, https://www.politico.com/magazine/story/2017/07/30/how-barbara-lee-became-an-army-of-one-215434.

3. Rep. Barbara Lee, "Rep. Lee Testifies on AUMF Sunset Amdt in Rules Committee," YouTube Video, 51:56, July 25, 2017, https://www.youtube.com/watch?v=BS51Lr0ibLc.

4. Thomas Carnan, *An Historic Description of the Tower of London and Its Curiosities,* (London: Londres, 1787, via Google Books), p. 47. This so-called "Collar of Torment" was on exhibit at the Tower of London in fall of 2017. It is described in colorful terms as an item that was once "used formerly to be put about the women's necks that made cuckolds of their husbands or scolded at them when they came late; but that custom is left off now-a-days, to prevent quarrelling for collars, there not being enough smiths to make them."

5. Jennifer Hansler, "A Brief History of Female Politicians Being Told to Smile," CNN.com, January 31, 2018, https://www.cnn.com/2018/01/31/politics/women-

politicians-told-to-smile/index.html. See also: Joe Scarborough (@ JoeNBC), "Smile. You Just had a big night. #Primary Day," Twitter, March 15, 2016, 6:10 pm, https://twitter.com/JoeNBC/status/70990 9770619248640.

6. Hansler, "Brief History of Female Politicians." See also: Chris Cillizza (@Cilliz zaCNN), "I think Nancy Pelosi looks like that all the time. I think she should smile a lot more often. I think the country would be better for it. She seems to embody the bitterness that belongs in the Democratic party," Twitter, January 31, 2018, 5:43 am, https://twitter.com/Cil lizzaCNN/status/958697219401682944.

7. Rodger Streitmatter, *Mightier Than the Sword: How the New Media Have Shaped American History* (New York: Routledge, 2018). See also: Elizabeth Johnston, "The Original 'Nasty Woman,' " *Atlantic,* November 6, 2016, https://www.theatlantic.com/entertainment/archive/2016/11/the-original-nasty-woman-of-classical-myth/506591/. And Mary Beard, *Women and Power: A Manifesto* (New York: Liveright, 2017).

8. Marjorie Spruill Wheeler, ed., *One Woman, One Vote* (Troutdale, OR: NewSage Press, 1995), p. 121.

9. Mary Beard, *Women & Power: A Manifesto* (New York: Liveright, 2017).

10. Joel B. Pollack, "The Naked Hillary Clinton Statues You've Never Seen — and Lived to Tell," Breitbart.com, August 21, 2016, http://www.breitbart.com/california/2016/08/21/naked-hillary-clinton-statues-youve-never-seen/. See also: Elizabeth Johnston, "The Original 'Nasty Woman,' " *Atlantic,* November 6, 2016, https://www.theatlantic.com/entertainment/archive/2016/11/the-original-nasty-woman-of-classical-myth/506591/.

11. Ian Schwartz, "Mnuchin vs, Waters: 'You Acknowledged I Shouldn't Interrupt'; Waters: 'I'm Reclaiming My Time!' " RealClear Politics, July 27, 2017, https://www.realclearpolitics.com/video/2017/07/27/mnuchin_vs_maxine_waters_you_acknowledged_i_shouldnt_interrupt_waters_im_reclaiming_my_time.html.

12. Sarah Taylor, "This Is Exactly Why Maxine Waters' Televised, Unhinged Threats Against Trump Need to Stop," TheBlaze.com, August 23, 2017, https://www.theblaze.com/news/2017/08/23/this-is-exactly-why-maxine-waters-televised-unhinged-threats-against-trump-need-to-stop. See also: Tony Lee, "Maxine Waters Unhinged: I'm Going to Take Ben Car-

son's A** Apart,' " Breitbart.com, July 3, 2017, http://www.breitbart.com/big-government/2017/07/03/maxine-waters-unhinged-im-going-take-ben-carsons-apart/.

13. "Trump-Loving Pastor Darrell Scott Comes for Maxine Waters, Calls Her a 'Crazy Aunt,' " TheGrio.com, February 2, 2018, https://thegrio.com/2018/02/02/pastor-darrell-scott-maxine-waters/.

14. Lindy West, "Brave Enough to Be Angry," *New York Times,* November 8, 2017, https://www.nytimes.com/2017/11/08/opinion/anger-women-weinstein-assault.html?smid=tw-nytimes&smtyp=cur&_r=0.

15. Andy B. Wang and Sean Sullivan, "Congressional Intern Suspended After Yelling Obscenity at President Trump in the Capitol," *Washington Post,* June 26, 2018, https://www.washingtonpost.com/news/powerpost/wp/2018/06/26/congressional-intern-suspended-after-yelling-obscenity-at-president-trump-at-the-capitol/?utm_term=.e6872a3b4676.

16. Author interview with Gloria Steinem.

17. Joanna Scutts, *Hotbed,* New York Historical Society, November 3, 2017–March 25, 2018.

18. Barry Michels and Phil Stutz, "The

Root of Anger — and Using Its Force for Good," goop.com, n.d., http://goop.com/roots-anger-using-force-good/?utm_campaign=socialflow&utm_source=twitter.com&utm_ medium=social-jp.

19. Matthew Biedlingmaier, "*Wash. Post*'s Achenbach: Hillary Clinton 'needs a radio-controlled shock collar so that aides can zap her when she starts to get screechy,' " *Media Matters,* January 8, 2008, https://urldefense.proofpoint.com/v2/url?u=https-3A__www.mediamatters.org_research_2008_01_08_wash-2Dposts-2Dachenbach-2Dhillary-2Dclinton-2Dneeds-2Da-2Dra_142081&d=DwMFaQ&c=jGUuvAdBXp_VqQ6t0yah2g&r=BL twNjxI6xU1TowZZXPw62rxL1h5Yh02O172-V1YNSunoH38hlyco6RBfK8BXD8O&m=sL2dj6nPNRrhSTnketBXS3yIKp1p_iNSqJEEq9TW4t8&s=APPmAsKAR38o3-gywLe-D5Cj0xCoFcoXx1XQq_L2Odg&e=.

20. Amanda Terkel, "Millbank Jokes That Hillary Clinton Should Drink 'Mad Bitch' Beer," ThinkProgress.org, July 31, 2009, https://thinkprogress.org/ milbank-jokes-that-hillary-clinton-should-drink-mad-bitch-beer-fa187583bd18/.

21. MoxNews.com, "Donald Trump 'I AM ANGRY,' " YouTube Video, 14:55, Janu-

ary 13, 2016, https://www.youtube.com/watch?v=v2dNzmaekmU.

22. Jonathan Martin and Patrick Healy, "In Democratic Debate, Candidates Clash on Money's Role," *New York Times,* February 5, 2016, https://www.nytimes.com/2016/02/05/us/politics/democratic-debate.html.

23. The Young Turks, "Hillary Having Problems Controlling THE VOLUME OF HER VOICE," YouTube Video, 2:54, February 4, 2016, https://www.youtube.com/watch?v=a5sXLoXxvBM.

24. Thomas Frank, "Donald Trump Is Moving to the White House, and Liberals Put Him There," *The Guardian,* November 9, 2016, https://www.the guardian.com/commentisfree/2016/nov/09/donald-trump-white-house-hillary-clinton-liberals.

25. Lisa Feldman Barrett, "Hillary Clinton's 'Angry Face,' " *New York Times,* September 23, 2016, https://www.nytimes.com/2016/09/25/opinion/sunday/hillary-clintons-angry-face.html.

26. "Michelle Obama: 'Angry Black Woman' Label Hurt," CNN.com, video, December 19, 2016, https://www.cnn.com/videos/politics/2016/12/19/michelle-obama-angry-black-woman-nr-sot.cnn.

27. I transcribed this interview immediately after video of the conversation ran alongside a story by Robin Givhan, reporting on the conversation. After a dispute about whether or not the conversation was on the record, the network, BET, which had supplied the video, pulled it from Givhan's story: Robin Givhan, "Michelle Obama Wanted to Gain the Public's Trust. So She Started With a Garden," *The Washintgon Post,* March 21, 2018, https://www.washingtonpost.com/news/arts-and-entertainment/wp/2018/03/21/michelle-obama-wanted-to-gain-the-publics-trust-so-she-started-with-a-garden/. See also: Danielle C. Belton, "They Said It Was Private. She Said It Was On-the-Record. The Reality? It's Complicated," *The Root,* March 23, 2018, https://www.theroot.com/they-said-it-was-private-she-said-it-was-on-the-record-1824024113.

28. Katy Guest, "Women! Reclaim Your Rage," Unbound.com, January 15, 2018, https://unbound.com/boundless/2018/01/15/women-reclaim-your-rage/.

29. Jason Le Miere, "Maxine Waters's 'Take Trump Out' Remark Was About 'Assassination,' Not 'Impeachment,' Says Fox News Guest," *Newsweek,* October 23, 2017, http://www.newsweek.com/maxine-

waters-trump-assassination-impeachment-690761.

30. Mark Swanson, "GOP Challenger Calls for Rep. Waters' Arrest After Trump Remarks," Newsmax, October 23, 2017, https://www.newsmax.com/politics/maxine-waters-omar-navarro-donald-trump-take-him-out/2017/10/23/id/821 549/.

31. Ian Schwartz, "Maxine Waters: Trump Supporters 'Not Accustomed' to a Black Woman 'Taking Leadership' to Impeach Him," RealClear Politics, October 24, 2017, https://www.realclearpolitics.com/video/2017/10/24/maxine_waters_trump_supporters_not_accustomed_to_a_black_woman_taking_leadership_to_impeach_him.html.

32. Ibid.

33. " 'Reclaiming My Time': Rep. Maxine Waters Interrupts Mnuchin's Roundabout Answer," *Washington Post,* video, August 1, 2017, https://www.washingtonpost.com/video/national/maxine-waters-reclaiming-my-time/2017/08/01/30fae7f4-76d4-11e7-8c17-533c52b2f014_video.html?utm_term=.e2dd5dd34636. See also IdolxNews, "Maxine Waters 'Reclaiming My Time' Performed Live — The View," YouTube Video, 1:54, August 4,

2017, https://www.youtube.com/watch?v=lRuRdEaatio.

34. Joe Concha, "O'Reilly Mocks Dem Maxine Waters for Wearing 'James Brown Wig,' " The Hill.com, March 28, 2017, http://thehill.com/home-news/media/326107-oreilly-mocks-maxine-waters-for-wearing-james-brown-wig.

35. Jamilah King, "Maxine Waters' Battle Against Powerful White Men Began When Eula Love Was Killed in 1979," Mic, April 26, 2017, https://mic.com/articles/174565/maxine-waters-battle-against-powerful-white-men-began-when-eula-love-was-killed-in-1979#.seD4bEkf9.

36. "Internetting with Amanda Hess: Episode 5: The White Internet's Love Affair with Digital Blackface," New York Times, November 28, 2017, https://www.nytimes.com/interactive/2017/11/28/arts/internetting-with-amanda-hess.html.

37. Audre Lorde, "The Uses of Anger: Women Responding to Racism," keynote presentation, National Women's Studies Association Conference, Storrs, Connecticut, June 1981, BlackPast.org, http://www.blackpast.org/1981-audre-lorde-uses-anger-women-responding-racism.

38. Angela Peoples, "Don't Just Thank Black Women. Follow Us," New York

Times, December 16, 2017, https://www.nytimes.com/2017/12/16/opinion/sunday/black-women-leadership.html.

39. Lori D. Ginzberg, *Elizabeth Cady Stanton: A Life,* (New York, NY: Farrar, Straus and Giroux, 2009); p. 91.

40. Adjua Fisher, "4 Philly Fitness Classes Where You Can Fully Express Your Rage," *Philadelphia,* November 9, 2016, https://www.phillymag.com/be-well-philly/2016/11/09/ boxing-classes-philadelphia/.

41. Regena Thomashauer, "Get Right with Your Darkness," MamaGenas.com, March 2, 2017, http://www.mamagenas.com/get-right-with-your-darkness/.

42. Richard Brookhiser, "The Happy Medium," review of *Other Powers: The Age of Suffrage, Spiritualism, and the Scandalous Victoria Woodhull* and *Notorious Victoria: The Life of Victoria Woodhull, Uncensored, New York Times Books,* March 29, 1998, https://archive.nytimes.com/www.nytimes.com/books/98/03/29/reviews/980329.29brookht.html?scp=9&sq=Napoleon%2520and%2520Josephine:%2520A%2520Love%2520Story&st=Search.

43. Marjorie Spruill Wheeler, ed., *One Woman, One Vote* (Troutdale, OR: New-Sage Press, 1995), p. 127.

44. Ibid., p. 126.

45. "Mother Bloor: U.S. Communist Heroine," *Life,* July 26, 1937, https://books .google.ca/books?id=pEUEAAAAMBAJ &pg=PA27&lpg=PA27&dq=grand+old +woman+of+the+U.S.+communist+ party&source=bl&ots=5SP8GXcvZf &sig=2lwUS5XCddb5z-6VAGT95wMG Z9I&hl=en&sa=X& ved=0ahUKEwiu6o fQrNLMAhXi44MKHYUtBrgQ6AEII DAC#v=onepage&q=grand%20old&f= false.

46. Mary Triece, *On the Picket Line: Strategies of Working-Class Women During the Depression* (Champaign: University of Illinois Press, 2007), p. 19.

47. Stephen Tuck, *We Ain't What We Ought To Be: The Black Freedom Struggle from Emancipation to Obama* (New York: Belknap Press, 2011), p. 189.

48. Marjorie Spruill Wheeler, ed., *One Woman, One Vote* (Troutdale, OR: New-Sage Press, 1995), p. 175.

49. Mamie Till Mobley, "The Untold Story of EMMETT LUIS TILL (Documentary 2005) by Keith Beauchamp," YouTube Video, 1:08:18, November 19, 2012, https://www.youtube.com/watch?v=bvij YSJtkQk.

50. David Deitcher (ed.), *The Question of*

Equality: Lesbian and Gay Politics in America Since Stonewall, (New York, NY: Scribner, 1996), p 67.

51. Manny Fernandez, "A Stonewall Veteran, 89, Misses the Parade," *New York Times,* June 27, 2010, https://www.nytimes.com/2010/06/28/nyregion/28storme.html?_r=1.

52. Alexandria Piette, "In Remembrance of the Stonewall Riots," *Women's Republic,* June 8, 2017, http://www.womensrepublic.net/in-remembrance-of-the-stonewall-riots-the-lasting-impact-on-the-lgbtq-community/.

53. Megan Garber, "All the Angry Ladies," *Atlantic,* November 6, 2017, https://www.theatlantic.com/entertainment/archive/2017/11/all-the-angry-ladies/545042/.

54. Meghan O'Rourke, "Mourning Trump and the America We Could Have Been," *New Yorker,* November 10, 2016, https://www.newyorker.com/culture/culture-desk/mourning-trump-and-the-america-we-could-have-been?irgwc=1&source=affiliate_impactpmx_12f6tote_desktop_Skimbit%20Ltd.&mbid=affiliate_impactpmx_12f6tote_desktop_Skimbit%20Ltd.

55. Lisa Feldman Barrett, "Hillary Clinton's 'Angry' Face," *New York Times,* Septem-

ber 23, 2016, https://www.nytimes.com/2016/09/25/opinion/sunday/ hillary-clintons-angry-face.html. See also: Mary Lay Schuster and Amy D. Propen, *Victim Advocacy in the Courtroom: Persuasive Practices in Domestic Violence and Child Protection Cases* (Boston: Northeastern University Press, 2011).

56. Leslie Jamison, "I Used to Insist I Didn't Get Angry. Not Anymore," *New York Times Magazine,* January 17, 2018, https://www.nytimes.com/2018/01/17/magazine/i-used-to-insist-i-didnt-get-angry-not-anymore.html.

57. Ibid.

58. National Woman Suffrage Association, "Declaration of Rights of Women of the United States," in *Selected Papers of Elizabeth Cady Stanton and Susan B. Anthony, vol. 3, National Protection for National Citizens, 1873 to 1880,* ed. Ann D. Gordon (New Brunswick, NJ: Rutgers University Press, 2003).

59. Nora Ephron, "Miami," *Huffington Post,* n.d., https://highline.huffington post.com/articles/en/ lets-go-full-crocodile-ladies/essay/.

60. Warren Weaver, Jr., "Schroeder, Assailing 'the System,' Decides Not to Run for President," *New York Times,* September

29, 1987, https://www.nytimes.com/1987/09/29/us/schroeder-assailing-the-system-decides-not-to-run-for-president.html.

61. Susan Ferraro, "The Prime of Pat Schroeder," *New York Times,* July 1, 1990, https://www.nytimes.com/1990/07/01/magazine/the-prime-of-pat-schroeder.html.

62. Robin DiAngelo, "White Fragility," *The International Journal of Critical Pedagogy,* Vol. 3, No. 3, 2011, http://libjournal.uncg.edu/ijcp/article/view/249.

63. Susan Ferraro, "The Prime of Pat Schroeder," *New York Times,* July 1, 1990, https://www.nytimes.com/1990/07/01/magazine/the-prime-of-pat-schroeder.html.

64. Ibid.

65. PBS, "Makers: The Women Who Make America," Season 1, Stop the ERA video: https://www.pbs.org/video/makers-women-who-make-america-stop-era/.

66. Susan Ferraro, "The Prime of Pat Schroeder," *New York Times,* July 1, 1990, https://www.nytimes.com/1990/07/01/magazine/the-prime-of-pat-schroeder.html.

67. "Hillary Clinton" (parody); "Let Me Remind You Fuckers Who I Am," *Medium,* July 25, 2016, https://medium.com/@shit

560

HRCcantsay/let-me-remind-you-fuckers-who-i-am-e6e8b297fe47.

68. "Hillary Clinton" (parody); "Are you Fucking Kidding Me," November 13, 2016, https://medium.com/@shitHRC cantsay/are-you-fucking-kidding-me-86 bdc2c638d6.

69. Robinson, Phoebe, *You Can't Touch My Hair (And Other Things I Still Have to Explain,* (New York: New York, Plume, 2016).

70. Nellie Andreeva, "Seth MacFarlane Opens Up About His 2013 Harvey Weinstein Oscars Joke, Condemns 'Abhorrent' Abuse of Power," Deadline, October 11, 2017, https://deadline.com/2017/10/seth-macfarlane-harvey-weinstein-oscar-joke-explained-1202186425/.

71. Megan Garber, "The Anger of Samantha Bee," *Atlantic,* October 11, 2016, https://www.theatlantic.com/entertain ment/archive/2016/10/the-angers-of-sam antha-bee/503612/

72. Callum Borchers, "Michelle Wolf's Caustic Comedy Routine at the White House Correspondents' Dinner, Annotated," *Washington Post,* April 29, 2018, https://www.washingtonpost.com/news/ the-fix/wp/2018/04/29/michelle-wolfs-caustic-comedy-routine-at-the-white-house-correspondents-dinner-annotated/

?utm_term=.2beb058203b6.

73. Masha Gessen, "Michelle Wolf Blasted Open the Fictions of Journalism in the Age of Trump," *New Yorker,* April 30, 2018, https://www.newyorker.com/news/our-columnists/how-michelle-wolf-blasted-open-the-fictions-of-journalism-in-the-age-of-trump.

74. Mika Brzezinski (@morningmika), "Watching a wife and mother be humiliated on national television for looks is deplorable. I have experienced insults about my appearance from the president. All women have a duty to unite when these attacks happen and the WHCA owes Sarah an apology," Twitter, April 29, 2018, 6:37 am, https://twitter.com/morningmika/status/990585968825597954.

75. Maggie Haberman (@maggieNYT), "That @PressSec sat and absorbed intense criticism of her physical appearance, her job performance, and so forth, instead of walking out, on national television, was impressive," Twitter, April 28, 2018, 8:14 pm, https://twitter.com/maggieNYT/status/990428993542414336.

76. "Can you Guess Kamala Harris' Favorite Curse Word?", *The Week,* July 6, 2017, http://theweek.com/speedreads/710360/guess-kamala-harris-favorite-curse-word.

77. Kristin Wong, "The Case for Cursing," *New York Times,* July 27, 2017, https://www.nytimes.com/2017/07/27/smarter-living/the-case-for-cursing.html.

78. Katie Hawkins-Gaar, "The Cohort: Don't Call Me 'Dear,' f**kface, and Other Ways to Approach Anger at Work," *Poynter,* August 31, 2017, https://www.poynter.org/news/cohort-dont-call-me-dear-fkface-and-other-ways-approach-anger-work.

79. Kristin Wong, "The Case for Cursing," *New York Times,* July 27, 2017, https://www.nytimes.com/2017/07/27/smarter-living/the-case-for-cursing.html.

80. Eric Grundhauser, "The Great Harvard Pee-In of 1973," Atlas Obscura, December 23, 2016, https://www.atlasobscura.com/articles/the-great-harvard-peein-of-1973.

81. Alice Kessler-Harris, *Out to Work: A History of Wage-Earning Women in the United States* (New York: Oxford University Press, 2003), p. 41.

82. Leigh Fought, *Women in the World of Frederick Douglass* (New York: Oxford University Press, 2017) p. 195.

83. Marjorie Spruill Wheeler, ed., *One Woman, One Vote* (Troutdale, OR: NewSage Press, 1995), p. 38.

84. Ibid.

85. Ibid.

86. "Transcript: Hillary Clinton's Full Interview with NPR's Rachel Martin," NPR.com, September 12, 2017, https://www.npr.org/2017/09/12/549430064/transcript-hillary-clinton-s-full-interview-with-npr-s-rachel-martin.

87. Harry Enten (@ForecasterEnten), "I cannot believe I did this . . . but! Per the 2016 CCES (again I can't believe I'm doing this), only 8% of black voters went for Trump. But among black men earing at least 100k a year, it was 15%. So Kanye isn't completely alone," Twitter, April 25, 2018, 1:18 pm, https://twitter.com/ForecasterEnten/status/989237343948328960.

88. Travis Deshong, "Diane Nash: An Activist's Lessons for a New Generation," *Yale Daily News,* January 27, 2017, https://yaledailynews.com/blog/2017/01/27/diane-nash-an-activists-lessons-for-a-new-generation/.

89. The Women's Convention, Women's Convention Schedule: http://www.womensconvention.com/schedule.html.

90. Kat Calvin (@KatCalvinLA), "This is actually true. A majority of our STV vols are white women who are going to homeless shelters every week, driving people they have never met and wouldn't nor-

mally speak to all over town, and are really putting their hearts into it. It's kind of amazing," Twitter, December 13, 2017, 8:31 am, https://twitter.com/KatCalvinLA/status/940982502126006272.

91. "Death of Fred Douglass," *New York Times,* February 21, 1895, https://archive.nytimes.com/www.nytimes.com/learning/general/onthisday/bday/0207.html.

92. Ta-Nehisi Coates, "Frederick Douglass 'A Woman's Rights Man,' " *Atlantic,* September 30, 2011, https://www.theatlantic.com/personal/archive/2011/09/frederick-douglass-a-womens-rights-man/245977/.

Part III

1. Joy Press, "The Life and Death of a Radical Sisterhood," The Cut, November 15, 2017, https://www.thecut.com/2017/11/an-oral-history-of-feminist-group-new-york-radical-women.html. See also: Roxane Gay, "Fifty Years Ago, Protesters Took on the Miss America Pageant and Electrified the Feminist Movement," *Smithsonian,* January 2018, https://www.smithsonianmag.com/history/fifty-years-ago-protestors-took-on-miss-america-pageant-electrified-feminist-movement-180967504/.

2. CBS This Morning, "Gayle King and Norah O'Donnell respond to Charlie Rose allegations," YouTube Video, 3:18, November 21, 2017, https://www.youtube.com/watch?v=-SIp6xSP7ds.

3. Bryn Elise Sandberg, "Sarah Silverman Addresses Louis C.K.'s Sexual Misconduct: 'It's a Real Mind — -,' " *Hollywood Reporter,* November 16, 2017, https://www.hollywoodreporter.com/live-feed/sarah-silverman-addresses-louis-cks-sexual-misconduct-a-real-mindf-1059117.

4. "To Tell the Truth," The Cut, video, December 20, 2017, https://www.thecut.com/2017/12/rose-mcgowan-harvey-weinstein-sexual-assault-and-harassment.html?utm_source=nym_press.

5. Marjorie Spruill Wheeler, ed., *One Woman, One Vote* (Troutdale, OR: NewSage Press, 1995), p. 38.

6. E. W. Capron, "Women's Rights Convention," *National Reformer,* August 3, 1848, http://facstaff.elon.edu/dcopeland/fourth%20hour/seneca%20falls.pdf.

7. Cecile Richards, *Make Trouble: Standing Up, Speaking Out, and Finding the Courage to Lead* (New York: Simon & Schuster, 2018).

8. Beverly Willett, " 'Feminists Love Divorce!' " *Huffington Post,* May 25, 2011,

https://www.huffingtonpost.com/beverly-willett/feminists-love-divorce_b_825208.html.

9. Jill Brooke, "Did Feminism Cause Divorce?" *Huffington Post,* May 25, 2011, https://www.huffingtonpost.com/jill-brooke/did-feminism-cause-many-d_b_836327.html.

10. Tracy Connor, "Larry Nassar Complains It's Too Hard to Listen to Victim Stories," NBCNews.com, January 18, 2018, https://www.nbcnews.com/news/us-news/larry-nassar-complains-it-s-too-hard-listen-victim-stories-n838731.

11. Havana Marking, "The Real Legacy of Andrea Dworkin," *The Guardian,* April 15, 2005, https://www.theguardian.com/world/2005/apr/15/gender.politicsphilosophyandsociety.

12. Lore Dickstein, "Street Fighting Feminist," *New York Times,* October 29, 1989, https://www.nytimes.com/1989/10/29/books/ street-fighting-feminist.html.

13. Jonathan Allen, "Pelosi Stumbles on Alleged Harassment in Her Own Ranks," NBCNews.com, November 27, 2017, https://www.nbcnews.com/politics/congress/pelosi-stumbles-alleged-harassment-her-own-ranks-n824041.

14. Dayna Tortorici, "In the Maze," *n+1,*

Winter 2018.

15. Jessica Campbell, "The First Brave Woman Who Alleged 'Sexual Harassment,' " Legacy.com, February 5, 2016, http://www.legacy.com/news/culture-and-trends/article/ the-first-brave-woman-who-alleged-sexual-harassment.

16. Kyle Svenson, "Who Came Up with the Term 'Sexual Harassment,' " *Washington Post,* November 22, 2017, https://www.washingtonpost.com/news/morning-mix/wp/2017/11/22/who-came-up-with-the-term-sexual-harassment/?utm_term=.d49729fcce2a.

17. Ibid.

18. Susan Brownmiller and Dolores Alexander, "From Carmita Wood to Anita Hill," *Ms.,* January/February 1992, http://www.nfwfwf.org/wp-content/uploads/2018/02/BROWNMILLER-ALEXANDER-MS-MAG-1992.pdf.

19. Megan Twohey, Jodi Kantor, Susan Dominus, Jim Rutenberg, and Steve Eder, "Weinstein's Complicity Machine," *New York Times,* December 5, 2017, https://www.nytimes.com/interactive/2017/12/05/us/ harvey-weinstein-complicity.html. See also: Irin Carmon and Amy Brittain, "Eight Women Say Charlie Rose Sexually Harassed Them — with Nudity, Groping

and Lewd Calls," *Washington Post,* November 20, 2017, https://www.washington post.com/investigations/eight-women-say-charlie-rose-sexually-harassed-them—with-nudity-groping-and-lewd-calls/2017/11/20/9b168de8-caec-11e7-8321-81fd63f174d_story.html.

20. Toni Morrison, "A Humanist View" as part of Black Studies Center public dialogue, Pt. 2, May 30, 1975.

21. Tom Bartlett and Nell Gluckman, "She Left Harvard. He Got to Stay," *Chronicle of Higher Education,* February 27, 2018, https://www.chronicle.com/interactives/harvard-harassment.

22. Gabriel Sherman, *The Loudest Voice in the Room* (New York: Random House, 2014).

23. Ella Nilsen, "Mark Halperin Once Downplayed Sexual Harassment Claims Against Trump. Now He's Facing His Own," *Vox,* October 27, 2017, https://www.vox.com/2017/10/27/16559880/mark-halperin-trump-sexual-harassment.

24. Manohla Dargis, "Harvey Weinstein Is Gone. But Hollywood Still Has a Problem," *New York Times,* October 11, 2017, https://mobile.nytimes.com/2017/10/11/movies/harvey-weinstein-hollywood.html?hp& action=click&pgtype=Homepage&c

clickSource=story-heading&module=first-column-region&region=top-news&WT.nav=top-news&_r=0&referer=https://t.co/Jl3eXTRHqT?amp=1.

25. Irin Carmon, "Porn Free: Talking to Andrea Dworkin," *Harvard Crimson,* March 22, 2002, https://www.thecrimson.com/article/2002/3/22/porn-free-talking-to-andrea-dworkin/?utm_source=thecrimson&utm_medium=web_primary&utm_campaign=recommend_sidebar.

26. Kyle Swenson, "Who Came Up with the Term 'Sexual Harassment,' " *Washington Post,* November 22, 2017, https://www.washingtonpost.com/news/morning-mix/wp/2017/11/22/who-came-up-with-the-term-sexual-harassment/?utm_term=.d49729fcce2a.

27. Raina Lipsitz, "Sexual Harassment Law Was Shaped by the Battles of Black Women," *The Nation,* October 20, 2017, https://www.thenation.com/article/sexual-harassment-law-was-shaped-by-the-battles-of-black-women/.

28. Cristela Guerra, "Where Did 'Me Too' Come From? Activist Tarana Burke, Long Before Hashtags," *Boston Globe,* October 17, 2017, https://www.bostonglobe.com/lifestyle/2017/10/17/alyssa-milano-credits-activist-tarana-burke-with-founding-

metoo-movement-years-ago/o2Jv29v6lj Ob-kKPTPB9KGP/story.html.

29. Jason Hancock and Bryan Lowry, "Missouri Gov. Eric Greitens Says He's Target of 'Political Witch Hunt,' Vows to Fight," *Kansas City Star,* April 27, 2018, http://www.kansascity.com/news/politics-government/article208615764.html.

30. Alan Feuer, "Lawyers for Two Schneiderman Accusers Brought Their Claims to Michael Cohen," *New York Times,* May 11, 2018, https://www.nytimes.com/2018/05/11/nyregion/eric-schneiderman-michael-cohen.html.

31. James Oliver Cury, "Charlie Rose's Life Now: 'Broken,' 'Brilliant' and 'Lonely,' *The Hollywood Reporter,* April 12, 2018, https://www.hollywoodreporter.com/features/what-happened-charlie-rose-we-asked-his-friends-associates-1101333.

32. Anna Graham Hunter, "How #MeToo Accusers Cope After Going Public: 'My Hatred Has Deepened,' " *The Hollywood Reporter,* May 9, 2018, https://www.hollywoodreporter.com/news/how-metoo-accusers-cope-going-public-my-hatred-has-deepened-1109891.

33. Isaac Chotiner, "Punishment Is Not Enough," *Slate,* December 11, 2017, http://www.slate.com/articles/news_and_

politics/interrogation/2017/12/the_limita
tions_of_punishment_in_the_metoo_mo-
ment.html.

34. "To Tell the Truth," The Cut, video, December 20, 2017, https://www.the cut.com/2017/12/rose-mcgowan-harvey-weinstein-sexual-assault-and-harassment .html?utm_source=nym_press.

35. Caitlin Flanagan, "The Conversation #MeToo Needs to Have," Atlantic, January 29, 2018, https://www.theatlantic.com/ politics/archive/2018/01/the-right-conver sation-for-metoo/551732/.

36. Laurie Penny, "We're Not Done Here," Longreads, January 2018, https:// longreads.com/author/pennyred/.

37. Annys Shin and Libby Casey, "Anita Hill and Her 1991 Congressional Defend-ers to Joe Biden: You Were Part of the Problem," Washington Post, November 22, 2017, https://www.washingtonpost .com/lifestyle/magazine/anita-hill-and-her-1991-congressional-defenders-to-joe-biden-you-were-part-of-the-problem/ 2017/11/21/2303ba8a-ce69-11e7-a1a3-0d1e45a6de3d_story.html.

38. Sarah Kendzior, https://twitter.com/ sarahkendzir/status/9963952828280913 92.

39. Susan Faludi, "The Patriarchs Are Fall-

ing. The Patriarcharchy Is Stronger Than Ever," *New York Times,* December 28, 2017, https://www.nytimes.com/2017/12/28/opinion/sunday/patriarchy-feminism-metoo.html.

Part IV

1. Amanda Litman, "I Wake Up and Go To Sleep Angry — And That's a Good Thing," *Women's Health,* October 17, 2017, https://www.womenshealthmag.com/life/a19948724/amanda-litman-run-for-something/.
2. Catharine MacKinnon, "Me Too Has Done What the Law Cannot," *New York Times,* February 4, 2018, https://www.nytimes.com/2018/02/04/opinion/metoo-law-legal-system.html.
3. "The Last 25 Senate Incumbents Defeated in Primaries (1962–Present)," NPR.com, April 28, 2010, https://www.npr.org/sections/politicaljunkie/2010/04/24/126248204/senate-incumbents-defeated-in-primaries.
4. Carol Moseley Braun, History, Art & Archives, U.S. House of Representatives, n.d., http://history.house.gov/People/Listing/M/MOSELEY-BRAUN,-Carol-(M001025)/.

5. LaurenUnderwoodwithAndreaCambron, WERA-FM,March21,2018, https://url defense.proofpoint.com/v2/url?u=https-3A__enlightenmeonwera.com_2018_03_21_3-2D21-2D18-2Dspotlight-2Dlauren-2Dunderwood_&d=DwMFaQ&c=jGUu vAdBXp_VqQ6t0yah2g&r=BLtwNjxI6xU 1TowZZXPw62rxL1h5Yh02Ol72-V1YN Sun oH38hlyco6RBfK8BXD8O&m=09_ aBCGDqXOZ9T8KMIoXJ04S8XPdJs7s cFA3SmWWjFU&s=9mru0fRfF–KXqr UJB0egkxipvH6SUIi3wTB9SsDehw&e=.

6. Dan Mangan, "Rep. Patrick Meehan of Pennsylvania Resigns After Sexual Harassment Case Forced End of Re-election Bid," CNBC.com, April 27, 2018, https://www.cnbc.com/2018/04/27/rep-patrick-meehan-of-pennsylvania-resigns-after-sexual-harassment-claim.html.

7. Natasha Bach, "This Woman Said Being Sexually Harassed by Trump Inspired Her to Enter Politics. Now She's Won Her First Election," *Fortune,* May 9, 2018, http://fortune.com/2018/05/09/rachel-crooks-trump-accuser-wins-ohio-pri mary/.

8. "She's the Ticket," Episode 104: Jennifer Carroll Foy, Topic, https://www.topic.com/she-s-the-ticket/she-s-the-ticket-episode-104.

9. Amanda Marcotte, "#MeToo Is Working: Now Data Shows Attitudes on Harassment Are Changing," *Salon,* December 7, 2017, https://www.salon.com/2017/12/07/metoo-is-working-new-data-shows-attitudes-on-harassment-are-changing/.

10. Ezra Levin (@ezralevin), "This piece by @CharlotteAlter is right on the money. Women are running indivisible groups at a 2-1 margin or more," Twitter, July 29, 2017, 5:33 pm, https://twitter.com/ezralevin/status/891456596647268352.

11. Vivian Gornick, "Who Says We Haven't Made a Revolution?; A Feminist Takes Sock," *New York Times,* April 15, 1990, https://www.nytimes.com/1990/04/15/magazine/who-says-we-haven-t-made-a-revolution-a-feminist-takes-stock.html.

12. Paul Schwartzman, "Why a Historically Conservative County in Virginia Is Making National Republicans Nervous," *Washington Post,* November 25, 2017, https://www.washingtonpost.com/local/virginia-politics/why-a-historically-conservative-county-in-virginia-is-making-national-republicans-nervous/2017/11/25/654a90f4-cbbb-11e7-8321-481fd63f174d_story.html?utm_term=.1b85f835d3da.

13. Amy Butcher, "MIA: The Liberal Men We Love," Literary Hub, February 27,

2018, https://lithub.com/mia-the-liberal-men-we-love/.

14. Vivian Gornick, "Who Says We Haven't Made a Revolution?; A Feminist Takes Stock," *New York Times,* April 15, 1990, https://www.nytimes.com/1990/04/15/magazine/who-says-we-haven-t-made-a-revolution-a-feminist-takes-stock.html.

ABOUT THE AUTHOR

Rebecca Traister is writer at large for *New York* magazine and a contributing editor at *Elle.* A National Magazine Award finalist, she has written about women in politics, media, and entertainment from a feminist perspective for *The New Republic* and *Salon* and has also contributed to *The Nation, The New York Observer, The New York Times, The Washington Post, Vogue, Glamour* and *Marie Claire.* She is the author of *All the Single Ladies* and the award-winning *Big Girls Don't Cry.* She lives in New York with her family.

The employees of Thorndike Press hope you have enjoyed this Large Print book. All our Thorndike, Wheeler, and Kennebec Large Print titles are designed for easy reading, and all our books are made to last. Other Thorndike Press Large Print books are available at your library, through selected bookstores, or directly from us.

For information about titles, please call:
(800) 223-1244

or visit our website at:
gale.com/thorndike

To share your comments, please write:
Publisher
Thorndike Press
10 Water St., Suite 310
Waterville, ME 04901